THE DIGITAL DISCONNECT

THE DIGITAL DISCONNECT

THE CAUSES AND CONSEQUENCES OF DIGITAL INEQUALITIES

ELLEN J HELSPER

SAGE

Los Angeles | London | New Delhi
Singapore | Washington DC | Melbourne

SAGE

Los Angeles | London | New Delhi
Singapore | Washington DC | Melbourne

SAGE Publications Ltd
1 Oliver's Yard
55 City Road
London EC1Y 1SP

SAGE Publications Inc.
2455 Teller Road
Thousand Oaks, California 91320

SAGE Publications India Pvt Ltd
B 1/I 1 Mohan Cooperative Industrial Area
Mathura Road
New Delhi 110 044

SAGE Publications Asia-Pacific Pte Ltd
3 Church Street
#10-04 Samsung Hub
Singapore 049483

Editor: Michael Ainsley
Assistant editor: John Nightingale
Production editor: Manmeet Kaur Tura
Copyeditor: Sarah Bury
Proofreader: Jill Birch
Indexer: Martin Hargreaves
Marketing manager: Susheel Gokarakonda
Cover design: Lisa Harper-Wells
Typeset by: C&M Digitals (P) Ltd, Chennai, India
Printed in the UK

Library of Congress Control Number: 2020942246

British Library Cataloguing in Publication data

A catalogue record for this book is available from the British Library

ISBN 978-1-5264-6339-5
ISBN 978-1-5264-6340-1 (pbk)

CONTENTS

LIST OF FIGURES

ABOUT THE AUTHOR

Ellen J. Helsper is Professor of Socio-Digital Inequalities in the Media and Communications Department at the London School of Economics and Political Science (LSE). Her research interests include the links between social and digital inequalities; vulnerability and discrimination in digital spaces; digital literacy; mediated communication and interpersonal relationships; and methodological innovation in quantitative and qualitative media and communications research. Her work is truly global in nature through her involvement in the From Digital Skills to Tangible Outcomes; Connected Communities and Inclusive Growth; YSkills; Global Kids Online; and World Internet research projects. She consults widely for governments, the third and commercial sector on issues to do with client and citizen (dis)engagement in increasingly digital societies. Organisations that she has worked with include the BBC, the European Commission, the International Telecommunications Union (ITU), OECD, and UNESCO.

Ellen holds and has held Visiting Scholar positions at prestigious universities and research institutes in Asia, Europe, Latin America, the Middle East and the US. She has a PhD in Media and Communications from the LSE and an MSc degree in Media Psychology from Utrecht University and worked in commercial market and audience research in Europe, Latin America and the US.

ACKNOWLEDGEMENTS

The journey to finishing this book was a long one, life and work frequently interfered. A continuous stream of research projects and international collaborations were a blessing, but also led to further delays. There was no way I could leave out all the exciting new ideas these brought! While I wrote the book, it is the result of a collective effort, the discussions and collaborations with these outstanding scholars. For this, my eternal gratitude goes to colleagues on the From Digital Skills to Tangible Outcomes (DiSTO) and the EU, LATAM and Global Kids Online projects, as well as to all those who shared their socio-digital life stories by participating in interviews, surveys, theatre plays, and other creative data-generating processes.

Closer to home, the 'Book club' provided critical and always spot on feedback on various drafts. Many of your books were finished before mine – this was great motivation, showing me that it could be done. I especially want to thank Sonia Livingstone, Peter Lunt, and Bart Cammaerts, who pushed me over the finish line, sacrificing their precious time, reading and commenting over lovely dinners. Without your insights and inspiration, this book would have lacked coherence and depth!

Similarly, Michael Ainsley, thank you for sticking this one out with me. Your patience and understanding about delays and eternal revisions were exceptional. Andrew Schrock, from Indelible Voice, what a godsend that I found you towards the difficult end. You performed a miracle and are a true editing wizard. The book is so much better (and shorter) because of your input. Without you, I would have given up with the finish line in sight and the book would never have materialised!

I want to thank all those who have accepted my distractedness and grumbles, continuing to believe in me and showing interest throughout. Special thanks to the West End girls and the Sunny escape crew for dragging me out, providing light relief and making sure I did not disappear into the pages of what seemed a never-ending story. A special shout out goes to Katka for tagging along on the ride and keeping me mentally and physically fit.

Last but not least, thanks go to my family. First, my parents and their partners, who always had a warm welcome and a cuppa at the ready. To my (great)aunts and uncles, in particular my aunt Marjan Lucas, for her moral support and help on international politics and how they are experienced from the bottom up. Special thanks to my brother, Charles Helsper, for listening while struggling with his own work–life balance and for providing the first reference to this book. And finally, to my nephews and niece for reminding me that there are more important things than writing a book. I am looking forward to living through an unpredictable future full of social and digital adventures with you!

This book is dedicated to my parents, Annelies Lucas and Hans Helsper. Without your unwavering, loving support and intellectual feedback, there would have been no book.

INTRODUCTION

Times change. Early in the 21st century, calls to bridge the digital divide were dismissed by people who saw internet access as a luxury. Two decades later, it is tough to find a policy maker, business leader, or academic arguing against the importance of high speed, broadband internet access. The internet and related Information and Communication Technologies (ICTs) have become household staples and are seen to have the power to transform lives for the better. In parallel, our understanding of the risks and opportunities of digitisation has matured. When I started writing this book, the language of 'divides' was still prominent, but has since been replaced by an outcomes-based approach that links social and digital inequalities (Helsper, 2012). These latter ideas frame this book, emphasising the consequences of digitisation in terms of well-being, health, and wealth – rather than digitisation itself.

With increased digitisation of society comes increased concern about who is left behind. Split realities might be emerging. In one reality, the social and digital seamlessly merge. In another reality, the digital is a hard-to-reach, inhospitable land with barely understood language and customs. Socio-pessimists fear that digitisation will perpetuate or amplify existing inequalities. From this perspective, technology adds an extra hurdle to full participation, further marginalising historically disadvantaged people and countries. Techno-optimists counter that connected technologies offer unprecedented opportunities to the same people, allowing them to 'catch up' and even overcome existing inequalities.

I am not the first to argue that digital inequalities are more complicated than a gap between the connected and disconnected. There are multiple layers and gradations of exclusion, not just 'haves' and 'have nots'. In this book, I go beyond describing who is disconnected, and look for explanations for why they are. In particular, I am interested in how social and digital inequalities are linked. By taking a fresh look at the quantitative and qualitative data collected in research done over two decades, I consider what the most likely causes and consequences are of being disconnected in different ways. I take the position that digital engagement for its own sake is not of interest. The digital gains relevance only if it results in tangible outcomes in people's everyday lives. In this sense, digital engagement is not an end goal, object, or artefact. It is a continuous process – a scene of constant struggle.

The structure of the book is inspired by my Corresponding Fields (CF) model (Helsper, 2012). I discuss this model in more detail in Chapter 2, but for this introduction the most important take away is that the CF model theorises the paths that different people take to reach different outcomes from ICT use. Their paths depend on the social and technological environment they come from and live in. The CF model unpacks how specific causes (i.e. offline domains of resources) are related to specific digital inequalities (i.e. digital domains of resources) and specific consequences of these inequalities (i.e. outcome domains). It hypothesises that links between social and digital inequalities are strongest for four similar corresponding domains of resources: economic, social, cultural, and personal. While I use the language of causes and consequences, and discuss these links in rather linear, sequential ways, the reality is that the social and digital are hard to separate. Therefore, I use the term 'socio-digital inequalities' instead of digital inequalities or divides.

To enrich my argument and illustrate my model, I weave in ideas from outside socio-digital inequalities research, policy, and practice. I hope this will inspire digital inequalities scholars and practitioners to broaden their horizon and expand their toolkit. The book starts with theories and ideas around traditional inequalities in Chapter 1. Since I also want this book to help expand the horizon of those who tackle traditional inequalities, the basic principles that underpin digital inequalities research are explained in Chapter 2. The 'disconnect' in the title refers to the potential disconnect of people from increasingly digital societies, and the disconnect I have observed between scholars and practitioners from different disciplinary and institutional backgrounds. Only by combining forces and knowledge, and tackling digital and social inequalities in conjunction, can we prevent inequalities from deepening and move towards a different status quo.

Part I of the book gives an overview of the past. It asks how we thought about inequalities before anything digital was on the agenda (Chapter 1). Subsequently, I delineate how socio-digital inequalities have developed (Chapter 2). In Part II, the book moves to the present. It explores what we know about, and how we can explain, current socio-digital inequalities. This part of the book starts with tried-and-tested areas of digital inequalities research, policy, and practice, relating to access (Chapter 3) and skills (Chapter 4). I then shift attention to a staple of traditional inequalities research by examining formal and informal civic participation (Chapter 5). Finally, I move to the lesser-explored frontiers of socio-digital inequalities, such as social engagement (Chapter 6), and everyday content creation and consumption (Chapter 7). Following the CF approach, these chapters link to corresponding economic, social, cultural, and personal domains of disadvantage. Chapters 3 and 4 follow the paths from traditional socio-economic forms of inequality (i.e. poverty and education) through ICT access and skills, and how they relate to socio-economic outcomes from ICT use. Chapter 5 adds inequalities in formal social resources and describes how active and passive digital engagement might lead to civic empowerment. Chapters 6 and 7 examine multi-layered, identity-based aspects of inequality, and how they correspond to inequalities in socio-cultural and personal well-being outcomes of ICT use. In the Conclusion, I apply the lessons from the rest of the book to suggest ways forward in research and practice and finish by considering what emerging technologies might mean for inequalities in future digital societies.

Throughout this book, quantitative data are supplemented by qualitative data. Chapters 3 to 7 are accompanied by vignettes of a person compiled from the experiences people have shared with me over years of research. These quotes and descriptions of people's everyday lives help animate statistics, demonstrating what life is like for people in very different circumstances around the world. The qualitative and quantitative data comes from the From Digital Skills to Tangible Outcomes (DiSTO) project and partner projects (DiSTO partners, 2020; Global Kids Online, 2020; Net Children Go Mobile, 2020), as well as publicly-available databases from organisations such as the OECD, World Bank, and the United Nations (OECD, 2019; World Bank & International Telecommunications Union, 2020). The qualitative data describe individual and personal experiences, while the quantitative data trace systematic, societal inequalities. This combination allows us to examine what is universal and what is unique in shaping socio-digital inequalities between certain regions and people.

Throughout this book, I advocate for more attention to meso-level social processes as drivers of inequalities. A meso-level approach augments current explanations focused on high-level societal processes or individual skills and needs. It helps us to better theorise how interactions with people, and the environments in which we live, shape how we think about ICTs. This is not to say that I ignore that technology can drive change. Just as our physical environments are constructed in ways that facilitate or hinder certain behaviours and interactions, so are our digital environments. Therefore, the book will point out how technological features can create exclusionary environments. In fact, because social and technological change are intertwined and mutually reinforcing, they potentially amplify inequalities. Nevertheless, the evidence presented shows that there are opportunities to break negative feedback loops through the cultivation of collective responsibility and individual agency in the communities in which we live.

I could have written a book on each of the chapters in this book, and look forward to exploring all these areas in more detail in years to come. I also hope that social and digital inequalities scholars and practitioners will be inspired to continue the dialogue, and design research and interventions that will help shape a better world. My wish is that this book will help readers understand that socio-digital inequalities are unjust and have real consequences. Only collective action by stakeholders across academia, policy, industry, and the third sector can ensure that a more digital future is indeed a future for all.

PART I

THE PAST: SOCIAL AND DIGITAL INEQUALITIES THEORIES

CHAPTER 1

SOCIAL WORLD: FROM POVERTY TO INEQUALITY

'Global inequality affects us all, no matter who we are or where we are from.'

United Nations (2018)

The second decade of the 21st century has produced numerous publications arguing that inequalities are on the increase (Piketty, 2020). Similarly, the above quote shows that inequality is high on the international policy agenda (United Nations, 2018). This rise in interest has come after decades of research that shows high levels of inequality have dire consequences for society at large – not just the less affluent. Societies with disparities between the wealthiest and the least well-off have higher rates of unemployment and poverty than more egalitarian societies. More unequal societies also have higher crime rates, worse health, weaker property rights, skewed access to public services, less influence on decision-makers, and are slower in transitioning to democracy (Held & Kaya, 2007).

In this book, I argue that understanding why inequalities endure requires analysing the interplay between traditional and digital inequalities. While, the link between traditional and digital inequalities is recognised, there remains a disconnect – people working in the field of digital inequalities draw on a very narrow range of traditional theories of inequalities. Part of this disconnect stems from the lack of understanding among digital inequalities practitioners and scholars about debates that traditional inequalities scholars have engaged with for decades. Digital inequalities literature, interventions, and policy making suffers from a narrow understanding and low integration of the knowledge gathered around traditional inequalities (Helsper, 2012). Understanding these debates is beneficial for digital inequalities researchers and practitioners searching for solutions. This book's goal is to inspire digital inequalities researchers and practitioners to employ a comprehensive range of approaches to participate more fully in these debates about inequalities. Therefore, I start by reviewing the concepts and theories of traditional inequalities. Specifically, in this chapter I explore how the conceptualisation of traditional inequalities has changed. I also ask which frameworks are most useful to predict the persistence of inequalities. This approach reflects the interdisciplinary and critical social science nature of my work. It reflects a need to integrate macro (or societal) explanations with micro (or individual) drivers of inequality by examining everyday contexts and realities.

What are we talking about? From poverty and absolutes to inequality and subjectivity

Many terms have been used to describe people who find themselves without power. This definitional variation reflects differences in thinking about the root of the problem. For example, speaking of 'exclusion' suggests to a top-down process imposed on people by a rich elite, creating divides between them and a poor underclass. By contrast, emphasising 'disadvantage' suggests a more agentic, dynamic process where persons and organisations in different positions can overcome inequalities through action. To emphasise agency, I draw on the term 'disadvantage' instead of 'exclusion' (or 'divides'). This decision reflects my constructivist and meso-level approach. That is, I do not assume inequalities are inevitable, because I contend that people collectively shape increasingly digital societies. Accordingly, in this chapter I examine why inequalities should be defined as relative and subjective rather than absolute and objective (Figure 1.1). Inequalities are typically defined according to economic resources and socio-cultural well-being models. I further discuss inequality of opportunities and inequalities in outcomes approaches. Synthesising this scholarship, I define inequalities as: systematic differences in economic, social, cultural, and well-being opportunities and resources between people from different backgrounds.

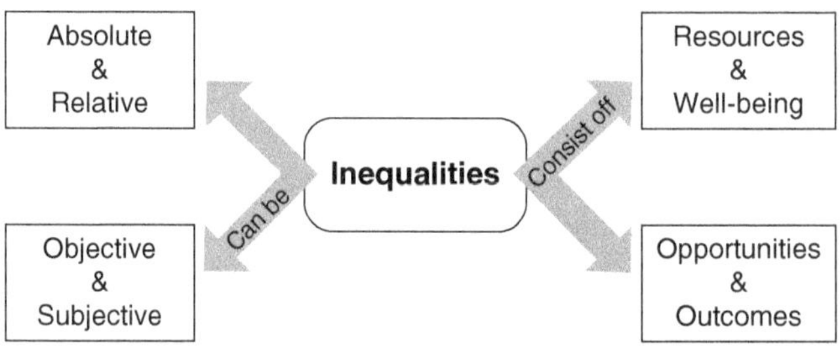

Figure 1.1 Definitions of inequalities

Absolute vs relative and objective vs subjective inequality

There is a long-running debate on whether poverty (i.e. absolute deprivation) or inequality (i.e. relative deprivation) matters most (Held & Kaya, 2007). Extreme poverty – people earning less than US$1.90 per day – is a form of absolute deprivation (World Bank, 2018). Those who argue that inequalities no longer matter focus on absolute deprivation rather than relative deprivation (Suttcliffe, 2007). In a sense, the absolutists are correct: there have been improvements in the human condition. Fewer people now live in poverty, and many enjoy longer lives. However, a closer look shows the shortcomings of an absolute concern with poverty at the expense of inequality.

A poverty perspective neglects contextual information of the country or region. For example, US$10 daily earnings provide a decent living in rural Malawi. Such a wage will not get you far in an average-sized Indian city, and would push you into homelessness in London. Economists often use a contextual 'basket of goods and services' approach to measure inflation. They define poverty as not being able to afford basic resources in a particular country and time. In 2020, smart devices were included and envelopes excluded from the UK basket (ONS, 2020). Whether a person is 'disadvantaged' depends on what counts towards inclusion in their society (Bossert, D'Ambrosio, & Peragine, 2007; Chakravarty & D'Ambrosio, 2006).

The Gini coefficient – a contextual, relative indicator of inequality – measures how much individuals contribute to the country's total income (Piketty, 2013). In a perfectly equal society, everyone contributes the same amount. In the most unequal society, one person earns all income and the rest earn nothing – a Gini value of 1. Alternatively, discussions in the early 21st century concentrated on relative inequality indicators that compare wealth accumulated by the very top with those at the very bottom. The increase in this type of inequalities in many countries is worse than when measured with Gini indicators, especially when comparing the top 1 per cent to the bottom 10 per cent in a country (Milanović, 2016; Piketty, 2013). Whether world-wide inequality has increased depends on the countries included in analyses. Inclusion of certain countries can bias statistical tests of inequality. For example, as soon as China is taken out of statistical tests, inequalities increase globally (Atkinson, 2015; Milanović, 2016).

While poverty and contextual inequality are important, they should be distinguished from systematic inequalities. Systematic inequalities refer to how people from certain backgrounds consistently have more resources than those from different backgrounds. Inequality is not simply determined by looking objectively at who controls resources. Relative Deprivation Theory (RDT) recognises that to mobilise against systematic inequalities, differences have to be seen as problematic (Smith & Pettigrew, 2015). There must be more than an acknowledgement of systematic differences between groups. There should be an affective component, such as feelings of anger and frustration (Walker & Smith, 2002). For structural change to happen, disadvantages need be considered subjectively relevant by individuals and society. Only then might structural disadvantages change through individual or collective action (Janmaat, 2013). To combat inequalities, we need to go beyond describing inequalities to creating public awareness about why they matter.

From money to capital to well-being

These rather abstract discussions about the absolute, relative, objective, and subjective nature of inequalities have been accompanied by fierce debates about which inequalities are most important. Generally, inequalities that were not translatable into employment or wealth opportunities were viewed as less relevant. Even Marxist scholars, who frame capitalism as positioning people in relations of exploitation, still focus on economic aspects (Hodgson, 2014). More recently, the 21st century has seen a growing interest in well-being, through 'objective' factors like life expectancy, and more subjective aspects like happiness (Held & Kaya, 2007). This shift came around the turn of the century, when 'social exclusion' emerged as distinct from 'poverty' in European policy making and academic literature (Chakravarty & D'Ambrosio, 2006; Hunt, 2005). Research on social exclusion successfully challenges purely economistic interpretations of inequality. It includes participation in social and political life in multidimensional measures of objective and subjective well-being (Thompson, 2007). Sadly, there is not enough agreement about factors in or reliable global data on well-being to draw conclusions about whether these inequalities are worsening.

Domains of inequalities

I draw from Pierre Bourdieu to justify my analytic concept of 'domains of inequalities'. Bourdieu (1986) inspires many who theorise inequalities beyond the goods we possess or our economic resources. He makes a distinction between economic and cultural and social capital. There is also symbolic capital, which refers to status and the power to define value derived from various other forms of capital (Lawler, 2011). Bourdieu makes a further specification between objectified capital (i.e. things we own) and embodied capital (i.e. the ways we think and behave) (Hesmondhalgh, 2006). While Bourdieu explicitly set out to counter purely economic definitions of capital, it remained the most important site for inequalities. Economic resources, such as employment, income, wealth, and possessions – the subject of Chapter 3 – allow a person to survive financially and have explicit economic value.

According to international bodies, education – the subject of Chapter 4 – refers to human capital captured in a certificate or a degree. Formal education translates to better employment and greater income. I follow this international guide and refer to education as an economic resource. Education in Bourdieu's framework is included within cultural capital because it is the main site for acquiring the kinds of value systems that shape a person's understanding of what has value. This interpretation of education as a cultural resource has gained traction in countries that have similar elitist education models to Bourdieu's France. However, in contexts with less class-based educational systems, education is foremost seen as an economic resource.

I employ the term 'cultural resources' in a broad anthropological sense derived from Bourdieusian cultural capital. Generally speaking, cultural capital involves the possession of works of art and membership in artistic organisations. Embodied cultural capital is produced by participating in the right hobbies, eating certain foods, and having ideological standpoints that are respected by powerful others (Bourdieu, 2010; Grenfell, 2014). It refers to the embodied and often-unquestioned behaviours, norms, and value systems acquired through socialisation (Maccoby, 2007; Straubhaar, Tufekci, Spence, & Rojas, 2012). These socialisations – akin to Bourdieu's habitus – take different shapes depending on a person's demographic characteristics and the society in which they live. Those with the 'right' kinds of cultural resources – the subject of Chapter 7 – have not only a greater sense of identity and belonging, they also have the power to shape others' ideas about them. I prefer the term 'resources' over 'capital' because resources refers to repositories we can build on to achieve certain outcomes, rather than simply what we possess.

Social capital is more widely referred to in research on inequalities, though its definitions vary. Bourdieu conceptualises social capital as being part of powerful networks. Coleman (1990) connects this idea with general relationships that give us access to novel resources. Drawing on these ideas, I think of political capital – the subject of Chapter 5 – as formal social resources that enable participation in public life and civic organisations. Putnam (2002) thought of formal social capital as membership in organisations and norms of trust in local communities. Separately, I follow the rough distinction Granovetter (1983) makes between bonding and bridging ties. Bonding capital refers to the ties we maintain through emotional and supportive interactions with people like us, often family and friends. Bridging capital refers to ties with diverse types of people who enable access to objectified and embodied resources (Williams, 2006). I consider these informal social resources, our more intimate relationships, in Chapter 6.

As a social psychologist, I am critical of the Bourdieusian scholars' failure to give individual traits a place within a capital model. Accordingly, my concept of 'personal resources' includes personality, intelligence, and problem-solving abilities which can be independent of a person's economic, cultural, or social background (Helsper, 2012). I come back to this in the nature–nurture discussion in the closing section of this chapter.

Capabilities and well-being

The frameworks discussed so far define inequalities as a question of resources. Sen's (1997) capabilities framework, on the other hand, emphasises what people are able to do or have the opportunity to do. This framework is used extensively in the digital inequalities literature related to development, but less so in inequalities research examining within country inequalities in the Global North. Sen (2004, p. 78) refuses to identify specific capabilities because 'pure theory cannot "freeze" a list of capabilities for all societies for all time to come, irrespective of what the citizens come to understand and value'. In Sen's capabilities framework, well-being is measured as which opportunities are important in the societies people live in, and whether they are unequally distributed.

Capabilities research goes a step further than RDT and forces us to grapple with why qualities and assets come to be valued differentially. Whether inequalities are seen as problematic – and if interventions are designed to combat them – depends largely on who is doing the evaluating. Do those in power consider rights, resources, talents, economic, or social opportunities to be worthy (Robeyns, 2005)? Capabilities scholars say that which opportunities matter should not be defined in this top-down way, because the experience of inequalities of opportunity does not necessarily overlap with the economic or material resource inequalities valued by the political and economic establishment. The prioritising of economic, physical, or psychological health risks in the COVID-19 pandemic emphasises that this debate is by no means resolved. The capabilities approach highlights that not all inequalities are about wealth and class, and that non-economic gains should be valued more because they provide paths to greater well-being (Burchardt & Hick, 2018).

Compound disadvantage

What we have, like, and can accomplish is always the product of combined economic, cultural, social, and biological factors – what I refer to as 'compound disadvantage'. While capabilities scholars are hesitant to give a list of opportunities, they concede that the ability to translate available opportunities into advantages depends on a combination of 'conversion factors'. These factors are categorised as personal (e.g. physical and mental abilities), social (e.g. laws, regulations, policies, social norms), and environmental (e.g. infrastructure, geographic isolation, climate) (Robeyns, 2005). Since structural inequalities shape how these factors come together, disadvantage is often compounded. Those who lack access to resources in one domain are likely to have similar problems in another domain too (Walzer, 1985). Nevertheless, someone can have many social resources without economic, cultural, or personal resources. These different domains of resources have different structural and cultural roots and should be tackled in unique ways. Therefore, it is important to conceptualise and study these resources separately without losing sight of how they interact (Fraser, 2007; Helsper, 2012).

Outcomes or opportunities?

Scholars debate the distinction between inequality of resources (Marxist and Bourdieusian approaches) and inequality of opportunities (capabilities approaches). As a framework to organise thinking and ensure no structural inequalities are overlooked, the Bourdieusian organisation of capitals is useful. Simultaneously, I agree with the position of capabilities scholars that what constitutes advantage or disadvantage should move away from detailed lists of resources normatively defined by elites. Nevertheless, a sole emphasis on opportunities is counterproductive when it comes to drawing conclusions about the existence of inequalities, evaluating interventions, and holding policy makers to account. There cannot be equality of opportunity if only particular people consistently transform opportunities and freedoms into more resources and greater well-being. Synthesising these perspectives in this book, I complement a Bourdieusian resource approach with the capabilities approach's emphasis on subjective well-being.

Causes, consequences, and solutions to inequalities

In the following section, I discuss the main approaches to explaining why inequalities persist. The idea that the causes of inequality are natural and inevitable permeates economic

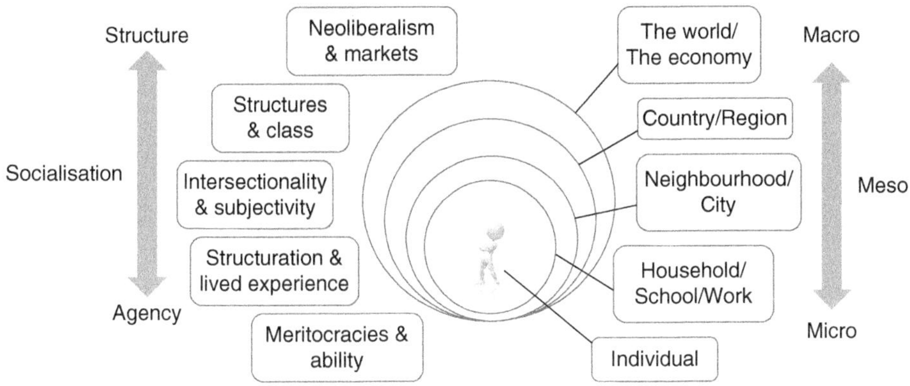

Figure 1.2 Theories (left) and levels of explanation (right) for the existence of inequalities

and sociological thinking, as well as related policy making. I will go through the optimistic neoliberal approaches to inequalities first and follow this up with the pessimistic, structural sociological theories. I make a distinction between explanations that focus on macro, structural components and those that emphasise micro, agentic drivers. I see the reality as being between these extremes: large-scale inequalities are driven by everyday meso-level, socialisation processes (Figure 1.2).

Systems and structures: Economic and capital-based explanations for inequalities

Markets and merit: Neoliberal explanations and solutions to inequality

At the beginning of the 21st century, neoliberalism has a strong presence in inequalities policies and practise. This strand of thought assumes inequalities are caused by 'morally neutral' market principles. In other words, inequalities are inevitable and desirable to innovate and keep society (i.e. the economy) going. Neoliberalism does not completely follow free-market principles; contrary to the richest-take-all principle of capitalism, neoliberalism rewards certain societal roles that require more investment and training. In the ideal neoliberal, meritocratic society, individuals who work and study hardest deserve to be rewarded. While societal change is driven by market demands, the state plays a facilitating role in making sure that the best and brightest flourish so they can contribute to future growth (Stiglitz, 2015).

Discussions around how to adjust to the increased importance of higher education in determining people's life chances in 'knowledge economies' show how a neoliberalist approach plays out. Individuals with access to particular knowledge (e.g. digital skills) have seen their incomes rise quickly. Incomes of differently- and lower-skilled workers, by contrast, have stagnated or declined. Neoliberals see this type of inequality as simply because market changes are driven by a natural evolution from labour to knowledge-based economies. Once the market and state have made sure that infrastructural and financial safeguards are in place, all have equal chances to succeed. Any differences in well-being are justified by a lack of intrinsic motivation and personal drive (Olssen, 2016). This is what neoliberal economists understand by equality of opportunity; they reject the notion of equality of outcomes (Cohen, 2008). Rawlsian (1971) principles permit the existence of inequalities if the more capable benefit in ways that also improve the circumstances of those who are not as fortunate – commonly known as the trickle-down phenomenon. Because neoliberalism justifies the idea of the 'deserving rich' and the 'undeserving poor', the justification of inequalities based on merit and lifting the boats for all is alluring. After all, 'why would anyone, and, in particular, the worst off, prefer equality to an inequality in which everyone is better off?' (Cohen, 1995, p. 162). Consequentially, neoliberal policies focus on absolute poverty reduction and increasing GDP, rather than tackling income inequalities and lowering the Gini coefficient.

The popular Kuznets curve reflects the neoliberal idea that an increase in inequalities is a fundamental part of a country's road to economic development (i.e. initially inequality and GDP go up, until a critical mass is reached, then GDP keeps increasing while inequality goes down). New resources coming into a country will initially be taken up by those who are best positioned to develop them further. The top 1 per cent in a country catches up with citizens in other developed countries, leaving the rest behind. After this initial growth spurt at the top, the rest will start to benefit because the systems the rich help create will produce equalising institutions akin to idealised European welfare states (Kuznets, 1955). However, the evidence is against this theory, just like it is against the so-called trickle-down principle. When analysing cross-national data, research finds nothing close to the inverted U curve proposed by Kuznets (i.e. inequality keeps increasing as GDP goes up) (Piketty, 2013; Stiglitz, 2015).

Capitalism and class: Marxist and Bourdieusian explanations of inequality

The Pareto principle, while different in origin, similarly assumes an economic inevitability of inequality. This principle has two components: 80 per cent of capital (i.e. land) is owned by 20 per cent of the population, and this type of inequality is consistent across time and nations (Hodgson, 2015). The Pareto principle is consistent across a variety of contexts. For example, the most disadvantaged 20 per cent of the population is said to use 80 per cent of social services (Caspi et al., 2016). Scholars critiquing the notion that inequalities are based on neutral market principles or merit concede that the Pareto principle exists. However, instead of concluding that this is justified as part of a natural equilibrium, they come to the opposite conclusion; according to Marxists, the main causes of inequality are wealth, class, and heritage, not market principles and merit (Hodgson, 2015).

There is transmission of resources across generations, through inheritance of material resources, learning environments, and genetic abilities and traits. As a result, inequality increases in the long run (Kanbur & Stiglitz, 2016). Creating a level playing field through, for example, a system of public education, does not suffice because 'aptitudes' and 'intrinsic motivations' are historically shaped and people come into these educational systems with very different resources (Goldthorpe, 1996). Bourdieu and Bourdieusian scholars are similarly wary of the emphasis on education or training as the great equaliser. They instead see education as the site for cultural 'indoctrination' into a class system, feeding false consciousness, and leading to reproductions of class inequalities (Bourdieu, 1990; Halsey, Heath, & Ridge, 1980). Formal education is also not the only site of socialisation into accepting inequalities. Elites get to set the agenda and determine which behaviours, types of knowledge, and skills get rewarded in spheres such as policy, regulation, and media discourse. The well-off gain more wealth to invest and more symbolic power to determine what and who is of value (Pogge, 2007). For these reasons, as inequalities increase, it becomes ever more difficult to reverse the rich-get-richer (or 'Matthew') effect.

To understand how material and symbolic power becomes entrenched, and how to dislodge it, we need to locate where it gets reproduced. Bourdieu emphasises that power/class structures inhibit turning opportunities into the achievement of outcomes. This inhibition happens through the formation of habitus – the internalisation of behaviours practised, and norms and values held, within a certain field (Grenfell, 2014). Bourdieu (1990) and associated scholars nebulously describe fields as the contexts in which individuals live and the positions they attain. This vagueness means that nearly anything – a school, industry, or country – can be a field. I do not find the Bourdieusian concept of the field helpful, because presence or participation in a field does not automatically translate into shared values and norms. Nor is the same symbolic capital assigned to all individuals in a particular field (Grenfell, 2014). Another problem with capitals theorisation is its emphasis on class. Private sites of reproduction, such as intimate relationships at home, are overlooked. I prefer to take domains of resources as a starting point for studying how inequalities are reproduced in everyday contexts and overturned in others.

This brings me to a final critique of Bourdieusian class-based explanations of inequalities. While expressions of class change, the emphasis is on how the underlying structures are reified and status is passed on to subsequent generations (Bourdieu, 2010; Gorski, 2016). This inevitable reproduction of inequalities through class-based inequality has led to Bourdieu being labelled a 'sociologist of inertia' (Friedman & Savage, 2019). Taking a compound approach that sees inequalities as rooted in a combination of factors, and not just as expressions of class, creates room for change. Such an approach believes people might be resource-rich in some domains, and not privileged in other domains. Viewing inequalities through a combined approach also allows for changes in non-class-based inequalities to drive class-based inequalities. For example, changes in gender inequalities have been shown to cause changes in broader economic class-based inequalities, rather than being the result of them (Walby, 2007).

Capabilities and agency: Opportunity-based explanations for inequality

Capabilities researchers explicitly put non-class-based inequalities centre stage. They emphasise how resource and 'existential' inequalities (i.e. well-being) are produced from the bottom up (Therborne, 2013). In capabilities research, it is common to see studies of 'horizontal' inequalities between people living together, rather than the 'vertical' inequalities between countries or upper- and lower-class individuals familiar to most inequalities research (Burchardt & Hick, 2018). Capabilities research adopts a less macro sociological view, regarding everyday environments where people live as providing opportunities for agency and the expression of preferences (Zimmermann, 2006). Solutions to inequalities, therefore, need to be sought through making opportunities available, rather than merely providing resources to establish equality of outcome.

Outcomes-based approaches risk creating top-down, paternalising, elitist ideas of what people should have. In response, capability scholars suggest that governance and economic systems should provide open structures that allow people to flourish in their local contexts, rather than push people to take up things that elites consider valuable. Ironically, this self-determination approach aligns with the neoliberal agendas discussed earlier. Both risk 'blaming the victim'. Either through choice or lack of merit, 'the poor's own attitudes and values are identified as the source of their poverty in a process of blaming them for their own condition' (Byrne, 2005, p. 25). By focusing on the choices people have in everyday living situations, the capabilities model also risks downplaying broader power relations and structural inequalities (Navarro, 2000). To bring structural factors back into how choices are determined, Nussbaum (2000) coins the idea of 'adaptive preferences'. This is close to Marx's idea of 'false consciousness', which postulates that people fail to recognise inequality because of public discourses that naturalise and legitimise its existence (Sen, 2002). It is also close to Bourdieu's idea of 'habitus achieved', where people are normalised into an unequal status through socialisation into a class system. Nevertheless, adaptive preferences are not shaped by elites through public discourse and education, but arise from what makes sense in the more subtle power struggles of everyday life.

The question becomes: what is to be done if all in a society accept that people from particular backgrounds are systematically paid less, discriminated against, socially isolated, or have lower levels of personal well-being? A capabilities approach might suggest that, given equality of opportunity, these are their choices/preferences and outsiders should not meddle in this society. This is where an opportunities or capabilities solution leads to complacency in policy making. As long as services and education are provided for people, then inequality is not considered an issue, even if it puts particular groups in harms way. I agree with capabilities scholars when they stipulate that we should consider the everyday context to understand which inequalities are important. Yet, when designing policies to combat inequalities and to hold stakeholders to account, we need to recognise inequalities in outcomes, and not just inequalities in opportunities (Milanović, 2016). To be clear, this does not mean forgetting about agency and reverting back purely to tackling elitist structures.

Structure and agency: Structuration explanations for inequality

Unlike capital and capabilities approaches, structuration is rarely used in socio-digital inequalities research. Structuration, more commonly found in qualitative research, is a process-based theory used to understand how inequalities might change through agency established within structural constraints (Parker, 2000; Stones, 2005). Structuration offers a way to engage with one of the most contentious questions in social science: whether human behaviour and thought is shaped primarily by structures (systemic approaches) or driven by individual agency (constructionist approaches). Two fundamental concepts stand at the heart of the debate. 'Structures' are the general economic, political, cultural, or social principles that organise societies and human collectives, while 'agency' consists of an individual's voluntary actions, resistances, and choices. To reconcile these ideas, structuration theory gives equal power to structure and agency. Unlike Bourdieusian scholars' emphasis on structure or capabilities scholars' concern with agency, structuration theory posits that agents have social structures within them. Structures consist of and are the product of practices of agents (Giddens, 1990). If we replace structure with systematic inequalities, historic inequalities are simultaneously the drivers of the actions and thoughts of individuals, and the outcomes of these actions.

Structuration theory has been accused of being both overly agentic or overly deterministic. The complication is that it tries to take a position between economic and political determinism which has as its only logical consequence the reproduction of inequalities and individualism, which leads to 'victim blaming' if inequalities continue to exist (Giddens, 1990). I believe, however, that Giddens' argument is more refined. Agents rely on their knowledge of structures either to conform to what is expected of them, or to resist them (Stones, 2005). This means that inequalities only continue to exist if enough people continue to behave in ways that support them. Counter to the 'victim-blaming' critique, structuration is not simply another way to tell people they just need to wise up and activate their rebellious selves. Structures restrict the actions of individuals because of how they shape their knowledge and capabilities. More than that, these are only activated and used when a situation arises in which they must be used. That is, a situation needs to arise where a person is made aware of these structures for them to be activated, driving them to exercise agency.

Giddens' structuration theory is a broad, rather abstract theory that does not define how these processes happen and for whom (Gregson, 1987). In this sense, his version of structuration theory is contextless; it does not explain why particular practices and norms exist for specific groups or how they can or might be challenged (Archer, 2010; Parker, 2000). Archer (2010) has argued that the lack of separation between structure and agency is theoretically valid but empirically problematic. This conflation does not allow us to understand when people are able to change the system and when they are not. In other words, it becomes difficult to study the historical and future developments of inequalities, unless we consider them part of sequential processes. Structure either predates agency, or agents interacting with these structures leads to reshaped structures. Others have said that conflating agency and structure ignores how not all agents or structures are the same. That is, the ability to take independent and voluntary decisions to either go with the flow or resist the system is not equally distributed. Some structures are more easily disrupted than others (Mouzelis, 1989).

What I will take forward in this book from structuration is the idea that everyday life is where structure and agency come together to shape action, inaction, opportunities, and constraints (Parker, 2000). I concur that absolute objectivism about structures and subjectivism about agents need to be avoided. What I like about structuration theory is that it is imbued with an optimist realism: a structure is not only a constraint but something that helps us to create a positive, collective sense of self. In this way, structure interacts with agentic action, making societal change possible (Hays, 1994). In the next section, I extend this line of thought by explaining how our lack of understanding of who can engender change might be helped by a stronger incorporation of intersectionality and relative deprivation theories.

Socialisation and context: Intersectional explanations and solutions to inequality

The idea of socialisation has come up in different guises in this book. It refers to people internalising the broader norms and values of the societies they live in through learning at home, school, work, and the media. Socialisation makes sure that individuals are 'socially integrated' (Parker, 2000). Capitals, capabilities, and structuration theories all assume that inequality continues to exist because we internalise and justify ideas about inequalities. The result is that we can feel better about how we fit into society, even if they disadvantage us personally. They also suppose that we can overcome inequalities by becoming conscious of these systematic inequalities, reflecting on them, and generating change (Risman, 2004). To study how socialisation might lead individuals to 'disadvantage' themselves does not mean denying that there are structures. Rather, socialisation research acknowledges that systematic power imbalances influence people's sense of self in ways that are not always rational, logical, or obvious (England, 2016).

Socialisation

In empirical research and practical interventions around inequalities, socialisation tends to be associated with understanding or changing how and what people learn about the characteristics of different socio-cultural and socio-demographic groups and how they should behave and think. For example, gendered socialisation refers to how people internalise ideas about what is appropriate for men and for women. Socialisation around sexual norms and behaviours refers to people picking up not only what 'normal' sexual behaviours and feelings are (e.g. heteronormativity), even as they might form ideas about what non-normative individuals and behaviours are like.

Marxist scholars emphasise political and economic structures as forming ideas about who deserves wealth, while Bourdieusian theorists see formal educational institutions as the main site for socialisation. Social psychologists, feminist, and communication scholars, on the other hand, take different routes to de-emphasise political and economic public structures as influencers. Social psychologists emphasise informal social relations, while feminist and communications scholars are concerned with representational aspects of cultural reproduction. Fraser (2007), in her cultural feminist critique of capabilities theorists that emphasises national politics and regulations, claims that we must go beyond thinking about states and traditional politics as the main structures that organise thoughts. The main site of power is in 'frame setting, denying voice to those who may be harmed in the process' (Fraser, 2007, p. 27). This is achieved through the implicit valuing of certain voices and recognising certain ideas and interests and not others, for example, in the mainstream media. This silencing can take place beyond political or economic lines, such as around gender and sexuality.

Intersectionality

Just as feminism was a reaction against gender differences being ignored in the experience of class, intersectionality was a reaction to feminist studies ignoring ethnicity, sexuality, and physicality as modifiers of gender (Clarke & McCall, 2013; Crenshaw, 1991). Black feminists foregrounded that inequalities experienced by black women were not comparable to 'simple' sexism or racism. The combination of race and gender needed to be understood as more than simply additive. They pointed out that multiple systems of oppression interact to reproduce inequalities in ways that could not be understood separately (Crenshaw, 1991; Robinson, Z.F., 2018; Walby, 2011). Gender, ethnicity, and other aspects of identity function in ways that are specific to the regulatory, legal, and cultural contexts in which the person lives so that no simple conclusions can be drawn about gender nor ethnic nor national inequalities.

In line with Collins (2015), intersectionality is approached here as the recognition that an interplay exists between physical limitations and internalisation of specific identities, the reactions of individuals within people's everyday life contexts to different aspects of one's identity, and how structures constrain possibilities for equality. Intersectionality forces us to think about gradations and shades of inequality or injustice, rather than absolute differences. It is anti-categorical, implying that inequality should always be studied at the intersection of different types of disadvantage. One cannot separate out the impact of economic, social, cultural, or personal disadvantages. Accordingly, we need to be conscious of how one type of disadvantage compounds and changes another type of disadvantage (Walby, 2011). This implies studying how disadvantage accumulates and concentrates over generations so that inequalities become entrenched over time in very particular communities or groups of individuals and how certain inequalities are more likely to change in a positive direction.

Several critiques have been levied against intersectional theories of socialisation and identity construction. The most important one is that it risks becoming a theory of the individual. Since everyone's life is seen as uniquely shaped by a combination of factors, structural inequalities based on particularly strong hierarchies might be overlooked. If all inequalities are conflated into a particular intersectional inequality for an individual, how one has more weight than the others might be ignored (Clarke & McCall, 2013). The danger here is relativism; if all inequalities matter equally and cumulatively, no one inequality really deserves attention. If inequalities are understood through detailed descriptions of specific intersections of ethnicity, gender, class, and ability, intersectionality reintroduces the problem of stasis – things are the way they are because of who someone is, without room for structural change. It seems the only way out of this is by rejecting the existence of dominant structures and categories. Walby (2011) suggests that this would be throwing the baby out with the bathwater, and that it is more useful to take complexity theory as a starting point. This approach assumes that it is possible to study one system of inequality (e.g. gender) separately and in conjunction with other systems of inequality (e.g. ethnicity, national politics) since they intersect with different effects. Complexity theory contextualises processes of inequalities, while still highlighting which phenomena are explained collectively by specific characteristics. In this book, I carry this idea forward to understand socio-digital inequalities by examining the universal and unique, using empirical evidence from different countries and people with different backgrounds.

Nature and nurture: Ecological explanations for inequalities

From an inequalities perspective, much of the above research remains descriptive of states that societies are in, rather than focusing on the processes that lead people to change themselves and alter unjust dynamics. These theories are often too macro, describing systems rather than people in everyday settings and networks that enable them to change power dynamics. They do not theorise the conditions that amplify individual or collective agency and potentially lead to social change. Everything seems set against changing structures and systematic inequalities, since our choices are internally constrained by the systems we live in and grow up with. Unless there is some horrific event that completely disrupts the status quo, inequalities can remain firmly in place.

There is some truth to this. Wars and pandemics, especially those that cross borders, have changed wealth distribution, and political and cultural systems. But no one would argue that the world we live in today is exactly the same as the world we lived in 20 years ago, even in relatively peaceful countries. Wealth inequalities increased in Europe and the US, even as their gender inequalities diminished and headway was made on ethnic inequalities. There is still much to do in these areas, and forces are at work to counter these improvements, but it is hard to deny that the opportunities I have had are quite different from those of my mother. She grew up in a small village in the Catholic south of the Netherlands. My mother had to go to Sunday school and could not get a place in day care for me because they did not expect her to finish university. She had to fight many battles to get her medical degree, none of which I experienced studying media psychology. My mother was too busy studying and taking care of a young child – acts of defiance in their own right – to be on the barricades for women's rights. However, she benefitted from the structural changes instigated by the feminist movement and changes in regulation, as I did many years later. So where did these feminists get their agency?

Nature: Biological and psychological drivers

Ironically, considering the supposed inevitability of the reproduction of inequalities, the possibility of change often leads researchers and policy makers back to individual merit. Merit is concerned with individual characteristics that allow people to persevere against the odds. We like the idea of David versus Goliath, of individual heroes who take risks and lead others to follow them even if it means facing violence. What forges this kind of counter status quo agency is not made clear in the theoretical or empirical frameworks I have already discussed.

How does a Muslim Kashmiri from rural India overcome a severe lack of opportunity? Why did someone like Martin Luther King stand up and lead change in a racist, segregated society? What was it about my mother that made her medical director of a regional diagnostic centre in the Netherlands? The responses to these questions quickly run into the nature versus nurture debate, the most controversial debate in social and natural sciences.

Those on the nature side argue that innate intelligence, particular types of personality, and physical and psychological strength allow people to overcome disadvantage. Numerous measurement instruments have been designed to measure these characteristics. IQ and personality tests are particularly popular with policy makers and industry actors. These tests are all assumed to measure genetically innate and stable individual characteristics. Some have argued that as societies become more equal in a structural sense, new inequalities based on these physical characteristics start to emerge because they turn out not to be equally distributed (Vuyk, 2017). This leads to the emergence of an elite intelligentsia that rules over those not as fortunate to be born with these characteristics. Over time, 'social sorting' has taken place where those with innate characteristics mate with those who have the same characteristics, creating upper- and underclasses through this homogeneity (Esping-Andersen, 2007).

From this perspective, because the 'underclasses' lack advantageous characteristics (e.g. IQ), they are less likely with each generation to be able to get out of this situation. When inequality was based on wealth, this was considered unjust or not deserved. Once societies figured out how to provide equal opportunities, any resulting inequalities based on innate differences in these traits should be considered just. That inequalities based on natural ability (e.g. intelligence, personality, physical strength) are problematic can be illustrated by the following example in a hypothetical equal opportunity knowledge-based society. Let's assume that to govern one should have a certain level of intelligence, an innate characteristic that you can do nothing about. In equal societies, people with high levels of intelligence will be able to go to university and end up making up 80 per cent of the government in a country where only 20 per cent of the people have this level of intelligence. The resulting differences in income, wealth, health, and power to define political issues would then be considered just. Those that are in power deserve to be there because they have what is needed to do the job. However, if you are not within the elite 20 per cent, that is just bad luck – the result of being dealt a weak hand.

This literature is heavily contested. The evidence that any of these factors are innate is debunked by the significant impacts of environmental factors. There is also sufficient indication that these 'traits' are not stable for individuals over time and across different situations (Fajkowska & Kreitler, 2018; Suzuki & Aronson, 2005). Furthermore, the tests that measure 'innate characteristics', such as IQ, are designed within a system that values the types of knowledge and skills prevalent among those who are successful. It is logical that those who do well on these measures at an early age go further within the systems that reward these types of knowledge or skills, but this does not mean that these traits are innate. It is impossible to evaluate these skills independently from the systems they are constructed in because we cannot check if the exact same person with identical characteristics growing up in different societies has different outcomes.

This does not mean that inequalities researchers should stop measuring biological and behavioural characteristics, because they can be useful to incorporate into the frameworks discussed earlier. Nevertheless, we should steer away of turning them into a justification of inequalities and turn towards seeing how they interact with the circumstances in which a person finds themselves. This will allow us to understand why such characteristics might be concentrated in certain groups and why certain individuals are able to create change against the odds.

Nurture: Ecological change and collective action

Social identity-based approaches provide ways to think about how supposedly innate traits change with circumstances. They teach us that how we perceive the world as unequal and act upon it depends on how we see ourselves. Further, how we see ourselves is shaped by particular, changing environments. As a result, identity and the resulting thoughts and actions that drive it are not fixed (Ellemers, Spears, & Doosje, 2002). For example, when I am teaching, it is the 'Professor' aspect of my identity that is most prominent. On panels about the future of digital societies, I am more aware that I am a woman because often all of the others are men. During field work, my university degree and foreign nationality are at the forefront. These different contexts shift attention to different aspects of my identity.

Ecological theory, a term coined by Bronfenbrenner (1979), emphasises our relationships and social context. Gibson (2015) and Barker (1968) emphasised that physical environments give us information about how to behave, shaping what we see as possibilities of behaviour (Heft, 2005; Kaminski, 1989). Such ecological theories help us to understand why we think and behave differently when we are with friends in a restaurant than with colleagues at work. Ecologies in these frameworks refer to both human, social and physical, and material environments. They bring together immediate micro, individual contexts with more macro, societal contexts by studying how agency and structure clash within these everyday interactions.

Ecological social psychologists explicitly study change, rather than the state a society is in. Howarth and his colleagues describe this perspective as 'both a focus on top-down and bottom-up planned change, as well as unplanned, emergent change' (Howarth et al., 2013, p. 375). These theories, and community interventions based on them, enable us to see how discrimination and stereotypes are formed, enacted, and influence individuals' behaviours in everyday life.

At the beginning of this chapter, I mentioned that Relative Deprivation Theory (RDT) suggests that we only undertake action to change an unequal situation if we perceive that unequal distribution exists and is unjust (Walker & Smith, 2002). RDT posits that whether we consider ourselves to be deprived is to a certain degree independent of our objective situation. Instead, it depends on our comparisons with what relevant others feel, have, and do. These relevant comparators are called referents, and make RDT a subjective, relative, and ecological approach to understanding change in inequalities from the bottom up. Besides the similarity of the comparator, environmental clues, such as the accessibility of resources or opportunities, inform our belief that we can change a situation. The relevance of the comparator and the ability of the person to undertake the required action will lead an individual to instigate personal change. For this to lead to more structural, systematic rather than personal change, one more step is required: the person has to realise that this unequal distribution in resources is unjust. This is the realisation that people who share an identity are systematically worse off than others who are not part of this group. This can lead to collective organisation, either by joining an existing movement or by starting one to find routes for systematic change. Only when the last step of collective consciousness or solidarity occurs will systematic change occur.

One of the problems is that structural contexts are embedded in everyday lives. The most comfortable and easy route is for people to go with the status quo (Cote & Levine, 2002). This means that it is easier to assume the referent object or person is not relevant and that there is not much that you can do. For higher status members of disadvantaged groups, this effect can work in interesting ways that are counterintuitive. Often elites see their success as due to their unique personal merits. In turn, they judge people who are like them, assuming they are (collectively) lazy or incompetent, which solidifies the lower standing of the group (Cote & Levine, 2002). For example, I might believe that if I achieve something or acquire a certain skill it is because I am intelligent and have a good work ethic. However, when another woman does not achieve the same, I may think it is because women in general are not smart or motivated enough. This 'meritocratic righteousness' is what Sandel (2020) blamed for a lack of solidarity with those who have less, leading to a turn away from collective action to combat inequalities.

In summary, ecological approaches propose that circumstances must come together to pave the way for individuals to feel that they have the agency to enact systematic change. Most importantly, these theories reinforce that real change is always collective. There needs to be a groundswell of individuals that agents can connect and feel close to, and a shared realisation that an inequality is relevant and unjust. Combatting inequalities requires a collective consciousness arising from individual changes in perspectives around the barriers that groups of people encounter in achieving beneficial outcomes, instigated through changes in people's everyday environments and networks.

The complexity of defining and explaining the causes and consequences of inequalities

I started this chapter with definitions and explanations for traditional inequalities because there is a general disconnect between these and the theories used to explain digital inequalities. Even theorists that are popular, such as Bourdieu, are often used in descriptive ways in digital inequalities research without a full grasp of the intricacies of these theories and their longstanding debates. Of course, it is impossible to summarise a field of such breadth and complexity in one chapter. Therefore, I restricted myself to the concepts and lessons learned from traditional inequalities literature that I will be relying on in the rest of this book. I propose that we understand inequalities to be:

- Compound and intersectional, with objective, economic, functional, subjective, social, and well-being dimensions.
- Systematic and structural, rather than as differences based on individual preferences or merit.
- Evaluated in terms of inequalities in outcomes rather than merely on the basis of inequalities in opportunities.
- Resisted only when there is a collective consciousness that inequalities are unjust.

Inequalities are increasingly seen as multiplex and compound rather than purely economic or based on a single identity category, such as gender. This broad conceptualisation of inequalities is inspired by the Bourdieusian strand of inequalities theory. Although it retains a Marxist concern with class as the cause of all sorrow, this approach conceptualises other aspects of capital based on social relations and cultural status. I use this framework and intersectionality to steer my conceptualisation of domains as economic, social, and cultural resources. To tackle the issue of a relative under-conceptualisation of agency, I add a fourth personal domain. This personal dimension is inspired by the capabilities and social-psychological approaches, which take a more subjective, bottom-up approach, prioritising well-being over material inequalities. The personal domain includes individual interests, skills, and health, which I relate to broader socio-demographic characteristics. I see these as distinguishing individuals but shaped by ecologies rather than genetics. These four domains comprise the conceptualisation of traditional inequalities in the Corresponding Fields framework that structures this book (see the Introduction and Chapter 2).

I am going to assume that nobody reading this book needs to be convinced that inequalities are problematic for society. Nevertheless, this is a view that is not shared by all. For example, neoliberal frameworks consider inequalities as justified because those who have risen to the top deserve to benefit from their hard work and abilities. There is enough evidence to conclude that this type of meritocracy does not exist, since inequalities have been replicated and are often more rooted in inherited structural advantages than effort and intelligence.

Thus, traditional inequalities are not about differences between individuals, but rather structural, systematic differences between groups of people. In the literature and policy making, recognising this distinction means shifting from a focus on absolute measures (alleviating poverty) to tackling relative differences (between top and bottom income earners, lowering Gini). To recognise the structural disadvantage of groups of people, we need to understand the causes and consequences of inequalities in separate domains. However, in everyday life people have multiple identities and live in multiple contexts. Therefore, we need to explore how the co-occurrence of different disadvantages leads to new social dynamics that are invisible when we focus on one isolated disadvantage. Therefore, I emphasised intersectional and ecological approaches that account for how people experience inequalities in everyday life, and how concurrent inequalities reinforce each other.

Solutions to overcome inequalities by changing economic or cultural systems cannot be sought at the structural, macro level. Nor can they be sought purely at the micro level in improving disadvantaged individuals' ability or opportunities. The meso level – the everyday social, physical, and technical environments in which people live their lives – must be incorporated into our explanations of inequalities and the policies and interventions we design. It is these subjective, everyday experiences and interpretations of inequalities that will move people to want to change societies, not their absolute existence.

As described in the next chapter, I will highlight the systemic nature of socio-digital inequalities and the importance of understanding who is disadvantaged in ways specific to where they come from and who they are. Following the Corresponding Fields model, the other chapters analyse the relationships between individual characteristics such as wealth, education, age, gender, and ethnicity with related types of digital inequalities. While everyday experiences of individuals with varying forms of disadvantage are used to illustrate how inequalities play out in digital societies, the solutions and policies to tackle these will have to be collective and the responsibility carried by society at large, not just by those who were unlucky enough to be born on the disadvantaged end of the scale.

CHAPTER 2

DIGITAL WORLD: FROM DIVIDES TO SOCIO-DIGITAL INEQUALITIES

> 'We are on the extreme promontory of the centuries! What is the use of looking behind at the moment when we must open the mysterious shutters of the impossible? Time and Space died yesterday.'
>
> The Futurist Manifesto (Marinetti, 1909)

While researchers and practitioners discussed in the last chapter were busy developing more nuanced and comprehensive theories of inequalities, the world changed. The internet, previously the realm of the military and scientists, became a public resource. The invention of browsers and interactive social media piqued the interest of users beyond geeky early adopters in the 21st century. Echoing Rogers' (1995) diffusion of innovation theory, many policy and academic briefs assumed an unescapable trajectory towards the uptake of these networked technologies. This optimism was driven by the idea that technology can open 'the mysterious shutters of the impossible' described in 'The Futurist Manifesto' (Marinetti, 1909). Accordingly, increased uptake of ICTs was thought to inevitably lead to positive outcomes for individuals and society.

These ideas – at the heart of imagining a digital future – are problematic. They overlook how digital inequalities link to historical social inequalities. Accordingly, in this chapter I will ask critical questions about the causes and consequences of digital inequalities. My critique touches on the history of definitions and theorisation, and questions how digital inequalities have been studied and tackled so far. This chapter connects with this book's concern with who benefits and who is disadvantaged by the increased digitisation of society. In it, I suggest we need not only to define and explain digital inclusion, but also to care about socio-digital inequalities.

I use the term 'socio-digital inequalities' to refer to the systematic differences in the ability and opportunity for people to beneficially use (or decide not to use) ICTs, while avoiding negative outcomes of digital engagement now and in the future. My definition critiques the simplistic notion that broad and frequent use indicates digital inclusion. This idea ignores more negative aspects of engagement, and the structural and societal factors that constrain beneficial outcomes. This is why I use the term 'socio-digital inequalities' instead of digital divides or inequalities. I am concerned with inequalities of outcomes in digital societies, not solely digital connection or engagement.

At the heart of this chapter is the question: What are socio-digital inequalities and why should we care about them?

To address these questions, this chapter discusses theoretical developments to understanding socio-digital inequalities over the last decade. This scholarship takes the perspective of the individual as embedded in social and societal structures. Here, I draw parallels with the history of theorisation of broader inequalities presented in Chapter 1, and critique previous writings on digital inequalities. Crucially, I contend that 'the distinction between the social and technical is not useful' (Couldry, Fotopoulou, & Dickens, 2016, p. 133). To connect digital and traditional inequalities literatures requires theorising and studying everyday tensions between the social and the digital.

Corresponding fields

In 2012, I wrote a paper on what I called Corresponding Fields (CF) – the links between social and digital exclusion (Helsper, 2012). When I wrote that paper, the digital inequalities literature under-theorised how amplification of inequalities took place in different areas of social and economic life. Scholars were aware of differences in engagement with ICTs, but did not theorise why these differences might change, or how to tackle systematic socio-digital inequalities. Many still take a descriptive Bourdieusian, rather than action-oriented, approach to differences between socio-demographic groups. They describe digital differences across historically-disadvantaged groups. Often, they argue that the digital is bound to replicate existing class, gender, and ethnic inequalities. Others take a more neoliberal approach on improving individual access and skills, seeking to create more prolific consumer-citizens. This approach focuses on the labour market without questioning the broader structural processes that reproduce inequalities. In response, this chapter builds on my earlier theorising by further integrating different disciplinary approaches to digital inequalities.

There remains significant confusion about the causes and consequences of social and digital inequalities. This disconnect reflects a split between techno-determinist and socio-constructivist paradigms in studies of technology and society. In response, in this chapter I continue to develop my CF model, which considers the digital and social as part of a continuous cycle of mutual influence. In many societies and peoples' lives, the online and the offline are intimately interwoven. Giving an answer to what comes first – social or technological change – becomes an unanswerable 'chicken and egg' dilemma. Instead, I adopt a realist-optimist view of how ICT-based interventions bring about social change. Realistically, the way ICTs are designed, acquired, and used is embedded in existing power structures and dynamics that privilege the advantaged over the disadvantaged. Optimistically, I believe that carefully-designed ICT-based interventions at multiple levels, implemented through policy and practice, can break this vicious cycle of reinforcement. But to discover how this is possible – and not to treat inequality as a simple matter of connection or engagement – we must first understand the theoretical history of digital inequalities.

What are digital inequalities?

Conceptualising digital inequalities has followed a similar trajectory to social inequalities from simple definitions to complex compound definitions. Many publications in the field still start by stating that the digital inequalities debate has moved from digital divides to gradations of exclusion as expressed in skills, motivation, engagements, and participation levels. In this chapter, I follow this trajectory by discussing first- (access), second- (skills and use), and third-level (outcomes) digital divides. A fuller discussion of these is necessary because an understanding of specific types and levels of inequalities remains narrow. The detailed conceptualisations that follow make clear that even those things that seem quite straightforward to define, such as access, are difficult to disentangle in everyday life. This complexity of all aspects of digital inequality demands care to be taken when they are operationalised for research or tackled through interventions. Although divide terminology is problematic, I adopt it for headings due to its common use, but talk about inclusion and inequalities (instead of simply 'divides') in each section.

Access and infrastructure inequalities: First-level divides

Definitions of digital inequalities started by describing differences between people who did and did not have access to desktop computers and the internet. Van Dijk (2020) uses 'material access' to describe this 'first-level' digital divide. High costs were thought to put devices and connectivity out of reach for those who were less financially well-off. At a more macro level, poor digital infrastructure in lower-income neighbourhoods and rural areas was another cause of digital exclusion. The discourse and the issues around digital inequalities during this period resonate with traditional inequalities literature's emphasis on wealth and income as the most important aspect of inequalities. Just as GDP remains the cornerstone of development indicators, internet adoption and infrastructure speeds dominate most digital agendas (Helsper, 2018; Hilbert, 2016).

Yet, the material aspect of digital divides demands a closer look, because it has been a difficult concept to define. Those who access the internet are included, while others are excluded. Nevertheless, what 'access' means and how it should be measured has evolved as the internet and other ICTs have advanced. In the second decade of the 21st century, high-speed broadband, mobile connections, and embedded technologies are necessary to consider for digital inclusion. Even these new definitions are continuously subject to updates. For example, the UK changed its definition of broadband under the Universal Service Obligation to 10Mb/s in their 2017 Digital Economy Act after it became clear that 2MB/s was not sufficient for the most common types of engagement (UK Government, 2017b). Mobile access is moving to 5G connections, Artificial Intelligence (AI) and the Internet of Things (IoT) are replacing access through devices such as PCs or phones.

Continuously redefining digital inclusion with every technological advance is not theoretically or empirically useful. Accordingly, I define access-based digital inclusion as high-quality, ubiquitous, and autonomous use of common ICTs. High speed and ubiquity are theoretically clear and measurable aspects of access. Autonomy refers to access that offers freedom to use ICTs without interruption or interference (Van Deursen & Helsper, 2015), such that the breaking or updating of a device does not necessarily lead to discontinued use. This allows playful use and learning through trial and error. However, to properly understand digital inclusion as defined earlier in this chapter, we need to go beyond use and non-use of devices or platforms and look at what people actually do with them.

Skills and use inequalities: Second-level divides

In research and policy around digital inequalities, we have to go beyond access to understand why certain people are less engaged with ICTs. Differences in use continue to exist in places where differences in access are small (DiMaggio, Hargittai, Celeste, & Shafer, 2004; Van Deursen & Van Dijk, 2015). As White (2016, p. 2) notes, 'the digital world has brought many opportunities for improved wellbeing through more personalised services, cheaper goods and products, more choice, wider connections with others and radically improved access to knowledge and communication'. However, if this potential only materialises for some, access is not the solution to digital inequalities. Early in digital inequalities research, just like in social inequalities literature, persistent inequalities in use prompted a broadening of scope. Social inequalities literature looked beyond economic approaches and formulated concepts that included human, political, and social capital and use of services (e.g. Sen, 1997) to explain autonomy and participation. The equivalent in the digital inequalities literature is the gradations of inclusion approach by Warschauer (2003) and Van Dijk (2020). Their more nuanced understanding of digital exclusion as consisting of levels and types, positioned against the more absolutist language of digital divides popular at the time, only found traction in policy and practice at the beginning of the 2000s. It reflected the growing understanding that people were (dis)engaged to various degrees rather than connected or disconnected.

Skills and literacy

Most digital inequalities scholars at the beginning of the 21st century focused on defining concepts such as digital skills and literacy. They generally agree that digital skills include technical know-how, and the extensive use of applications and platforms is seen as an indicator of skilled use (Zillien & Hargittai, 2009). Others refer to literacy instead of skills.

They see digital literacy as the ability to create high-quality content, critically evaluate the trustworthiness and accuracy of content, and to understand commercial, political, and social interests of content producers (Buckingham, 2005; Jenkins & Carpentier, 2013). Theoretically, it is important to disaggregate different skills because operational, information processing, social, and creative skills have different predictive capabilities for different uses of ICTs (Van Deursen, Helsper, Eynon, & Van Dijk, 2017). In addition, while digital skills are often studied on their own, they are now seen as key parts of so-called 21st-century skills, such as problem-solving and collaboration skills (Van Laar, Van Deursen, Van Dijk, & de Haan, 2017).

Digital literacy is a broad, multidimensional, and dynamic concept. In an ever-changing world that is increasingly digital, the continuous upgrading of our skills becomes necessary. To stay 'equally included' we need to commit to lifelong learning that allows us to undertake (or reject) the next new activity in ways that benefit us. Important discussions are taking place around which skills allow us to engage with a broad range of activities relevant to our current everyday lives. To keep up with technological advances, we should also be concerned with transferrable skills that allow us to adapt to new contexts. This time period is similar to the era when decisions were made around which subjects should go into core or nationally integrated school curricula in the mid-20th century (Beane, 1997; Short, 1986).

Content: Engagement and interests

Warschauer (2003) and Van Dijk (2020) conceptualise different gradations of engagement with technologies. From this theorisation follows that access and skills alone are insufficient to understand how people are digitally connected (Livingstone & Helsper, 2010; Van Deursen & Van Dijk, 2014). Therefore, this book is organised along the five engagement types that have received the bulk of academic, policy, commercial, and third sector attention: economic, educational, political/civic, social, and creative/leisure uses (Blank & Groselj, 2014; Van Deursen & Van Dijk, 2014).

Some consider engagement of the first three types to be more beneficial because they offer users chances and resources in career, work, education, and societal advancement, unlike the latter two, which are perceived as merely consumptive or entertaining (Arora, 2012). Nevertheless, mirroring the debates around conceptualisations of traditional inequalities, it might be impossible to give an upfront definition of the activities that constitute inclusion. Some argue that the criterion for inclusion should be people's own estimates of what it means to be included. For example, whether they are satisfied with the activities that they undertake online, or feel that a technology is useful in relation to what they need (Selwyn, 2006). Straubhaar et al. (2012) use the term 'techno-dispositions' to describe what use we think ICTs (should) have. Techno-dispositions are shaped by our histories and experiences, meaning digital engagement and motivations or attitudes are difficult to separate. They shape our decisions about getting access, confidence in using technologies, and our ideas about what to use ICTs for. This conflation means that a lack of engagement within certain activity domains might be perceived as unproblematic. For example, someone can be disengaged from social activities online that others consider beneficial for civic engagement, but not perceive this as a problem because they do not see the point of engaging in this way. Further, subjective evaluations of how technology 'should' be used are unequally distributed. Those in already-privileged positions often 'choose' to undertake activities that strengthen their position of dominance. Subjective understandings of use thus pit privileged, top-down definitions of what constitutes appropriate engagement against bottom-up choices about what people want and need to do online.

In Europe, the activities considered productive and proper by policy makers, commerce, and the third sector are not those which are undertaken most by internet users. For example, social uses of the internet and video-based entertainment are part of the digital diet of three quarters of European internet users (Eurostat, 2019a). Granted, so do reading news and finding information about goods and services. However, formal learning activities and participation in political activities or discussions are restricted to around 10 per cent of internet users. No more than one in five of European internet users has made an appointment with a practitioner or looked for a job online.

In this book, I take a broader perspective and treat inequalities in different types of use as important, even those considered 'undesirable' (for a discussion of undesirability, see Livingstone & Millwood-Hargrave, 2006). Incorporation of a full range of activities is important because even engagement with 'unproductive' online activities, such as gaming or aimless browsing, might have desirable effects in domains of traditional inequalities, such as the establishment of social networks and increased self-confidence (Arora, 2012; Cole & Griffiths, 2007).

Outcome inequalities: Third-level divides

The implicit assumption in most research, policy, and digital inclusion initiatives is that increased and broad uptake of ICTs automatically leads to universally positive outcomes. Alexander van Deursen and I (2015) adopted the term 'third-level' digital divide to describe systematic disparities in outcomes that people obtain from engaging with ICTs (see also Wei, Teo, Chan, & Tan, 2011). In societies with near-universal internet access, there are important inequalities in the use of ICTs to achieve specific objectives that cannot be fully explained by differences in skills or use (Amichai-Hamburger, McKenna, & Tal, 2008). There are third-level digital inequalities in the outcomes that people achieve, even among those who have similar usage patterns and enjoy relatively autonomous and ubiquitous access (Van Deursen & Helsper, 2015). Yet, the emphasis on digital skills training as the solution to broader inequalities is also problematic because it might mask long-term inequalities in outcomes. I am not arguing that skills training and education are useless. However, it is risky to assume that all those who engage in, for example, online learning will go on to get a degree at LSE or MIT.

Third-level digital inequalities are not about people doing different things online benefitting differently from ICTs. Rather, they are about how different individuals get different outcomes from doing similar types of things online (Van Deursen et al., 2017). The CF classification positions different internet uses and outcomes within corresponding domains in the social exclusion literature. As in traditional inequalities literature, the digital inequalities literature tends to situate particular types of outcome as more 'worthy' than others. The prevalence of neoliberal market economy approaches in policy and interventions means that evidence for socio-digital inequalities in economic and formal participatory outcomes dominates (see Chapters 3 and 4). There is much less attention paid to and, consequently, less evidence for systematic differences in types of engagement, such as online social networking and content creation, and associated outcomes which are considered less important for society, such as self-actualisation, creative expression, and personal well-being.

It is important to separate these different outcomes domains, because research has debunked the notion that someone who has managed to achieve a particular outcome of ICT use is able to achieve outcomes in other domains (Van Deursen & Helsper, 2017). For example, someone who can save money online does not necessarily achieve positive health outcomes from using ICTs. Positive health outcomes might rely more on using ICTs' social and communicative functions. Similarly, someone who has positive interactions with others online does not necessarily achieve valuable learning or economic outcomes. What you can do with and get out of digital engagement depends on the offline resources that you have and the online resources you use. Individuals should always be conceptualised within broader social and societal contexts that shape their engagement with ICTs and constitute socio-digital inequalities.

A model of digital inequalities

I integrate the three levels of digital inequalities described above as follows. I critique economistic, functional approaches to socio-digital inequalities – in line with Sen's capabilities

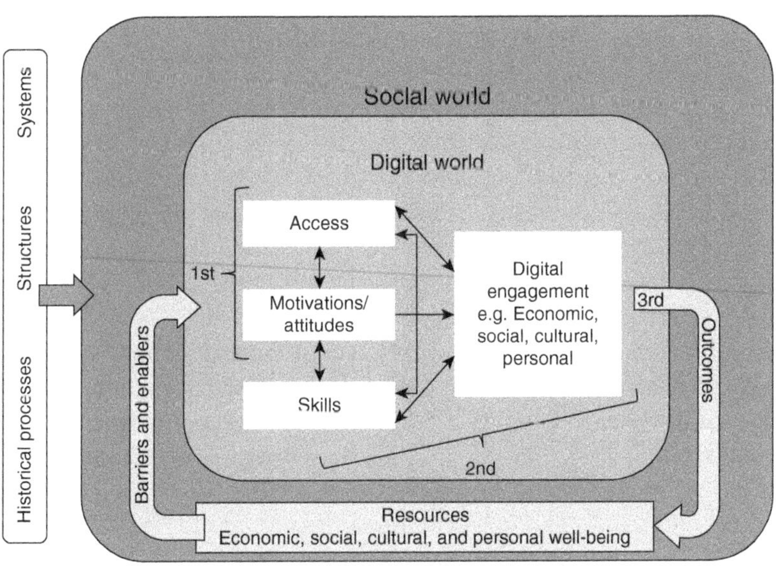

Figure 2.1 Model depicting first-, second-, and third-level digital inequalities

framework (1997, 2008) – by foregrounding well-being outcomes across all domains, and respecting bottom-up definitions of what is important for full participation in society. However, I diverge from Sen's conclusion that we must look at equality of opportunities and not at inequalities in outcomes, since outcomes are where structural inequalities manifest (Chapter 1). If opportunities are systematically not taken up by people from different backgrounds, there must be underlying structural causes. This means we cannot avoid defining outcomes. I do this in the broadest way possible by grouping them into four domains of resources (Figure 2.1), and ground them in the traditional inequalities literature as presented in Chapter 1. What constitutes these resources and their explanatory weight can be different for different individuals and contexts. Nevertheless, all individuals and communities have a right to high-quality outcomes in all these equally-valued domains (Helsper, 2012).

Why should we care? Explaining socio-digital inequalities

Differences in ICT access, skills, and use are not what primarily matters when it comes to inequality. The real issue is the continuation or exacerbation of existing inequalities in everyday life that impact our well-being. ICTs have the potential to open up a world of knowledge, leisure, and connection to those who would not otherwise have these. We need to understand how this potential can become reality. Hence, my continued insistence on shifting from ability and opportunity to outcomes. At the moment, digital and social inequalities seem caught in a vicious cycle, commonly described as the Matthew or rich-get-richer effect. Consequentially, 'those who already have a head start in possessing particular resources benefit more from a new resource than those who are behind and already have some disadvantage' (Van Dijk, 2005, p. 225).

Therefore, I prefer the term 'inequalities' over gradations of inclusion and divides. Simple differences between individuals in ICT access, skills, motivation, and engagement do not constitute inequality. Socio-digital inequalities are persistent, systematic differences between groups that give individuals in them different societal status and power. In the rest of this chapter, I will look at the theories that have been used to explain why these systematic differences exist and which processes could counter rich-get-richer effects accompanying the increased digitisation of society (Norris, 2001). First, let me present four scenarios for more equal socio-digital futures.

As illustrated in Figure 2.2, the most pessimistic amplification model posits that differences between the disadvantaged and advantaged will increase over time. That is, the disadvantaged might see an increase in how they take up opportunities and have access to information, education, and income. However, those who started advantaged are able to take up opportunities to a greater extent and the disadvantaged fall relatively further behind.

Others envision a different, less pessimistic future. The stratification model predicts no change in the difference in well-being and opportunities between the advantaged and

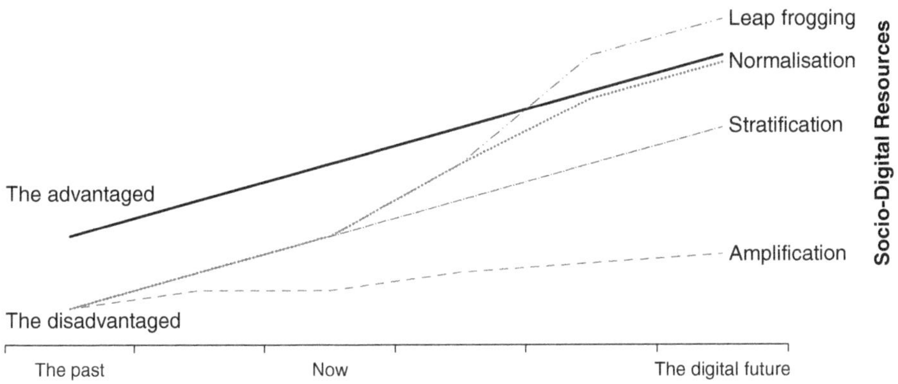

Figure 2.2 Four models of future (in)equalities in digital societies

Source: Adapted from Norris (2001)

disadvantaged over time. Both increase their socio-digital resources over time at the same pace. While the disadvantaged are able to acquire access and skills and use ICTs in ways that improve their situation in absolute terms, the advantaged are able to do so at the same pace. Since their starting level is higher, the disadvantaged never catch up, thus maintaining the status quo. In between lies the normalisation model, which relies on the assumption that ICTs do the same thing for all individuals, and that once there is widespread diffusion, there will be equality that was not possible before because of a lack of access to resources among the disadvantaged.

The leapfrogging model is the most optimistic model, spiked with techno-determinist discourse. It predicts that the widespread availability of ICTs will give the disadvantaged access to resources that allow them to tap into a theretofore unrealised potential and avoid some of the problems that the advantaged have encountered in their use and take up of technologies. The disadvantaged thus surpass the achievements of the previously advantaged.

In what follows, I will start with micro-level explanations about the individual, and emphasise choice and awareness as being at the basis of socio-digital inequalities. I then move on to widely-used societal-level theories that emphasise structure and status. I conclude with the less-explored theoretical area at the meso-social level where agency and structure come together. These digital inequalities theories rely heavily on the underpinnings of traditional inequalities detailed in Chapter 1, but there are some key theories discussed here that digital inequalities researchers infrequently use, even though they would be useful.

Linking digital inequalities and social inequalities approaches

The digital inequalities literature shows some similarities with the traditional inequalities literature. It tends to position a neoliberal, utilitarian economic perspective against a more critical, societal perspective. The neoliberal perspective regards free markets and individual agency as conduits for change. Scholars using this perspective take an individualistic approach that echoes the meritocratic ideals of neoliberalism. They suggest that to overcome socio-digital inequalities, the attitudes and skills of those who are disconnected have to be improved. The latter, more critical, scholars rely on Marxist and Bourdieusian models of inequalities. They argue that the only way societies will become more equal is by changing how inequality is embedded in social structures and economic systems. Less explicitly linked to the traditional inequalities literature are the meso-level, community approaches, which take the everyday as their point of departure. They see neighbourhood and networked changes in socialisation as the most effective way to combat inequalities, following structuration and relative deprivation approaches. As of yet, very few studies take an intersectional approach to understanding socio-digital inequalities, with ecological approaches coming closest.

Individualism and agency

There are roughly four dominant frameworks in the individualistic approach to explaining digital inequalities: Uses and Gratification (U&G), Technology Acceptance Models (TAM), Diffusion of Innovation, and Competencies approaches. The U&G and TAM frameworks do not explicitly refer to inequalities, while the others implicitly envision a more equal future. The idea is that, since there are no structural barriers, interventions at the individual level will lead to a reduction of differences between people and that normalisation will be the result (Figure 2.2). Here, a limited review of the main theoretical assumptions of these approaches and how they have influenced policy and intervention decisions will set the stage for the remainder of the book.

Rogers' (1995) diffusion of innovation model was popular when first-level digital inequalities were high on everyone's agenda. It is used to describe the logical and natural progression in uptake of new ICTs within a society, with pioneers adopting them first and others following. Eventually, all but a few luddites will use the next new communication technology after the innovators and early adopters motivate the later adopters to adopt. The underlying assumption is that availability and economies of scale drive uptake, meaning the proposed solutions to getting the disconnected online are: improving infrastructure, increasing the availability of ICTs or applications, and designing interventions around influencers. In countries with low levels of diffusion, this thinking continues to influence policy decisions (Chapter 3), but it is also still present in higher diffusion countries.

Uses and Gratification is used extensively by media and communication scholars (Cho, Gil de Zúñiga, Rojas, & Shah, 2003; Ruggiero, 2000). The framework's main premise is that individuals use media – including ICTs – to gratify intrinsic needs. People have different personalities and interests that can be clustered into different user types. A 'disconnected' individual is either not aware that a technology can satisfy a need that they have or the content and the types of engagement of interest are unavailable. The U&G framework is used to explain second-level digital inequalities. Solutions to getting people online include making sure content is available for different types of people, and making individuals aware of opportunities. For example, public awareness campaigns are a favourite vehicle for policy makers. The U&G literature has produced different classifications of use and user types. It shows a consistent clustering of uses or users around six areas: entertainment and leisure; information and learning; communication and interaction; commercial and financial; creative and productive; and societal participation and engagement (Cho et al., 2003; Papacharissi & Rubin, 2000).

Thiessen and Looker (2010) point out that ICTs are expected to bridge inequalities of distance and geography. The U&G approach would predict that people in rural and distant communities who do not have access to resources will rally around ICTs. This digital diversity approach 'predicts that even with equal material access to ICT, young people with different life interests will use this technology for distinct purposes' (Thiessen & Looker, 2010, p. 61). Thiessen and Looker are critical of the idea that individual interests form the foundation of digital inequalities and take a non-agentic approach. Nevertheless, this quote illustrates how access and availability might not lead to equality of use, but can guarantee equality of opportunity. That is, once access has been acquired, people can take advantage of online opportunities, satisfying needs that they have not been able to satisfy before.

Researchers using the Technology Acceptance Model (TAM) in their research come to similar conclusions as U&G researchers in terms of the causes and potential solutions to digital disconnects. TAM scholars assume it is not only awareness of the opportunities or availability of content that makes a difference; practical barriers and cost–benefit analyses of the effort needed to engage also dictate uptake (Hong, Thong, & Tam, 2006; Venkatesh, 2000). Rather than focusing on individual needs and personality types, they explain inequality through general attitudes towards technology. From a TAM perspective, a person is likely to be offline if they have generally negative attitudes towards technology and innovation. Another possibility for disconnection is that they are pressed for time or do not consider the benefits of ICTs worthwhile when weighed against the costs. People can be brought into the digital fold by gaining easy access, acquiring skills, and changing attitudes to and perceptions of technology. Equality of opportunity is based on an individual's ability to make informed choices to disengage after a cost–benefit analysis of what it means to be online.

The last framework that I will discuss under the individualistic approach is based on competencies. While there is ample emphasis on skills in societal and social constructivist approaches to digital inequalities (Chapter 4), much skills-based research and interventions do not dwell on the social aspects of inequalities. They assume that differences in digital engagement can be fully explained by differences in skill levels (Saranto & Hovenga, 2004). Subsequently, solutions to digital disconnect include national IT skills curricula, formal training, the provision of online educational materials, and the construction of support networks. When problems continue to exist, this is often blamed on people not taking courses, and educators not reaching people who might need more extensive training. Tufecki (2012), for example, argues that interventions and programmes accept only the most qualified. By ridding themselves of tougher cases, they seem successful. Many interventions merely measure whether a person entering the programme has acquired skills, not what they do with them. Several authors suggest that it is optimal, targeted, and effective access and use that leads to positive and beneficial outcomes, not just intense and general use (Dixon et al., 2014; Thiessen & Looker, 2010). In other words, looking at how people 'choose' to use technologies should not overshadow a concern with outcomes of use.

Research and interventions that advocate increased skills training and ICT use as the solution to inequalities risk overlooking structural constraints and systematic patterns behind inequalities in use. In ascribing differences in use to a diversity of needs and interests, they give too much weight to agency and choice. As a result, they ignore how uses are systematically unequally distributed among different groups of people (Davies, Eynon, & Wilkin, 2017; Helsper & Reisdorf, 2017). Kuttan and Peters (2003) caution against dismissing IT-based programmes altogether; while technology might not solve all problems, solutions will be slower without technology. This consideration helps to avoid the pitfall of saying that the only explanation for inequalities are social and that digital societies just replicate the old status quo – a common view among those who take a societal, social constructivist perspective.

Societal structure and capitals

This discussion brings us to the theoretical approaches that have historically run in parallel to the above individualistic approaches. Just as in the traditional inequalities literature, there is a split between scholars who take a more neoliberal perspective and those concerned with societal processes that lead to inequalities.

Neoliberal economistic approaches

While policy often recognises the role of the state, discourse around digital inequalities mostly builds on neoliberal ideas. This is especially the case in historically capitalist countries. In these countries, concern revolves around loss to the economy due to access gaps and the resulting unrealised potential of ICTs to overcome inequalities related to poverty, employment, and wealth. This overlooks that diffusion – even with state intervention, such as subsidies – follows the Pareto principle. It plateaus, leaving the most disadvantaged disconnected. The neoliberal inequalities literature presents this as natural phenomena that cannot be prevented (Houston & Erdelez, 2002).

Numerous indexes use access and skills to rank order and benchmark countries against each other to describe the digital readiness of economies and their citizens, including the World Bank (2016), the ITU's *ICT Development Index* (2017a), and the EU's *Digital Economy and Society Index* (European Commission, 2020). The global market is seen to drive digital growth in these documents and indices, leaving governments to step in when the market does not cover demand or conditions are not right for innovation (Luyt, 2006; Thurow, 2000). These state-supported markets aim to neutralise existing economic inequalities, and are supposed to lead to whole nations leapfrogging others, benefitting disadvantaged individuals within them (Alzouma, 2005).

The neoliberal undertone of interventions becomes apparent in relation to the digital skills gap, where the need for education and training is linked to work in the tech industry.

During the digital revolution, formal educational institutions are to provide digital factory workers and managers. These workers are better able to deal with automated processes, rather than improve general well-being or seek equality (Olssen & Peters, 2005). The teaching of technical skills such as coding is necessary to supply workers for a brave new world in which all work will be digital (Friederici, Ojanperä, & Graham, 2017). In this vision, digital inclusion is seen only in terms of outcomes for the economy, where increasing jobs and employment in the digital sector is seen as an unquestioned benefit for society. Growth of digital infrastructure, development of a tech market, digital upskilling, and increased employment in this sector have well-being as a logical, inevitable outcome – if individuals can get up to speed.

This debate continues in relation to artificial intelligence and the skills employees will need to be able to accommodate robotised labour. Critics of this neoliberal approach argue that there is nothing inevitable about a digital future where humans have no choice but to adapt. Rather than assuming that technological progress and the associated skills and activities are unavoidable and a neutral outcome of 'natural' development on the road to a digital society, one needs to look at the persistent structural inequalities that shape which skills and types of participation in society are valued, and how this shapes our vision and design of ICTs and digital economies (Mansell, 2012).

Societal capitals approaches

Advocates for a social constructivist perspective argue that because ICT use is driven by societal processes, digital inequalities will continue to exist unless social structures change. That is, it is not just access and economic drivers to acquire skills that increase digital engagement (Drabowicz, 2017; Robinson, Wiborg, & Schulz, 2018). The most popular theoretical approach to describe how societal inequalities are related to digital inequalities is the appropriation of Bourdieu's theory of the unequal distribution of capitals related to social class (Chapter 1). Mirroring an emphasis on the multimodality of social inequalities, digital inequalities scholars argue that differences in economic, social, and cultural capital may all explain the causes of digital inequalities. However, Bourdieu's emphasis on class is not as prominent in these discussions (Ignatow & Robinson, 2017; Zhang, 2015). Digital inequalities scholars rarely incorporate Bourdieu's theorisation of fields as located in specific sites or networks, and instead use general social categories as expressions of habitus. While not explicitly mentioned, the distinction these scholars make between access, skills, and engagement levels in definitions of digital inequalities mirror the distinction between internalised (ability and aptitude) and externalised (access) resources (Kvasny, 2005; Ragnedda & Muschert, 2018).

A Bourdieusian approach takes inequalities in the distribution of capitals as a cause rather than as a consequence of digital inequalities. This influenced me to map different online activities in my CF framework onto economic, social, and cultural capitals. Extending Bourdieusian approaches to socio-digital inequalities, I hypothesised that engagement feeds back into historically unevenly distributed capitals. This distinction between the different domains of digital engagement forces people to examine which inequalities are subject to amplification, stratification, or leapfrogging processes as societies digitise. We must also recognise that traditional inequalities re-emerge in the translation of this use into tangible outcomes (Figure 2.1). Specifically, the model hypothesises that the links between social and digital inequalities are strongest between corresponding domains of offline and digital resources. For example, those with high levels of economic resources are likely to use ICTs for economic purposes and increase their wealth, but do not necessarily increase their social capital. Due to processes of concentration of resources, it is likely that those who have economic capital also have higher levels of social capital. Nevertheless, research shows that it is important to separate these out to clarify the relationships between social and digital inequalities (Van Deursen & Helsper, 2017; Van Deursen et al., 2017).

Most Bourdieu-inspired socio-digital inequalities research does not acknowledge other theories that look at the individual within social structures such as structuration or social psychological approaches. This is why, in the CF model, I added a domain of personal resources to the economic, social, and cultural domains (Figure 2.1). In addition, Bourdieusian digital inequalities research often has a very narrow, descriptive empirical approach. It relies on quantitative methodologies such as factor and cluster analysis that describe how patterns of digital and social disadvantage group together. It is less helpful in explaining how the processes of replication and entrenchment in specific classes work in everyday life.

Theorisations of capitals based on Bourdieu's original framework have been accused of using a kitchen-sink approach, creating and defining new capitals for every new interest of researchers. Similarly, in the digital inequalities field, scholars have debated whether digital capital is distinct from other forms of capital, or whether we should map digital onto traditional capitals (Ragnedda, 2018). Still others contend it is not a primary capital at all but a secondary form of capital, similar to objects or status (Villanueva-Mansilla, Nakano, & Evaristo, 2015). I follow the approach that ICTs are secondary aspects of capital. High-quality access is, therefore, not a separate digital capital, but a secondary capital that individuals have mostly because of their economic capital (e.g. wealth). It can also be an outcome of cultural capital, if aspects of their upbringing have socialised them into perceiving technologies to be important. This is how this book is organised, each chapter discussing one specific aspect of primary traditional capital as related to specific types of secondary digital capital in terms of access, skills, and uses of technologies.

The question remains whether the digitisation of societies changes which forms of capital are important to achieve high status. Kreckel (2005) argues that subjective aspects such as attitudes and status are more important, now that power, knowledge, and wealth are not exclusively based on the scarcity of goods. Status, in his interpretation, is how capitals are expressed and felt by people in their everyday lives. This means that whether having broadband or being skilled with ICTs is desirable and resource-enhancing depends on whether others confer status on those aspects. It also means that Bourdieu's theory of taste and status is more relevant than his theory of capitals, as used in many of the digital inequalities studies. This leads me to a critique: one problem with Bourdieusian approaches is that it is difficult to separate out the different capitals and fields in everyday life. Status, and therefore inequality, is built in people's everyday realities, which are messy. Our lives take place across a variety of contexts simultaneously, making it hard to use Bourdieu's terminology of status within fields. Many Bourdieusian socio-digital inequalities studies ignore that private lives of individuals are inherently social and privilege public and formal institutions over the home and community where status and inequalities are constructed.

Situated socialisation and ecological approaches

Theorisations have produced abundant descriptive work about digital inequalities. Socio-digital inequalities scholars tend to emphasise the macro (e.g. markets) or the micro (e.g. individual skills) as the level where digital inequalities can be found. Most current interventions blend the two. With an awareness that there are structural factors lying behind inequalities, they instigate change at the individual level through the provision of courses, curricula, and public awareness campaigns. Yet, in socio-digital inequalities theorisations, the middle is largely missing. Relatively few scholars incorporate the networks and communities where people live their everyday lives. Empirical research and interventions that use community and family-based approaches are more common. In this last section, I will discuss the theoretical frameworks that fill this missing middle and show promise in accounting for the meso-level causes and consequences of socio-digital inequalities. This level is mostly concerned with socialisation: how behaviours, norms, and values around the importance and the use of ICTs are learned and expressed in everyday interactions. Theories at this level are established in the general inequalities literature, but are less common in digital inequalities. Three concepts – intersectionality, relativity and network effects – are important to understand this meso level. Here these will be discussed to prepare for a deeper dive in the conclusion chapter.

Intersectionality

Digital inequalities researchers define social inequalities along a spectrum of economic, social, and cultural capitals. They also integrate resources and digital inequalities along a continuum of access, skills, and types of use (Alper, Katz, & Schofield Clark, 2016; Kvasny, Trauth, & Morgan, 2009). For example, Fuchs (2009) argues that access to ICTs is shaped by the interaction of socio-economic, political, cultural, social, and technological factors. Together, they counter 'technological determinism, economic reductionism, and linear trend projection in the digital divide debate' (Fuchs, 2009, p. 41). Nevertheless, gender, education level, race, and class are mostly studied as isolating groups of individuals. As a consequence, individuals within these social categories are implied to be a homogeneous group. For example, research based in theories of digital inequality that examines gender differences is often blind to race. Feminist scholars see intersectionality as a framework to study inequalities in the design and production of ICTs, most of which is conducted in very particular contexts of the Global North (Elwood & Leszczynski, 2018; McMillan Cottom, 2017). However, intersectionality is still largely absent in digital inequalities research (see Alper et al., 2016, for an exception). This is against evidence that disadvantaged people experience oppression in a variety of compounded ways. For example, lower educated and unemployed individuals with health problems who have low levels of skill and access are the most marginalised and vulnerable to exclusion in digital societies. How intersections of different types of disadvantage influence a person's position in a digital society depends on how and when these different aspects of their identity are emphasised (or considered important) in the communities in which they live. Clearly, this needs to be studied more extensively.

Relativity

We live in a world where digital skills and engagement are fundamental for employment, health, and friendship. I argued in my relative digital deprivation paper (Helsper, 2017a) that it was not the absolute but relative level of skill or engagement that made the difference in terms of our well-being and ability to participate as citizens. For this reason, it is important to look at relative, subjective aspects of digital inequalities. This approach is accepted in the general social exclusion and inequalities literature, but not in digital inequalities scholarship. Nevertheless, the four models of possible future digital inequalities (i.e. leapfrogging, normalisation, stratification, and amplification) align with relative subjective approaches.

In light of how fast ICTs and digital engagement change, the prevalence of absolute digital deprivation indicators – with fixed levels of connection speed and skill or use – is an oddly static approach and likely to produce short-lived policies and interventions. The finish line in the race for digital equality is continuously moved. Some have a head start, better shoes to run in, and more enthusiastic supporters. Even if all eventually reach the original finish line, they will find the goal posts have been moved. Digital inclusion is, therefore, best defined relative to a particular time and place. The equivalent in traditional inequalities research was when theories focused on poverty as the indicator of deprivation. They neglected to look at inequality in terms of how an individual was positioned within a country in relation to other individuals, in terms of their wealth and income (e.g. focusing on GDP instead of indicators such as Gini) (Ravallion, 2003).

Additional methodological problems for digital inequalities research have emerged. Creating digital Gini and odds ratio measurements was easier when the discussions of digital inequalities centred on access, which has a natural saturation point of 100 per cent. Now we are including different skills and uses, measurement has become more complicated since there is no maximum level of skill or engagement. This means lifelong learning will be necessary in digital societies. But it also means that digital inequalities theorists have an important task ahead in studying and understanding how these processes of socialisation take place across a variety of settings. How do others around us in the different settings of our everyday lives influence what we perceive to be the norm? How will we act in digital societies? The socio-digital ecologies approach, which I describe below and in more detail in the Conclusion, addresses these questions.

Ecologies and subjectivity

Theorisation of digital inequalities should recognise that for change to be driven by more sustainable bottom-up actions by individuals rather than top-down policies, it should be relative and subjective (Chapter 1). Socio-digital inequalities research, especially the qualitative research done using domestication frameworks, has been looking at these subjective aspects of digital disadvantage. Domestication theorists argue that the households and communities where people live determine how a person is socialised in the digital world. Subsequently, they shape how a person feels they should engage with ICTs (Cummings & Kraut, 2002; Haddon, 2011). While they started with a concern with how family give meaning to technologies as artefacts, they later expanded domestication to include spheres such as work (Haddon, 2011). Domestication theorists' most important contribution is their social, contextual approach which counters the material, individualistic approach that dominates digital inequalities research.

I have argued (Helsper, 2017a) that for subjective relative digital deprivation to exist, individuals should be aware of absolute inequalities and they should consider digital engagement important for their everyday lives. This echoes Sen's (2002) capabilities approach, but addresses critiques that it emphasises freedom to decide for yourself what is valuable over inequalities in achieved functionalities (Olsaretti, 2014). I differ from Sen when I say we need the difficult, normative debate about what to do when 'freedom of choice' leads to the amplification or stratification of systematic inequalities in resources vital for participation and survival in digital and 'analogue' societies alike (Arora, 2012). I find it difficult to talk about 'free' choice if already-disadvantaged groups are systematically not taking up digital opportunities because they do not consider them to be relevant to them, or when they feel negative outcomes in ICT use are part of the price of being online.

The previously-mentioned frameworks – including my own CF model and Bourdieusian frameworks – incorporate socialisation to explain inequalities in choices people make and attitudes people hold. However, they do not clearly theorise where and how this process takes place. How do longstanding patterns of social inequalities get translated into digital inequalities in everyday life? What are the sites for the creation of what Nussbaum might call digital adaptive preferences, and Marxist scholars would label 'false consciousness' (Grenfell, 2014; Nussbaum, 2000)? Formal education and training are seen as important sites, but this ignores informal sites of social learning. The socialisation frameworks that look at people's everyday lives show that behaviours, attitudes, and preferences are mostly shaped by social interactions that transmit societal norms (DiMaggio & Garip, 2012). Sometimes these reflect broader social stereotypes or are very specific to the community where a person lives. At other times, the socio-cultural identity of the individual is less important than their personal interests or expertise. This is why Servon (2002) argues that we should not ignore personal and meso-level social resources; loneliness and social isolation are relevant as are social networks and interactions.

Theories such as domestication look at how perceptions and uses of ICTs are shaped by home, school, and work environments. This approach emphasises continuity of social relationships and contexts over mobility and change. Largely missing are more flexible approaches that define an individual's socio-digital environment as fluid. Who people are surrounded by and what they consider to be the norm for digital engagement, changes as people move between physical locations and social situations. Network and neighbourhood effects approaches are starting to be applied to explain socialisation within the context of socio-digital ecologies (Kral, 2014; Mossberger, Tolbert, & Lacombe, 2021). It is likely that in the coming era of the Internet of Things (IoT), where engagement with ICTs is less formal and more embedded in actions, these theoretical approaches will become more valuable. Individuals' adoption of ICTs will be even more likely guided by observing how others around them use technologies, rather than obtained through formal education.

The complexity of socio-digital inequalities

I started this chapter on the history of conceptualisations and theorisations of digital inequalities by asking: What are digital inequalities and why should we care about them?

I conclude that socio-digital inequalities should be defined as inequalities in the achievement of positive outcomes and the avoidance of negative outcomes of ICT use in digital societies. Socio-digital inequalities are systematic differences between individuals from different backgrounds in the opportunities and abilities to translate digital engagement into benefits and avoid the harm that might result from engagement with ICTs. To understand the barriers and enablers to overcoming socio-digital inequalities requires taking a compound approach that includes access, skills, attitudes, and different ways of engaging with ICTs. This approach must be relative, understanding how the economic, social, and cultural environments in which a person spends time shape their perception of how important digital engagement is.

The answer to why we should care comes from normative questions about who gets to decide what being digitally included means, and if we should desire a society where everyone does everything online. By way of an answer, I made the distinction between individual-level theories, based on differences in needs, abilities, and interests, and societal-level theories, which are heavily influenced by market-based neoliberal approaches and Bourdieu's ideas of class and capital. Existing models theorise from a macro or a micro perspective. As a result, decisions about the most useful ways of engaging are made through top-down or bottom-up valuations of what technology should do for a person. Unfortunately, structuration and social psychological approaches, which focus on processes of socialisation at the level of the everyday life, are less frequently used. These would emphasise that decisions about what digital inclusion means and why it is important depends on a combination of characteristics of the individual and the particular situations in which they find themselves. Socio-digital inequalities are intersectional, meaning the experience of disadvantage is specific to a person in the same way that traditional inequalities are.

The more controversial argument I made in this chapter is that inequalities in outcomes that people achieve from ICT use are problematic, even if disadvantaged people do not view these as problematic. We cannot be content that we have done enough if providing access, skills training, and content for all still produces systematic inequalities that replicate or amplify traditional patterns of inequalities. Policy makers and other stakeholders who say they are interested in reducing inequalities in digital societies need to be held to account for outcomes of ICT use. As a guide, I use the Corresponding Fields framework I developed in 2012. This framework hypothesises that as people build on their strengths, they are more likely to build up resources through ICT use in domains that correspond to their offline resources. These domain-specific feedback loops lead to the amplification of inequalities unless the environments in which digital interventions are introduced are better understood.

There is a persistent critique that the overemphasis on skills and access in many policy interventions and theorisations do not account for social factors. There is empirical evidence that access and skills have different consequences for different people, depending on their situation. At a global level, evidence exists that high-income countries reap positive benefits of widespread diffusion of ICTs. However, in low-income countries, the poorest households might not benefit to the same extent as richer households. As a result, the negative and positive effects of ICTs depend on who you are and where you live. The rest of this book will delve deeper into this empirical evidence and illustrate this for economic, social, and cultural domains of resources.

The question about why we should care is also a question about what awaits us in a digital future, a question about the historical links between social and digital (or technological) inequalities. Techno-utopian and techno-pessimist imaginations of the future are not new. We see arguments and mistakes repeated due to a lack of knowledge around what inequalities really are and how they have come to be (Burke & Briggs, 2001; Eubanks, 2011; Joinson, 2003). In this book, I respond to Marinetti's (1909) provocation in 'The Futurist Manifesto' about what the point of looking behind is. When living in a brave new world where radical technological change seems to be happening in front of our eyes, we should learn from the past and existing theories of inequalities. We should not get carried away, thinking each new ICT is going to destroy us or, conversely, lead us into a more equal future.

In trying to imagine, based on existing research, what the digital future might be like, I fall into neither the techno-determinist nor the socio-determinist trap. I define the social as the physical, ideological, and social environments that shape our everyday lives, as well as the resources we have and the ways in which we act, think, and feel about all of these. The digital consists of our ICT access, skills, use, and the attitudes we have towards the digital. In this book, the social is both the cause and the consequence of the digital. In turn, the digital is the cause and the consequence of the social. Both are caught in eternal feedback loops. To counter amplification or rich-get-richer effects – often observed in relation to digital inequalities research and interventions – we should take into account social and digital contexts. That is, the social cannot be understood without the digital, and vice versa. This is why I use the term 'socio-digital inequalities' and not digital inequalities. In this book, I will paint the picture of how the social and the digital mix to create a diverse and complex landscape of inequalities, and how this shapes our future in increasingly digital societies.

PART II

THE PRESENT: LESSONS LEARNED ABOUT THE CAUSES AND CONSEQUENCES OF SOCIO-DIGITAL INEQUALITIES

CHAPTER 3

ECONOMIC INEQUALITIES IN DIGITAL SOCIETIES

> 'Countries cannot hope to compete in the global marketplace of ideas if their business communities and broader populations are not online.'
>
> (Global Commission on Internet Governance, 2016, p. viii)

Without access there is no digital engagement. This means a lack of access, or abysmal digital infrastructure, is the most basic form of digital disconnect. There was a period when access was seen as a luxury good. For example, Michael Powell compared broadband-related inequalities to a 'Mercedes-Benz divide' during his first press conference as chairman of the US Federal Communications Committee (cited in Cooper, 2010). He argued that it would be a nice, though not essential, to have toy for those who could afford it. This attitude would be unimaginable now there is broad agreement that access is a basic right. High-speed, widespread internet infrastructure is of the utmost priority for countries, and individuals, that want to participate in digital society. As in this chapter's opening quote, improvements in infrastructure and access are seen as vital to competing in the global digital economy.

In this chapter, I walk through why equality of opportunity in high-quality, ubiquitous access is important, and the economic causes and consequences of inequalities in this area. I emphasise empirical evidence for differences between individuals from different backgrounds both within and across countries. There is accumulating evidence for a rich-get-richer (or amplification) effect, but also for the effectiveness of technological interventions.

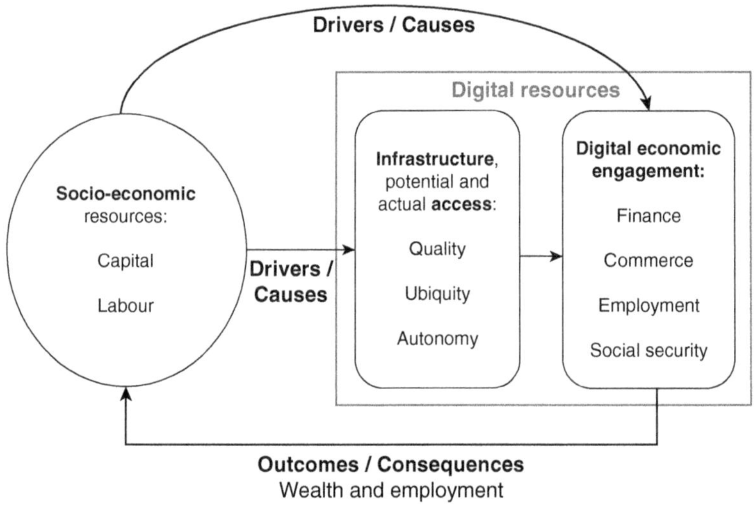

Figure 3.1 Links between traditional and digital socio-economic inequalities

This chapter is organised around two key questions about socio-economic inequalities, and the causes and consequences of inequalities in ICT access and use (Figure 3.1):

- Why should we (still) care about inequalities in access?
- Which types of inequalities in access exist and are problematic?

I will show that access needs to be thought of in a more nuanced way than is usual in research and policy making. Using the definition of access described in Chapter 2, I will look at the data for the diffusion of different types of access. I then propose a new framework to describe what Van Dijk (2005, 2020) labels 'material access' by examining the evidence for inequalities in quality, ubiquity, and autonomy of access. This will be done by exploring the economic domain of inequalities and what the causes and consequences of digital inequalities in this area are (Figure 3.1). This chapter follows the Corresponding Fields (CF) model in hypothesising that the strongest links will be between socio-economic inequalities and digital inequalities in access, infrastructure, and the economic uses of ICTs, and subsequently with the economic outcomes or consequences of these inequalities in digital resources (Chapter 2).

This chapter's follow up question is: What has and can be done to counter inequalities related to access and socio-economic engagement with ICTs?

Even when it comes to something as relatively simple as access quality, policies and research have a hard time dealing with an ever-moving target. This requires constantly catching up with new devices, platforms, and activities that require ever increasing speeds and data storage capacity. Consequently, interventions in this area focus on quality of access and infrastructure. Other aspects of access that determine use, such as ubiquity and autonomy, remain under-explored.

Chapters 3 to 7 will be illustrated by vignettes – individual case studies composited from different individuals I have met through my research. In this chapter, Ben, a middle-aged British man, is used to illustrate how inequalities in wealth and ICT access limit full participation. This is true even in countries where ubiquitous, high-quality access is readily available.

Case Study: Ben

Ben is 42 years old and lives in a small town in England. He completed secondary-level education and worked on and off ever since. For almost six months now he has been unemployed and is in quite a bit of debt. While he would like a stable job in construction, he will take anything, including temporary or zero-hours contract work. He divorced a year ago and now lives in a small room above a bakery, with an uncomfortable bed. His clothes barely fit in his closet, and he shares a bathroom with a malfunctioning power shower. He is not unhappy. He counts himself lucky that he has a place to live and good friends, especially when he compares himself with his neighbours, who fight continuously. He has barely been able to pay the very low rent, and is eating into his savings, but friends are helping him out. His ex-wife lives in a city far away with their daughter. He does not have much contact with the other people who live in the building or with the landlord, but he goes to the local pub with his mates on a regular basis to chat.

Ben has a mobile phone but no data plan, a television with access only to public channels, and gets the free newspaper from the bus stop or the pub where people often leave it behind. The following statement sums up what he thinks about ICTs: 'Technology moves so fast I think tomorrow there'll be something else we have to learn. And you're always going to have to upgrade your phone. They always want you to buy something new because this one can do more. You feel like you're behind already ... because tomorrow it's going to be something else.'

Why should we still care about inequalities in access?

In the literature on digital inequalities, there is plenty of evidence that those without access or those with lower-quality access to ICTs have historically been economically disadvantaged. This is true for countries and individuals alike: for example, comparing countries in the Global South to countries in the Global North, and comparing those people who live in poverty with those who are wealthier. To understand inequalities in access, we need to look at the consequences and the likely future implications of these inequalities. The main issue is that the services that people use to acquire, accumulate, and consolidate wealth are now 'online mostly or only' through 'digital-by-default' policies (Yates, Kirby, & Lockley, 2015). UK-wide, estimates of £1.8 billion (Cabinet Office & Government Digital Services, 2012) and £146 per person (CEBR, 2018) would be saved if transactions moved online. The Pareto principle (Chapter 1) is particularly stark when it comes to access; the 20 per cent of the population that would benefit most by accessing services is least likely to be online. However, governments often seem more concerned with cost savings than service provision.

Ben is a good example of how a lack of quality access can lead to increased economic disadvantage. If he was better connected, he could circumvent the humiliating job centre and receiving his unemployment benefits would be easier. In addition, because his phone is so old, the online banking app does not work and he has a hard time keeping track of accumulating debt. Perhaps more immediately relevant to him, he missed out on an offer at his local pub for meals and drinks at half price.

There is a clear chicken and egg problem (Schwabach, 2014) in these discussions about the causes and consequences of inequalities in access and infrastructure. Whether inequalities in access are discussed as causes or consequences of socio-economic inequalities depends on one's position. Some argue that inequalities in wealth cause access inequalities, because financial resources allow people to acquire better access and benefit from it. Others argue that socio-economic inequalities are the consequence of inequalities in access. They believe that improved infrastructure and high-quality access will inevitably lead to economic benefits and growth for all. Social scientists and the non-profit sector generally believe in the first, while governments and commercial sectors advocate for the second.

Ben's case illustrates these two perspectives. Those favouring the consequences perspective would argue that if only he got properly connected, he could get a job. He would then discover his rights for renting the flat, and save money when shopping online. From this perspective, Ben is economically deprived because he does not have access to online opportunities. If he got connected, he would be able to overcome economic disadvantage. The inverse cause perspective is that Ben does not have the economic resources to obtain high-quality access. This 'wealth inequalities as a cause' reasoning emphasises that even if connected, he would not economically benefit from the internet similar to affluent others. There are few opportunities for someone like him to buy cheaper things, save money, find a job, or pay his rent. In the consequence scenario, providing access and improving infrastructure improves socio-economic inequalities in digital societies. Under the cause scenario, increasing Ben's wealth and economic capital is required for him to access the beneficial opportunities available online.

Whether socio-economic inequalities are a cause or a consequence of digital inequalities matters for effective interventions. The answer indicates what our digital future might look like when more and more people get connected. However, this debate is not as relevant when deciding whether ICT access is important. Without fast and affordable access, Ben cannot take advantage of the opportunities that ICTs offer and will become more entrenched in his economic exclusion. This is why inequalities in access matter; they are systematically linked to traditional forms of disadvantage, potentially leading to the emergence of a digital 'underclass' (Helsper & Reisdorf, 2017).

What do we actually mean by access (inequalities)?

In early days, access was defined as black and white. Someone had access and was included, or did not and was excluded. Access seemed straightforward to define as whether someone has access to the internet/ICTs or not. Similarly, the level of digital inclusion of a country was captured by the proportion of individuals or households that have access to the internet/ICTs somewhere. At the beginning of the 21st century, simpler definitions were scrutinised as distinctions were made in terms of speed and types of access (mobile/PC). Types of access are now diversifying rapidly. Broadband connections and laptops with WiFi have emerged, and tablets are no longer a novelty. Increasingly sophisticated and data-heavy smartphones come out regularly. Smart devices measure and upload everything, from the temperatures of our bodies to the security of our houses. The Internet of Things (IoT), Embedded Reality (ER), and Artificial Intelligence (AI) are populating policy and commercial agendas.

To address these challenges, my definition of access inequalities distinguishes access from infrastructure. 'Access' is individual or household access to the internet and other ICTs, while infrastructure is the general availability and quality of connectivity in an area. Ben might have a smartphone to access the internet, but it becomes useless if the infrastructure in his neighbourhood is bad. 3G data is the maximum he can get nearby, while other areas have 4G, and in the large city there's 5G. Not that that matters since he cannot afford a monthly data plan and would rely on WiFi. In his case, the WiFi signal he could get through the copper wire connection at home would have inconsistent, slow signal speeds. Fibre in the ground or bits in the air do not necessarily mean that individuals have access to it.

For access to be a true indicator of inclusion in digital societies, it should be high quality as well as ubiquitous (omnipresence and mobile), and there should be autonomy in use (Helsper, 2012). Quality of access refers to the speed, type, and consistency of the connections and functioning of devices. Ubiquity refers to ICTs being available in all physical spaces you move through, including the possibility to take devices or platforms with you wherever you go. I use autonomy as a broader concept than being able to personally afford, own, and update a device. It denotes freedom to use devices in ways that allow learning through trial and error (Van Deursen & Helsper, 2015).

Data gathered for research and policy focuses mostly on quality (i.e. speed and type) of access, rather than ubiquity or autonomy. Large-scale surveys ask individuals about access to the internet and type of connection. Similarly, international comparative data include quality of infrastructure and access. The International Telecommunications Union (ITU) (2015) and Eurostat (2019a) measure multiple indicators. These indicators need to qualify even simple things, such as a dialup connection, showing that defining quality of access and infrastructure is complicated. Sometimes questions hint at ubiquity and autonomy by asking about which devices people use to access the internet. The assumption is that laptop use provides more autonomy and mobile phones give ubiquity. These types of question are mostly classified as use, but since they only ask whether the person has used a device to connect to the internet, I consider these types of question an indicator of access.

More in-depth academic studies also measure the locations where individuals access the internet, which reflects my ubiquity concept. The range of access types that allow people to use ICTs include those that a person has access to without having to ask for permission. They comprise access at places like home, work, school, other people's homes, and public access points. Ben's case shows why ubiquity is important in terms of autonomy.

The library is the only public place he has access to a device to write a CV or browse for information. However, at the library his browsing time is restricted, and it is not a space where he feels comfortable. He associates the library with learning and education, full of people who remind him he is at the bottom of the socio-economic ladder. If there was better internet access at the pub, he might use it. He would also feel more comfortable exploring if he could get a cheap device and a WiFi connection at home, instead of relying on his expensive mobile phone with a small screen and intermittent signal.

In summary, I distinguish three levels and three aspects of access (Figure 3.1). To be connected there first needs to be infrastructure. A person then needs to have a device to access the internet, and then they need to use it to access online services and content. Infrastructure with access gives potential access, but without use this would still mean a person is not actually accessing ICTs. Under the definition of this book, they remain socio-digitally excluded. It is also useful to distinguish quality (i.e. functionality and speed of connectivity), ubiquity (i.e. availability at locations and devices accessible), and autonomy (i.e. affordable, sustainable ownership and private use) across these three levels of infrastructure, access, and use. Next, I will review the history of diffusion of high-quality, ubiquitous, and autonomous access for these three levels, before moving on to discuss the evidence for inequalities in this diffusion process.

Diffusion of different levels and aspects of access

Global infrastructure data is hard to obtain, perhaps with the exception of the global maps of undersea cables. Submarine Cable Maps (Telegeography, 2019) suggest that data

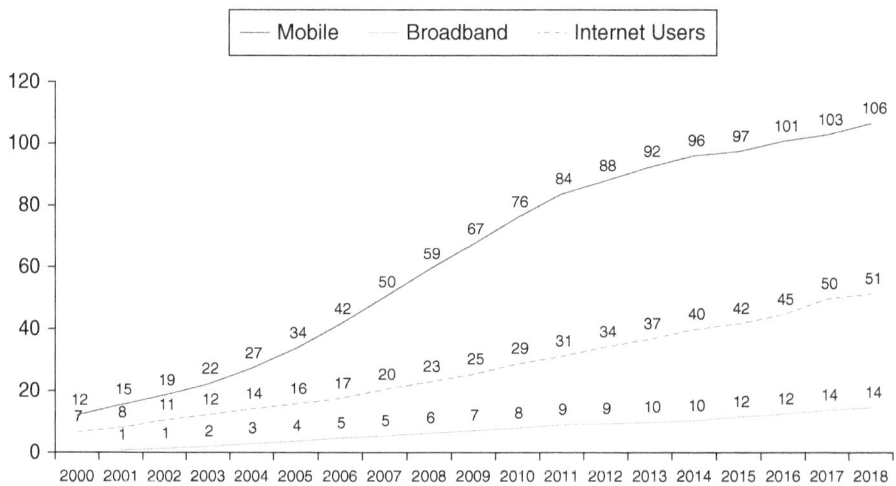

Figure 3.2 Global increases in mobile and broadband subscriptions and internet users

Source: World Telecommunication/ICT Indicators database (World Bank & International Telecommunications Union, 2020).

Data: Mobile cellular subscriptions (per 100 people), Internet users (per 100 people)*, Fixed (Wired) Broadband subscriptions per 100 inhabitants.

transportation infrastructure diffusion over the last decade has grown rapidly. However, these maps also show that some regions are far more connected. For example, connections between continents in the Global South were only recently added. The World Bank and ITU provide global data on diffusion of the quality, ubiquity, and use aspects of access. Their data suggest impressive changes in connectivity over time, although they caution that they assume some overestimation since they rely on industry and national statistics agencies reporting.

Over the last decade, the steepest increase in global ICT access has been in mobile phone diffusion. Increases in internet users and fixed broadband subscriptions have been more gradual, with about a 2–3 per cent increase each year (Figure 3.2) (World Bank & International Telecommunications Union, 2020). The future of mobility and ubiquity of connections thus seems to be bright. Led by improvements in infrastructure and affordability, mobile phones now outnumber humans on this planet. Nearly all people (95 per cent) live in areas with mobile signals, and most households (80 per cent) use mobile phones. People are starting to rely on their mobile phones for internet access (World Internet Project, 2018). In Europe, mobile devices dominated from 2016; 80 per cent used a mobile phone to browse the web, compared to 64 per cent on a laptop, 54 per cent on a PC, and 44 per cent on a tablet. Eurostat (2018b) data similarly show that 69 per cent used mobile data or WiFi to access the internet on the move in 2018, almost doubling in six years (36 per cent in 2012). In Britain, a country with a history of fixed line subscriptions, 'mobile mostly users' rose from 15 per cent to 48 per cent. The percentage of those who use a laptop/PC to access the internet dropped from 78 per cent to 58 per cent (Ofcom, 2019).

However, data on what people actually do with their mobile phones are scarce for developing economies. It is unclear if people use mobile phones in these countries to access online services (ITU, 2016). Perhaps most surprising to many who read this book, half the world has never used the internet. This suggests caution in drawing conclusions about availability and how people use these connections and devices. World Internet Project (2018) findings indicate that if individuals access the internet on more than one device, the PC (desktop or laptop) is the primary way of connecting. This suggests that there is added value to use on these devices for those with a choice. ITU (2016) data have evidence that mobile phone access is often shared among the youngest and oldest generations. From qualitative research, we know the costs of maintaining technology is a persistent worry, creating a situation where use becomes unsustainable.

As should be clear, ubiquity of infrastructure does not mean actual access. Worldwide, fewer than one in eight have a fixed broadband subscription at home – one of the highest-quality and autonomous forms of internet access (Figure 3.2). Data on where individuals use the internet in Europe further complicates confidence in the ubiquity of actual access, rather than potential access (Eurostat, 2019b). Almost half of working Europeans did not access the internet at work, and almost the same percentage of school-age Europeans did not access it at school in 2013. Where people use the internet counters easy conclusions that ubiquitous connectivity is on the rise. In addition, quality might be diminishing since what individuals can do with mobile phones is more restricted than on PCs (Donner, 2015; Napoli & Obar, 2014). People may also have their ability to experiment and expand their

ICT use constrained. In the creation of immersive, autonomous digital ecologies, availability of connections in multiple places is important. Ben definitely does not enjoy this connectivity as seamlessly integrated into the fabric of everyday life. He has to embarrass himself to get access. Last week he did 'sneak outside my friend's house, and just sat on their wall for five minutes using their WiFi'. There are still gaps in the data around high-quality, ubiquitous, and autonomous use of infrastructure. The next section turns to the question of how this type of access is distributed.

Regional inequalities in access and infrastructure

Patterns of regional inequalities between resource-rich and resource-poor areas are replicated in infrastructure, access, and use. Here, I will explore the evidence for differences between and within countries and within cities.

Between-country inequalities

While infrastructure in the Global South has improved over the years, the global picture remains familiar: high levels of connectivity in Europe, the US, and China, with lower levels of connectivity in Africa, Latin America, and South East Asia (Telegeography, 2019). Increases in the use of broadband connections in the Global South have not kept pace with the Global North. Nevertheless, ITU data show that in the 'developed world', the proportion of overall internet users has steadily increased from around 51 per cent in 2005 to around 81 per cent in 2017, while the increase in the developing world also keeps a steady pace, rising from around 8 per cent to around 48 per cent (ITU, 2017c). The internet use

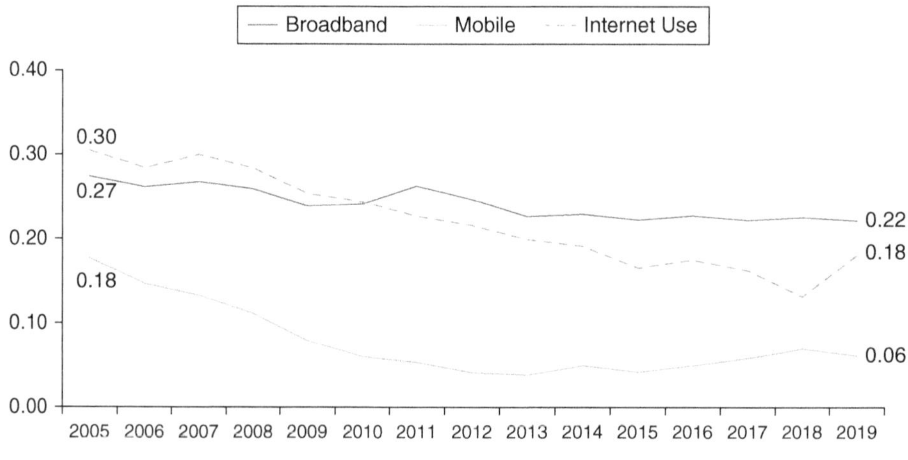

Figure 3.3 Correlations between GDP and broadband, mobile, and internet use penetration

Source: World Telecommunication/ICT Indicators database (World Bank & International Telecommunications Union, 2020).

Data: Fixed (Wired) Broadband subscriptions per 100 inhabitants, Mobile cellular subscriptions (per 100 people), Internet users (per 100 people), Country's current GDP in US$.

gap between the Global North and South has remained constant (43 percentage points difference in 2005 and 2017), even though there is now a one-to-one ratio of mobile phones to people in the developing world. Thus, wealthy countries with high GDPs tend to have better digital infrastructures (Norris, 2001), but there is much excitement about mobiles and smartphones helping developing countries to leapfrog in the race towards a digital society (James, 2016).

When looking at the relationship between ICT infrastructure and use and its relation to country wealth, a pattern emerges that stresses the importance of distinguishing quality and other types of access (Figure 3.3). In the last decade, there has been very little change in the trend of countries with higher GDPs having a larger proportion of the population on high-quality connections. That is, a higher percentage of broadband subscriptions is still related to more wealth in a country. While in richer countries more people are internet users, the difference between high GDP and low GDP countries has become smaller. In contrast, the correlation between GDP and mobile phone use has always been smaller and declined exponentially to a point where there was little correlation between country wealth and mobile phone subscriptions in 2014, although it increased minimally in 2015–2016. This means that a country's wealth no longer tells you much about how many mobile phones there are. Perhaps more importantly, the reverse is by definition also true: higher levels of mobile phone use are not linked to greater wealth in a country. While none of these data can prove causality, it does show that mobile phones are not the solution to solving inequalities in actual access. Mobile phones have not yet produced the economic leapfrogging that people have hoped for. Further evidence suggests inequalities in the quality and ubiquity of mobile connectivity. Active mobile broadband subscriptions still show a gap between developed and developing countries (98 per cent versus 48 per cent of residents) (ITU, 2017c). Other research demonstrates that mobile phone inequalities in actual access or use are larger than those for potential access (Donner, 2015).

While we should take a nuanced approach to inequalities and gradations of inclusion, it is important to remember that gaps in internet use remain significant between countries, even in highly connected regions. In 13 of the 21 European Member States, more than one-fifth of the population were non-internet users (Eurostat, 2019b). In Bulgaria, Bosnia-Herzegovina, and Romania, around one-third of people never used the internet. In Iceland and Denmark, these non-users are almost unnoticeable at 2 per cent. Ben lives in Britain, a country at the more included end of these European extremes (5 per cent were never-users). He cannot afford data, even if it is cheap in comparison to countries with similar GDPs, such as the US. In other words, he cannot convert the potential access he has through his mobile phone into actual access. If he lived in the Global South, data traffic would be exponentially more expensive, and he would likely restrict his mobile use to messaging. Still, a Ben of the Global South has more alternatives in informal and non-digital access to services, and he would be less disadvantaged in comparison with his connected peers than a Ben of the Global North.

To sum up, wealthier countries have better infrastructure and populations with higher-quality access. Citizens are more likely to turn this potential access into actual access, even though differences in more basic mobile forms of access between wealthy and poorer countries have almost disappeared. However, access to services in developing countries is less restricted to the digital world. Lower levels of access put the disconnected at less of a disadvantage than their counterparts in countries where the only option is to go online. Less access does put these countries globally at a disadvantage, since their citizens are less likely to benefit from the global resources available to more connected citizens in other countries.

Within-country inequalities

Regional inequalities are not restricted to those between countries. Within countries, there is often concern about digital inequalities between rural and urban areas. This differential again mirrors traditional inequalities in wealth. The correlations between rurality in a country and access are all significant, the highest correlation being between rurality and internet use (r=.66), followed by rurality and broadband penetration (r=.55), and mobile cellular subscriptions (r=.45) (World Bank, 2017). At the regional level, in general access goes down as regions become more rural, although in South Asia internet use (30 per cent) and mobile take-up (87 per cent) are higher than would be expected based on rurality. In the Middle East and North Africa, internet use and mobile penetration are lower than expected. Pew data show that in the US, 58 per cent of rural households has a broadband connection in comparison to 70 per cent of the urban population (Anderson, 2018). Interestingly, the differences in mobile broadband use between rural and urban areas in the US are explained mostly by household demographics rather than infrastructure. In other words, it is because rural areas are poor that they have poorer connectivity, and not because they are difficult to reach (Prieger, 2013).

In China, actual access is approximately 72 per cent in urban and 37 per cent in rural areas, with very little change in rural access since 2010 (Statista, 2018). In Europe, there is a significant difference in high-quality infrastructure: 39 per cent of households in rural and 76 per cent in urban areas are covered by high-speed fibre. There are again considerable country differences in these regional inequalities (European Commission, 2017). In the Netherlands and Malta, rural coverage is over 90 per cent and in the UK, it is around 78 per cent. However, in Croatia, Finland, and Greece, it is below 10 per cent.

What that means for people living in these countries can be explained by returning to Ben. He does not live in a large metropole but neither does he live in the countryside. While Manchester is a relatively short train ride away, he hardly ever goes there. The town he lives in is pretty typical of a post-industrial city which has seen better days and is digitally comparable to a smaller rural British village. The speed and accessibility of public WiFi in town is not great. His local pub has inconsistent WiFi. In any case, it is primarily a place where he hangs out with friends. He is not going to check his benefits or finances there. The only place where he can access a good PC with a high-speed connection is at the library, not his favourite place and a little out of the way. The few times he has gone there, he could go online for only 30 minutes and he had to sit in an uncomfortable booth where others could see his screen. He was not able to finish writing and uploading his CV in the time allocated. If he lived or worked in the city, surrounded by tech start-ups and hipsters, there would have been more possibilities to buy cheaper phones and access the internet.

Within-city inequalities

Patterns of inequalities are replicated within cities. Mossberger, Tolbert, and Lacombe (2021) have shown a pattern for poorer inner-city and wealthier urban areas, which mirror our analyses of neighbourhoods in Los Angeles (Galperin, Bar, & Kim, 2017). There are several forces that link the wealth of the individuals that live in an area and the digital infrastructure available to them, such as demand from jobs and lives. Wealthy citizens move into suburbs where quality digital infrastructure is available. Subsequently, it becomes more attractive for companies to invest in higher-quality infrastructure in those areas, creating a reinforcing cycle between supply and demand. This cycle of 'human–infrastructure migration', noticed by Servon (2002) in the early 2000s, does not help the areas that have poor infrastructure and connectivity. It results in inner-city deprived areas having less leverage for high-quality access, leaving them in a situation of infrastructure poverty. Ben's 'problem' is not only that he does not have the money to get access, he also lives where infrastructure works against him. The only copper wire connection that he could get would not provide speeds sufficient to stream video services on YouTube or Netflix. No people or businesses in his neighbourhood are demanding higher speeds.

Cities like Los Angeles are more connected than they should be, looking at their income levels. In comparison to the richest areas in LA, such as Bel Air, South East LA is considerably poorer but has almost equal levels of people with ICT access (Galperin et al., 2017; Helsper, 2019b). These areas have seen an influx of young people employed in the tech sector or who have just finished higher education. The same effect can be seen in Hackney in London, a historically poorer, migrant area that has recently seen gentrification (Helsper, 2019b). Not all are equally connected within these areas. For example, in our study with people experiencing homelessness on Skid Row in LA, there was clear evidence that they were marginalised even in this highly digitally-resourced area (Galperin, Bar, & Helsper, 2019).

Research shows that regional differences in infrastructure do not impact all individuals equally. That is, the gaps in access between rural and urban areas are largest for the poorest households. The poor are proportionately better off in terms of access when they live in wealthier urban areas than when they live in rural or inner-city areas (Prieger, 2013). Nevertheless, this also means that a poor person in a large metropolitan area is comparatively more disadvantaged than their counterpart in a rural village. The poor urbanite is competing for jobs and resources with others who are much more connected than individuals in the village. While infrastructure is best in suburbs in most US cities, in many other parts of the world this distribution is different. In Sao Paolo, for example, the exact opposite pattern can be observed: the outskirts of the city are poorer and worse connected (NIC.br, 2019). However, US cities and Sao Paolo similarly have broadband speed distributed in patterns that reflect real estate prices (Mossberger, Tolbert, & Franko, 2013; NIC.br, 2019).

In summary, those in the Global South, in more remote regions, and poorer urban areas live in less dense digital ecologies. To them, high-quality, ubiquitous, and autonomous access is the preserve of the wealthy. Interestingly, this might mean that there are fewer disadvantages to being digitally excluded in terms of access for those living in those areas than for those living in richer, more digitally dense ecologies. Next, I turn to the question of how inequalities are perpetuated on an individual level.

Individual inequalities

Wealth, education, and employment status predict having high-quality, ubiquitous, and autonomous access better than residential location. Researchers have shown that at the individual level there is a strong relationship between income, employment and home access/speed, locations, platforms, and mobility. If the only thing we knew about Ben is that he was in debt, unemployed, and has only finished secondary-level education, you could have predicted that he would not have a laptop, home broadband, or the latest model smartphone with a data plan, even if you did not know where he lived.

To understand whether access inequalities might normalise or amplify in the future as societies become more digital, it is useful to look at trends in the quality and ubiquity of access over time. In the UK, high-quality access has increased for all groups (Figure 3.4). However, the gap in broadband access between people both without employment and with low levels of education and those with high levels of education and employment gradually increased too (ONS, 2003–2014). To understand what this comparison means, think in betting terms. Imagine you placed 'who has broadband' bets in 2003 and now on Ben or his old schoolmate Jake, who has an MBA and is managing his dad's business. The bet on Jake would be more likely to get you a pay-out now than then, because someone like him was much less likely to have access to broadband in 2003 and is almost certain to have it now. Similarly, knowing that Ben is unemployed and has a lower level of education helps to predict how (un)likely he is to have high-quality access better now than 15 years ago. This is because

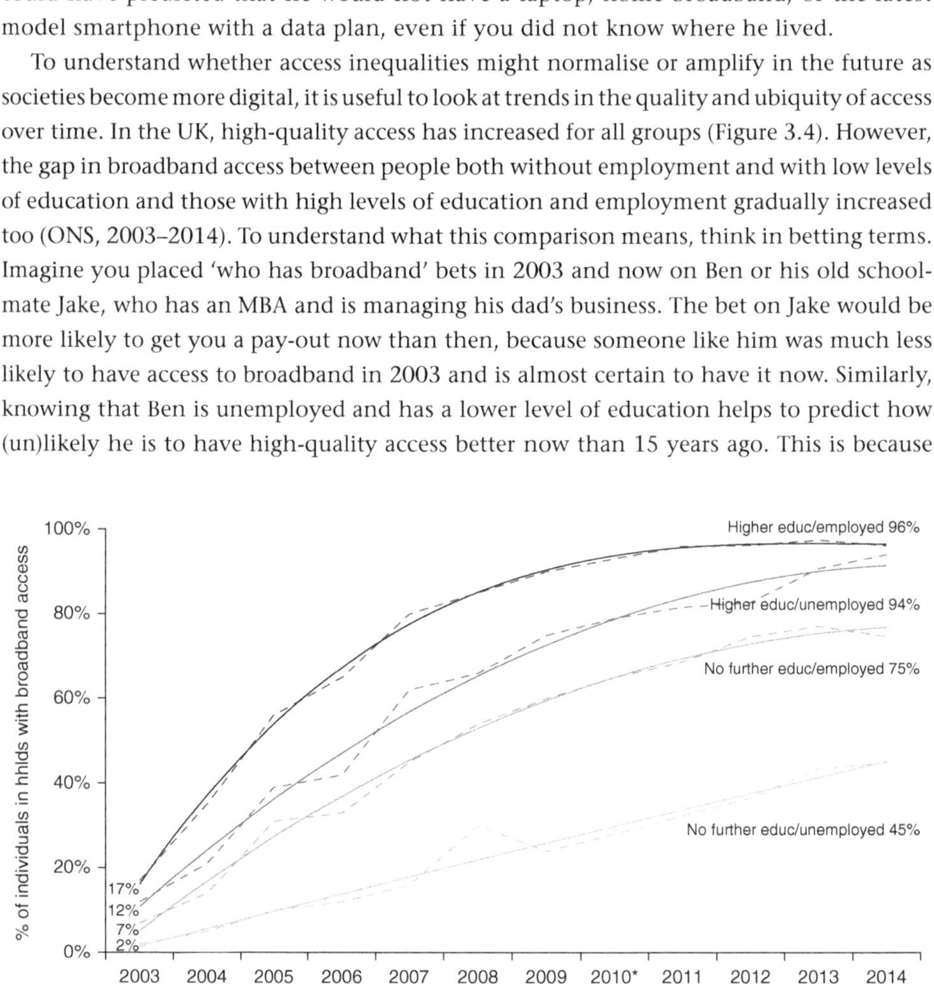

Figure 3.4 Broadband access in the household via mobile or fixed lines (UK) by employment and education level

Source: ONS Omnibus Surveys (ONS, 2003-2014).

Base: Adult Internet Users (Household survey).

* Issues in compatibility when ONS switched to a different survey to collect internet access and use data in 2009 distorted results and 2010 data were estimated based on the mean difference between 2009 and 2011. The smoothed trendlines are more likely to be accurate.

the better off and the disadvantaged were both unlikely to have broadband access in 2003 and thus knowing someone's socio-economic status was irrelevant in predicting high-quality access.

A person's job type could be more important in terms of obtaining actual access than their income (Gonzales, 2016; Mendonca, Crespo, & Simoes, 2015). In high-diffusion countries, most companies and organisations now provide access to the internet, even if the time available to employees is limited. In addition, people who work are likely to be surrounded by others with access. Through them, they can indirectly access opportunities offered by ICTs. Unemployment restricts spaces and platforms to engage with ICTs, as well as making home or personal mobile access less affordable. Ben is in a catch-22 situation. Getting a job could help him to access the opportunities offered by the internet. A job could provide him with potential ICT access on the job and income to acquire better connectivity. Nevertheless, having high-quality access is needed to find and get a job with access to ICTs. This leads him down an 'analogue' path for job searches: 'I'm only going to find the local jobs and then I'll go into the place and hand in my CV and stop there.'

This is why we must look not only at access to, but also at actual use of devices. Martin and Robinson (2014) analysed data from a National Telecommunication and Information Administration (NTIA) report using odds ratios of the likelihood of individuals with certain backgrounds having computer ownership and using the internet. The NTIA's analyses suggested diminishing gaps in access between rich and poor. However, in more precise analysis, Martin and Robinson showed that use was spreading more slowly among poorer households than among richer households. If trends continue, poor households will eventually have the nearly universal levels of computer and internet use currently seen among richer households. However, this 'catching-up' could take two decades, as with broadband uptake by the unemployed and lower educated in the UK (Figure 3.4). The catch-up narrative also assumes that there will be no change in the kinds of access needed to fully participate in digital societies. A move to embedded technologies would mean people like Ben have to start all over again in the race to catch up. Ben would say: 'The tech stuff has got an edge over you, because as you're trying to keep up with it, there's always something else coming out.'

Access does not necessarily correspond to use. In 2014, 45 per cent had broadband access at home (Figure 3.4). Of those who were unemployed and lower educated, only 35 per cent used the internet (Figure 3.5). This difference was much smaller for the highly educated and the employed, who enjoyed near saturation rates for broadband access and internet use. For use, the gap between those with compound economic deprivation and those who are better off will remain almost equal. Nevertheless, when it comes to access, there is a steeper increase in take-up among the unemployed and lower educated, which means that the gap in access is getting smaller and normalisation might be occurring. Ben, living in a wealthy, high-diffusion country, is a typical example of someone who shows up in country statistics as having a mobile phone and a reasonable digital infrastructure in public spaces, but who cannot be said to have high-quality actual access. As many others in similar position to him, he is vulnerable to technology breakdowns and reliant on others to help out (Helsper & Smirnova, 2016). He recounts what happened last year: 'My phone smashed in,

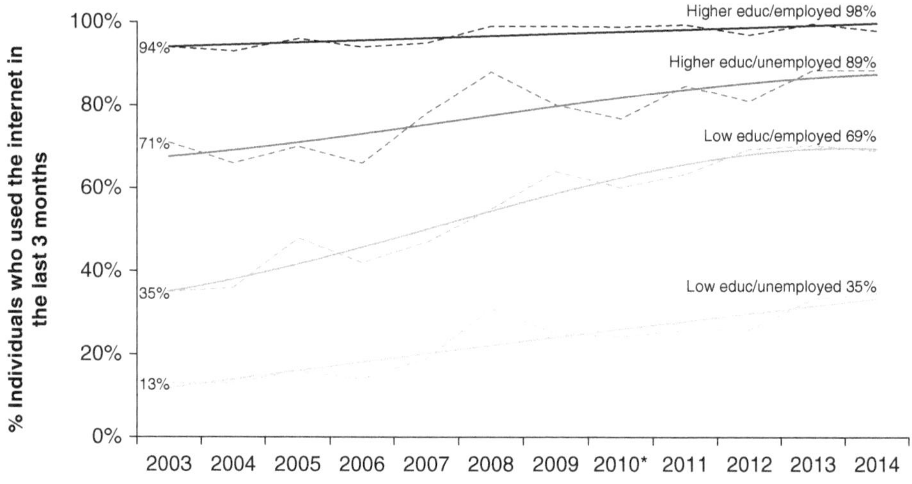

Figure 3.5 Internet use in the last three months over time by education and employment levels in the UK

Source: ONS Omnibus Surveys (2003-2014).

Base: Adults in the UK (household survey).

* The rise in 2008 and the slight dip in use in 2010 might be explained by a switch in the survey that data were collected from. Trendlines are more likely to be accurate.

my friend broke it, then she gave me another phone, and then that phone smashed as well. So then we had no phones.'

Throughout this discussion there has been an underlying difficulty of understanding whether the lack of high-quality, ubiquitous, and autonomous access that people like Ben have is a consequence of his socio-economic situation, or whether his digital disconnect can be considered a cause of him being less well off. This is important for the design of interventions, because if a socio-economic situation is the cause of digital disconnect, then the socio-economic aspects need to be confronted. However, if the digital disconnect itself causes marginalisation, then interventions that change the technical landscape will help (Figure 3.1). In the next sections, I will look at theories about whether social inequalities cause or are the consequences of digital inequalities.

Causes of inequalities in access

If economic resources are a strong predictor of high-quality, ubiquitous, and autonomous access to ICTs, the main barriers to getting online should be costs and a lack of infrastructure in areas where poorer individuals live. People who live in good infrastructure areas where connectivity costs are low should be online. Strong support for this idea in policy is demonstrated by high levels of investment in the rollout of broadband to rural areas, and the regulation of markets to ensure inexpensive, high-quality connections. The reasoning is that once infrastructure improves and prices go down, people will flock to ICTs. This creates a critical mass of connected consumers who require improvement in infrastructure, and a further reduction of prices in order for demand–supply market principles to take hold. However, this ignores the 'upgrade issue'. The ITU's *State of Broadband* report shows that affordable tablets are relatively basic in their functionality and capacity to go online. As a result, they are used far less by their owners than the latest, more expensive, high-end versions (International Telecommunications Union, 2014, p. 25). There is of course value in policies and interventions that lower costs of infrastructure and quality connections. Indeed, lowering the costs and increasing the take-up of smartphones has been the focus of countries in the Global South.

People with fewer economic resources are likely to 'chose' to only or mostly use mobile phones for intrinsic and extrinsic reasons. Extrinsically, users are forced by financial circumstances, being unable to afford other devices (Ofcom, 2016a). Intrinsically, users stick to phones because they evaluate them to be sufficient to meet their needs. Nevertheless, intrinsic drivers are shaped by people's environment and experiences. They push people towards mobile-by-default. For example, in the UK, mobile phone-only use is five times as high among individuals of the lowest socio-economic group in comparison to those in the highest group (Blank, Dutton, & Lefkowitz, 2020). Many of Ben's friends chose to have only a smartphone, not seeing investment in a laptop or PC as worth the money. A smartphone lets them interact with friends, contact their boss, and get daily news. Ben barely has the money for a data plan and would definitely not be able to afford a laptop. Jake might decide he does not need a new laptop because his new fancy smartphone manages all his needs. However, Jake and his friends do not go mobile only because they cannot afford something else and will remain connected at work and at friends' houses through a range of devices.

The pattern in non-use of the internet, and the reasons people give for this disconnect, does not simply correspond to increased ubiquity and dropping prices (Kuttan & Peters, 2003). In analyses using World Internet Project data, we examined the reasons non- and ex-users gave for not being online (Helsper & Reisdorf, 2017). In a country with better infrastructure (i.e. Sweden), a lack of access remained important. In a country with lower-quality infrastructure (i.e. Britain), lack of access decreased in importance as a reason for disconnect. The same study showed that not having access was more important for ex-users than for never-users, even though the infrastructure for both was the same. However, a lack of interest was the only reason for non-use that increased in importance over time, becoming the most important reason. Ben likes messaging his friends and checking the weather every now and then. His phone is old, but does what he needs it to do. He has other problems he needs to deal with and he feels he can use his money more wisely than to buy a new expensive phone he will not really use. That said, changes in Ben's life might motivate him to get a proper internet connection at home. For example, if his daughter comes to live with him or he seeks further education, these factors are likely to push him to get a home connection. The lesson here is: if there are no clear benefits from using ICTs, then it is unlikely that people will acquire better access. They will stick with familiar, trusted offline interactions. This takes me to the next step in the cycle of inequalities in access in my

Corresponding Fields model: the transition from ICT access to how this influences specific uses of ICT and their associated outcomes.

Consequences of inequalities in access

When developing the CF model, I sought to trace the barriers and enablers of engagement in the digital world. I was concerned with what prevents individuals from achieving the benefits from engagement with digital media in their everyday lives. Thus, I examine not just people's digital opportunities, but also what they do with them to achieve tangible outcomes (Helsper, Van Deursen, & Eynon, 2015). The economic domain is where these processes from causes to consequences of disconnect have been studied most. Accordingly, in the remainder of this chapter, I will focus on economic outcomes. Economic outcomes are where policy and industry reports abound, mostly propagating normalisation: potential and actual access will automatically lead to the take-up of economic activities and benefits online.

The idea that universal access will solve economic woes is widespread, not only the preserve of the Global South or the neoliberal right. In the UK's 2019 elections, the Labour Party promised free broadband for all to guarantee an equal future (Labour Party, 2019).

These reports also tout employment benefits. Getting connected is regarded as the best way for countries and small and medium enterprises to improve productivity and for individuals to increase employment. Increasing broadband penetration and speeds is generally associated with GDP growth. Estimates of the impact of broadband on employment gains range from 2.5 to 4.0 additional jobs per additional broadband connection (Kelly & Rossotto, 2012). Katz (2009) calculated that closing the broadband gap of 11 million broadband connections for 12 Latin American countries would create 378,000 jobs. At the individual level, Kuhn and Mansour (2014) calculated that unemployed individuals find a job 25 per cent quicker when they use the internet. Nevertheless, the evidence is mixed and the economic impact of broadband is not always significant, especially in developing countries (Glaumann & Bohlin, 2013; Minges, 2015). There is growing evidence that suggests amplification effects when it comes to who is able to take up the economic opportunities online.

Research shows that people eligible for benefits are among the least likely to access information and other opportunities online. This is true even when those who are unemployed, unwell, and/or on a low wage access ICTs for other activities (Buchanan & Tuckerman, 2016). Mossberger, Tolbert, and McNeal (2007) found that actual access at work correlates with higher income, while more economically-disadvantaged groups benefit the most, relatively, from work access. This is the digital version of the Pareto principle, whereby 'underserved people often require a greater degree of public information and services than the more affluent sections of society' but are the least likely to access it (Mervyn & Allen, 2012, p. 1126). That potential access is not enough is also reflected in Ofcom's (2016a) finding that, in the UK, internet users who are forced to be mostly mobile rely on and trust face-to-face or telephone services more to claim benefits and access services. Ben echoes this sentiment. When looking for jobs, he would 'rather have them walk up to me, have them look me in the eye so I can say: listen I want the job!'

Van Deursen and van Dijk (2014) showed that people with lower levels of education and disabilities were spending more of their spare time online than those with higher educational attainment or employment. However, the former gravitated more towards social interaction and gaming than economically 'productive' activities such as personal development and financial transactions. Arora (2012) found that in the Global South, leisure uses are more common than the socio-economic activities hoped for by organisations investing large funds into digital interventions. She also critiques the judgemental undertones of this research and related policies. People from higher diffusion countries are held to less exacting standards for 'beneficial use'. She sees this as a moral discourse that gives more agency to those in advantaged positions. The privileged get to decide what is 'good for them' while those in disadvantaged positions get told what they need technology for. This often prioritises economic over personal and social well-being uses for the disadvantaged.

The cause and effects issue discussed earlier is particularly problematic in the economic domain. For example, you are much more likely to look for a job if you do not have one. This means that the unemployed are more likely to look for a job online, simply because they are looking. Therefore, the unemployed are more likely to find a job through their internet use. There is a flipside to this, though. The kinds of temporary, zero hours, day-off hire jobs people like Ben are looking for are not readily available online. In other words, Ben is more likely to be looking for a job online than an employed person but is much less likely to find one than someone like Jake, working in administration or management. Ben's frustration is summed up as follows: '...when you're applying for jobs or benefits, you email somebody and you don't get any responses, they don't even acknowledge you.'

Longitudinal research shows that employment correlates with frequent use of the internet for financial activities (White & Selwyn, 2013). This is probably because you need money to be able to save money by buying goods or investing in property online. Ben is a good example. If he wanted to financially benefit from using the internet, he could spend the 30 minutes of internet access at the public library trying to buy something and save money. But at the moment, he can barely afford to buy his friends a pint of beer in the pub. The value of that pint in the company of his mates is far higher for him than saving money. There is little intrinsic motivation for Ben to overcome his disconnect, since the jobs he is looking for are not online and he has no money to buy anything. Similarly, when Ben still had a job, he considered taking a course to become a supervisor in construction, and considered using the internet for education. However, once he got fired, he figured he was too old to learn more. He switched to using his phone only for communication with friends and checking football scores.

DiSTO studies across generations confirm Ben's experience is not unique. ICT use for a particular economic purpose does not lead to associated outcomes for all. In DiSTO research with disadvantaged young people, we found that 88 per cent of the young people surveyed who did not have a job looked for a job online. Nevertheless, only 46 per cent of these found one and only 33 per cent of those who tried managed to upload a CV (Helsper & Smirnova, 2018). In DiSTO (2020) projects with adults, we ask questions about using the internet for work and saving money. Our research shows that the achievement of economic benefits from using the internet is unequally distributed in comparison to other types of activities and their associated benefits (Helsper, Van Deursen, & Eynon, 2015).

This is partly due to an unequal distribution of skills between different socio-economic groups, but not completely. Wealth, education, and employment were also related to the individual economic uses of the internet and the benefits they reap from it. That is, no matter how digitally skilled someone is, if they are poorer or lower educated, they are less likely to achieve high-quality financial and education outcomes than those who are economically better off.

The Corresponding Fields framework was supported more than we expected, even in a country like the Netherlands, with low levels of socio-economic inequalities and high diffusion levels (Van Deursen et al., 2017). Income and employment status strongly related to achieving high-quality economic outcomes in both 2015 and 2018. While achievement of work-related outcomes was higher for the unemployed, satisfaction with the jobs they found was lower for the unemployed than the employed. In general, as I will show throughout this book, inequalities in the quality of outcomes are even more striking than for the achievement of outcomes (Van Deursen & Helsper, 2015). To demonstrate, let's return to Ben, who is unemployed but entitled to benefits. Earlier I explained how it is difficult to achieve financial outcomes because his unemployment benefits go into paying his debts. Additionally, he cannot go online to check whether he is getting the right benefits. A little money is coming into his account every month, so he assumes it's OK.

This is the vicious cycle in the economic causes and consequences of digital disconnect. People with the most economic resources are most likely to live in good infrastructure areas and have high-quality, ubiquitous, and autonomous personal access. They frequently engage in online activities that build these resources, and are more likely to accrue economic benefits from this use (Van Dijk & Hacker, 2003). This suggests that the gap between the economically rich and poor is likely to become larger over time, unless interventions can break this cycle.

What should be done about inequalities in access?

This chapter has shown that improving ICT access remains key to tackling inequality in increasingly digital societies. Improving infrastructure and access are rightly high on the agendas for growth and inclusion of the majority of national government agendas. However, in many digital agendas, access provision problematically remains the sole focus (Helsper, 2018; Whitacre, Strover, & Gallardo, 2015). In addition, digital agendas and industry reports are concerned with economic benefits for the country and society. They tend to ignore other types of inequalities that might arise with further digitisation (Arora, 2012). Discussions about these other types of digital inclusion and outcomes make up the next chapters of this book. In this section, I will examine whether policies and interventions that try to create equal opportunities in access and subsequent beneficial economic outcomes are likely to be successful. This is where the issue of cause and effect is extraordinarily prescient, because how inequalities in digital societies are understood determines the effectiveness of interventions and policies.

Digital agendas are often embedded in economic development, growth policies, and infrastructure policies. As a result, agendas are based on pillars of universal access to transport and telecommunications infrastructure. Policy makers reason that these guarantee the human rights of freedom of movement, free speech, and education. The language used in their documents suggests that by improving and investing in ICT infrastructure and access to devices, economic development of countries will follow (Helsper, 2018). Politicians and stakeholders emphasise that being online is needed to achieve cheaper travel, better jobs, and access to government services. They believe that organisations would save money if all services were provided online and their employees were connected (e.g. Digital Europe, 2019). As a result, programmes are oriented towards disadvantaged or remote areas with poor infrastructure and access and not at those where actual access (i.e. uptake) is the problem. They emphasise that these inequalities cause inequalities in wealth and resources. This implies that providing accessible and affordable infrastructure and access will alleviate inequalities, since all will benefit equally from going online.

Industry and consultancy documents similarly prefer the language of inclusive growth. Very rarely do they acknowledge that digitisation might be linked to increased socio-economic inequalities. Channelling diffusion of innovation approaches, they instead emphasise the potential for ICTs to change things for everyone (Friederici, Ojanperä, & Graham, 2017). Using macro-economic assessments, the optimistic techno-determinist argument goes that ICTs will allow countries to join the knowledge economy, sparking positive developmental outcomes from an open and accessible internet. The One Laptop per Child (OLPC) programme, popular at the beginning of the 21st century, is an example of this. Negroponte aimed to give all children access to low-cost laptops in participating countries (Kraemer, Dedrick, & Sharma, 2009). They soon came across political and social obstacles, as well as the earlier critiques about the effectiveness of these interventions in fostering education and learning. Around 3 million laptops were handed out, mainly in Latin America. The much smaller final scheme became a shared laptop at schools rather than a one-per-child scheme. Its proponents blamed its failure on political and economic policies that limited rollout and the potential impact of these programmes. However, interventions that were more successful in rolling out the programme showed that, even under those conditions of equal access opportunities, benefits were unequally distributed.

Many digital agendas and consultancy documents glaze over historical and geographic contexts, assuming a universal effect of connectivity. They have little consideration for how access might benefit the rich more than the poor. Friederici et al. (2017) warn that policy and industry documents are often written by those that benefit from increased ICT diffusion and use. Therefore, it is not strange that they see ICTs as the main sites for interventions and solutions. This is evidenced by the push from companies like Facebook and Google to take over what should be government initiatives in providing phones and internet connections in the Global South (Shahin, 2018).

Digital inclusion policies and third-sector initiatives take a slightly more nuanced approach. They explicitly orient themselves towards reducing economic as well as infrastructure and access inequalities. That is, they see inequalities in access as a consequence of and contributor to inequalities in wealth and resources. While this social-digital feedback loop is recognised in their understanding of inequalities in digital societies, the design of interventions is still mostly focused on ICT provision rather than creating accountability structures around the reduction of socio-economic inequalities as a result of this provision.

A sole concern with access, instead of embedding ICT policies into social policies, limits the effectiveness of interventions. Ineffectiveness is compounded by a narrow understanding of access. Unless policies and initiatives start to incorporate potential and actual access, and take quality, ubiquity, and autonomy of use as desirable outcomes, interventions are less likely to be effective. For example, relying on smartphones and public access points to get the most disadvantaged connected is problematic. While smartphones seem to increase ubiquity and autonomy, in reality they fail because they provide lower-quality and restricted ubiquity and autonomy. For example, paying for a data plan is difficult, so people rely on WiFi to connect, reducing ubiquity. Phones are often shared, which limits autonomy. In addition, the quality of actual use suffers even with a high-speed connection. Uses of smartphones are narrower, and it is difficult to create content like CVs or professional videos on a phone. Truly effective interventions need to be contextual, taking these constraints into consideration. They should measure success by sustained use that provides high-quality outcomes for all and not by devices handed out.

Inequalities in infrastructure, access, and use are easier to intervene in than poverty or education. No wonder that providing tablets, free or cheap mobile phones, and public WiFi access is enthusiastically embraced. It is vital that this is done. Nevertheless, we cannot sit back and relax once a platform has been rolled out. There is contradictory evidence about the ability of ubiquitous infrastructure and lower costs to solve digital inequality, let alone socio-economic inequalities. Over time, the gap between rich and poor in actual access has increased, even though prices have plummeted and infrastructure has improved. More affluent people are able to benefit more from improved infrastructure and lower costs than the poor. Kuttan and Peters (2003) argued that focusing on providing affordable access to ICTs that are cutting-edge at a certain point in time is not sustainable. What type of connection and equipment are needed for efficient and effective digital engagement changes over time.

Returning to Ben, he would appreciate a free or low-cost tablet. However, in a year's time, the provider will probably come out with a new model. Apps will require more memory and only run on the latest operating system, which he cannot download. 6G might be in place while he still has only 4G. Unless his economic situation improves or he sees the value of investing in a tablet, the provision of cheap access will only be a temporary solution to his digital disconnect.

Beyond a potential for ICTs to phase out, we should scrutinise autonomy of use in platform provision interventions like the OLPC. Looker and Naylor (2010, p. 174) caution that interventions positioning public ICT access as an agent of change to support transitions out of poverty may only lead to 'a short-term relief of misery'. Due to circumstances of compound socio-economic exclusion, relief cannot be sustained outside the particular situation where access is provided by external parties (e.g. the library). In addition, access interventions are often subject to the 'lower hanging fruit' phenomenon; their success and uptake are higher among the more easily reached and advantaged. The harder to reach and more disadvantaged are left behind by these programmes (Araque et al., 2013). While providing high-quality access at low cost is important, ensuring these connections are ubiquitous where individuals live their everyday lives in is even more important. These locations should be convenient for and already frequented by individuals, such as work, schools, gyms, pubs, community centres, or libraries. This will merge people's social and digital ecologies. Ideally, people would enjoy use at these locations without restrictions or supervision, but with support.

In a future where the Internet of Things is a reality, merging ecologies will be even more important to prevent the already disconnected from falling further behind, because they move and live in parallel disconnected universes with very different socio-digital ecologies. Tackling labour, wealth, and other inequalities alongside digital inequalities will be the only way to prevent a socio-digital underclass from emerging (Fuchs, 2009; Helsper & Reisdorf, 2017).

Conclusions: Economic inequalities in digital societies

Universal ICT access and infrastructure is an essential step towards diminishing inequalities in an increasingly digital world. High-quality access gives people an economic advantage over those with no or low-quality access. Therefore, it is no surprise that access and infrastructure inequalities – also referred to as the first-level digital divide – have long been prioritised on research and policy agendas. This is why we should still care about inequalities in access, although not just any access will do. Most research and policy making uses simplistic definitions of access. These have caused all kinds of problems when predicting who might be disadvantaged in increasingly digital societies, and designing effective policies. If we understand inequalities through what Van Dijk (2020) called material access, we cannot be satisfied by just asking whether someone has access to ICTs. Responding to my question posed at the beginning of this chapter, I define access across three levels:

• Infrastructure such as fibre cable, broadband speed • Devices to connect to the available infrastructure	} potential access
• Use of devices and infrastructure to access content	} actual access

At each level, three factors determine its quality:

- Quality – the speed and features of the infrastructure, devices, and websites visited
- Ubiquity – access is available whenever and wherever needed
- Autonomy – the opportunity to use without reliance on, or control by, others

Most theorisations and interventions involve only improvements in potential access and quality of connectivity. However, ubiquity is increasingly part of national policies, and industry and third sector initiatives. Notwithstanding these initiatives, often led by big tech companies in the Global South, the relationship between wealth and access has not decreased. Inequalities in high-quality potential access, such as having broadband at home, and actual access have increased between countries and between individuals. The hope that smartphones and tablets will solve inequalities in access should therefore be tempered with the evidence presented in this chapter.

Smartphones' capacity for varied, autonomous use is limited. Reliance on these devices has been linked to more narrow actual use and fewer benefits, especially for the more socio-economically disadvantaged. Cheap smartphone connectivity and public access points are certainly better than nothing. Nevertheless, if phones and access points are the sole emphasis in interventions, those who can afford the latest technology and have the socio-economic resources to take advantage of high-speed services will rush ahead at greater speeds than those who cannot afford to update continuously. A neoliberal, demand-driven infrastructure and access model will inexorably produce increasing inequalities. Caught in a vicious cycle, those who do not have economic resources to acquire quality ICT access are less likely to translate their use of ICTs into improvements in their socio-economic situation.

The answer to my question about what can be done about socio-economic inequalities in access seems straightforward: provide affordable, universal access to those who cannot afford it. A misplaced, techno-utopian, 'access drives economic well-being' idea has accompanied almost all past ICTs. Consistently, equality of opportunity through the improvement of infrastructure and provision of access to the latest device does not translate into equality of use. Even worse, such approaches rarely translate into equal socio-economic outcomes for people from different backgrounds. Complex interlinking means that economic and digital inequalities need to be tackled in parallel through multi-stakeholder approaches to prevent the amplification of traditional inequalities based on capital and labour. In other words, to obtain a good return on investments in infrastructure and access, we need to ensure that potential benefits exist for everyone, and relevant content and services are accessible for the disadvantaged. Setting up funding and accountability structures based on improvements in sustainable socio-economic outcomes for access-based interventions will help to achieve this goal.

There are other important causes for digital disconnect, such as a lack of skills and relevant digital content and services for the disconnected. Access interventions can overcome extrinsic barriers, such as not being able to afford devices and a lack of network availability in areas where people live. Nevertheless, intrinsic barriers, such as people's perceptions that ICTs have nothing to offer to them, are often more important to steering people away from ICTs. People with higher education and children in their household are more likely to value access, independent of their income. It has further become clear that objectively lower-quality access does not always mean someone is worse off than their peers. The value of access depends on where you live, what you do, how connected everyone else is, and what the alternatives to the digital in your environment are.

To address these issues, the next chapter will look at how access interventions cannot be implemented separately from literacy and awareness training. The subsequent chapters propose that initiatives should situate ICT use within existing needs, interests, and motivations of individuals within their social and cultural contexts.

CHAPTER 4

SKILLS AND LEARNING INEQUALITIES IN DIGITAL SOCIETIES

> 'ICT skills determine the effective use that is made of ICTs, and are critical to leveraging their full potential for social and economic development. Economic growth and development will remain below potential if economies are not capable of exploiting new technologies and reaping their benefits.'
>
> ITU (2016)

The previous chapter discussed research, policy, and interventions in access and infrastructure. Framed within the paradigm of first-level digital inequalities, Ben illustrated the link between a lack of high-quality and ubiquitous access to ICTs and outcomes. It turns out that access alone is not sufficient to tackle inequalities in opportunities in digital societies. Research that defined inclusion as access to ICTs found individuals who were 'unexpectedly excluded' – they had access to the internet but did not use it or did so in very limited ways. From this research, the idea emerged that a lack of digital skills could explain this phenomenon. The idea that digital skills were key to unlocking 'economic potential', as expressed in this chapter's opening quote, drove interest in defining and measuring digital skills and literacy at the beginning of the 21st century. Interest in skills was accompanied by a boom in online resources for online learning. Wikis, newspapers, online learning platforms, and instructional YouTube videos found mass appeal, teaching nearly anything: hard-core coding, origami, and professional make-up. This led to optimism around the learning and knowledge acquisition opportunities through access to ICTs for the traditionally disadvantaged. Access would help them overcome inequalities in socio-economic and personal resources that restricted their access to formal and informal education.

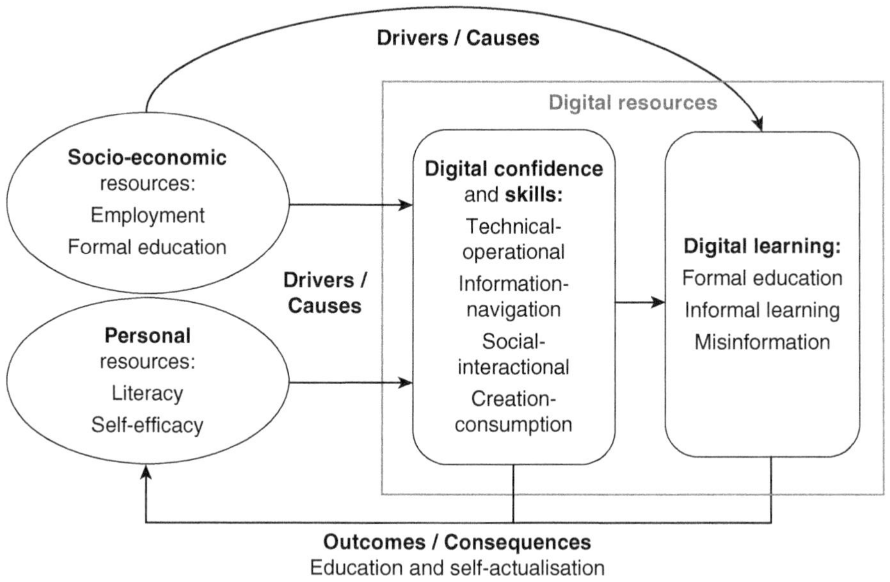

Figure 4.1 Links between traditional and digital socio-economic and learning inequalities

In this chapter, I follow the Corresponding Fields (CF) model path from socio-economic and personal resources to the digital skills and learning that augment these resources (Figure 4.1). Definitions and understandings of digital skills and digital literacy have changed considerably. This chapter, therefore, discusses definitions and the measurement of digital skills, and how shifts in both continue to influence the design of policies and interventions. I define digital skills as: the abilities that allow someone to make the most out of their use of ICTs by taking up opportunities and avoiding harms. Inequalities in digital skills, defined in this way, are core to understanding inequalities in digital societies. To understand whether ICT access will help traditionally disadvantaged people catch up, I respond to two key questions related to socio-digital skills and inequalities:

- Is the abundance of learning opportunities online taken up equally by all once they have gained access to ICTs?
- How are ICT-based knowledge acquisition and learning outcomes linked to inequalities in traditional socio-economic and personal resources and digital skills?

This chapter will show that socio-economic resources and educational background drive inequalities in digital skills between and within countries. Fortunately, the heightened attention and concern around digital skills – as an indicator of progress and 'future readiness' – has driven a relative abundance of global measures of digital skills. Indexes like the ITU's ICT Development Index (IDI) benchmark countries and push industry and policy makers to ensure those who lag behind 'catch up' (ITU, 2017a).

In this chapter, Ana's vignette illustrates how inequalities in digital skills connect with traditional inequalities and how they relate to inequalities in the outcomes of the use of ICTs. For the purpose of this chapter, I will emphasise resources and outcomes of formal and informal learning, because they are of pressing concern. I will also touch on the importance of digital skills in relation to other domains, such as socialising and general well-being. Like Ben in the previous chapter, Ana's experiences are a compilation of stories shared with me by the people I have had the pleasure to meet through my research.

Case Study: Ana

Ana is 28, has dropped out of school, and lives in Los Angeles (US). At the moment she has a job as a cashier in a supermarket and earns a bit of extra money as a cleaner for friends, with which she is able to survive financially. She has a small apartment. Her parents live nearby and help her out in taking care of her son while she and her boyfriend, who works in the kitchen of a fast-food restaurant, are at work. Her parents did not finish school either. Her dad works hard as a bus driver. Her mum used to work as a waitress at a local diner but stopped working a few years ago to take care of her mother. Ana and her parents have lived in the same neighbourhood for 22 years. She would like to get out of the neighbourhood and find a different kind of job. She is looking for opportunities to go back to school and learn a new set of skills that would allow her to move on professionally. Ana has a smartphone and a computer that is connected to broadband at home.

Here is how she would describe herself in terms of her use of technologies such as the internet and mobile phones: 'I'm really clumsy with them. I ask my boyfriend who is more up to date with these things, and my son too, he's really on board. I need to know at least enough to take care of myself, for example, when I need to find directions. I focus on what I really need to know!'

This chapter is organised around Livingstone's (2013) challenges for media literacy. The 'why should we care about skills?' section emphasises skill over access when it comes to socio-digital inequalities, and looks at the policy discourse. Then I tackle Livingstone's 'what?' question about the challenges of assessing progress when there are gaps in the definition of literacy and no clear metrics for success. Subsequently, the 'whether and who is digital literacy for?' questions will be addressed through illustrations with data about who tends to lack which skills with what consequences. I conclude with questions about who is responsible for digital upskilling, and how interventions can be effective. Importantly, a lack of digital skills and ability to learn using ICTs is very present in Ana's generation of supposed 'digital natives' – not just older people (Helsper, 2019a). This means that if no solution is found to the unequal distribution of digital skills and online knowledge acquisition, socio-digital inequalities will continue well into the future.

Why should we care about digital skills inequalities?

The discourse around leapfrogging is omnipresent when it comes to the opportunities for disadvantaged individuals and countries. They are often told they can acquire the knowledge and skills to propel themselves into a brighter future through connected devices. Ana was forced to drop out of school because her home lacked educational resources, and she had to take care of her young child. The experiences she did have with the formal education system were frustrating: a fixed curriculum with irrelevant examples. Now she has been out of formal education, she would not feel comfortable going back to school. In this context, the potential of digital technologies appears limitless. They give her access to educational materials at institutions that she could never have imagined attending, and personalised learning tailored to her pace of learning and interests.

This techno-optimist discourse – still prevalent in many parts of the world – emphasises access provision as the solution to problems of exclusion and inequality (Friederici et al., 2017; Helsper, 2018). Yet, the previous chapter shows that access alone is not enough to proliferate use of technologies by all. A lack of skills is now widely seen as the most important barrier to fruitful engagement. For Ana, access is really not the issue; she has a smartphone and a home PC connection and there is plenty of public WiFi to go around where she is. Another problem is that she does not know how to navigate the digital world to find the information she needs, and she becomes frustrated with application forms and confusing websites.

Let me draw an analogy with a traditional medium through which many generations have learned – books. Simple access to books through schools and libraries has never created equality of opportunity in learning or employment. Literacy is fundamental to taking in knowledge through texts. Knowing how to read and write are skills learned and practised at home, at work, and when walking down the street. Ana's traditional reading level in English can be described as functional; she will be able to follow instructions from a manual, but is not as confident in more formal settings. Her day job involves very little writing or reading beyond the information that appears on her cash register. She uses Spanish – in which she is more proficient – in her everyday relationships, exchanging texts with her family and posting updates on social networking sites. As a result, it is unlikely that she will learn advanced literacies 'on the job' or in her everyday life.

I am not the first to argue that digital skills are key to digital inclusion, which Hargittai (2002) labelled as the second digital divide. I am not comfortable with using the term 'divide' because it implies that people either have or lack skills. I prefer to imagine gradations of skills. Still, I align myself with researchers who emphasise that inequalities in the take-up of opportunities in digital societies cannot be understood without incorporating skills into the toolkit (Litt, 2013; Van Deursen & Van Dijk, 2014). Digital skills are also high on the political agenda, evident in policy documents. They express concern about the 'digital skills gap' or 'skills deficit' assumed to be holding countries, businesses, and individuals back. Explicitly linking digital skills to traditional literacy, these organisations emphasise 'the importance of bolstering students' ability to navigate through digital texts [but first] all students need to be equipped with basic literacy and numeracy skills so that they can participate fully in the hyper-connected, digitised societies of the twenty-first century' (Van Deursen & Van Dijk, 2014, p. 204; OECD, 2015b). In this area, Europe is leading with its DigComp framework, which informs the New Skills Agenda (Vuorikari, Punie, Carretero Gomez, & Van Den Brande, 2016), and the UK has established a specific Digital Skills and Inclusion Policy (UK Government, 2017a). A report by Doteveryone, one of the partners in the UK government's multi-stakeholder Research Working Group on Digital Inclusion, estimated an annual price tag of £744 per person resulting from a lack of basic digital skills and not using the internet (R. Newman, 2017).

The emphasis has shifted from access provision to skilled uses of technologies. Scholars, including me, have long argued that this shift is necessary to truly tackle digital inequalities. Nevertheless, the debate around digital skills is still heated. Often, there is a lack of nuance and clarity about how digital skills relate to and are different from use or confidence, particularly as employed in large-scale surveys. A lack of precision in defining digital literacy hinders robust evaluations of digital policy and intervention effectiveness in achieving a sufficient level of skill. In the next section, I will look at why a nuanced conceptualisation (and measurement) of skills is so important, building on work from the DiSTO projects and the extensive literature on digital literacy and inclusion.

Defining skills/literacy and 'educational' uses of the internet

A substantial body of literature now describes how digital skills and literacy can be defined and measured. From the beginning of this debate, distinctions were made between different elements of digital literacy. The first distinction was between self-efficacy (i.e. the confidence people have in themselves) and skills. This distinction is important because self-efficacy and confidence are often expressions of general social position (e.g. gender, race) and associated status in society, rather than whether someone can actually do a task. Self-efficacy is important in stimulating people to learn and try out things, driving risk taking and learning through trial and error (Gecas, 1989). However, while self-efficacy often increases with skills, the reverse is not necessarily true; higher levels of self-efficacy with lower levels of skill might prevent a person from understanding what they are not able to do (Broos & Roe, 2006). Ana, who lacks confidence, is more likely to blame herself, her lack of skills, or her inability to learn about ICTs. Yet, she is quite good at managing personal relationships online, keeping different types of relationship separate and protecting her privacy. She has problems with information navigation, which prevents her from finding information on health care. As a result, she uses social apps extensively but is hesitant to look for information online.

What do we mean by digital skills? The skills debate has been dominated by an applied sciences approach from computer science and education. This dominance has resulted in an emphasis on technical competencies related to operating devices and using software. On the higher end of the spectrum, they include programming and coding. More recently, there has been a move towards an integrated skills framework that includes increasingly important 'softer' skills (Helsper & Van Deursen, 2018). This distinction between technical and social is important even with online activities that do not seem intuitively based on these types of skill. Consider informal learning online; people will often rely on their ability to understand social conventions and structures of the internet. Knowing how to network and how to decide who to trust and what is appropriate are all important in relation to informal online learning. In addition, learning which interactivity is effective, how to exchange ideas, and understanding why information is shared are all relevant for online learning.

Thinking ahead, technologies are becoming embedded into our bodies and the objects around us, and decision-making is made by algorithms and artificial intelligence (AI). It might seem that digital skills will become less important. This is the same argument that arose with tablets, since they are so much easier to use. Yet, Van Deursen and Mossberger (2018) have argued that, while a lack of technical skills will become less of an issue, critical information and social and content creation skills will become even more important in digital societies where ICTs are increasingly invisible.

Simultaneously, an important parallel discussion is taking place about the distinction between skills and literacy. The latter builds on a long tradition of critical, creative, and interpretative media literacy research. In media literacy, digital literacy links to empowerment and resistance against ideological and commercial content and production processes that serve elites. There are clear parallels here with thinking about print literacy. For example, Freire & Macedo (1987) criticised the understanding of literacy embodied in conceptualisations of basic and functional literacy. He argued that the latter limit literacy to the passive consumption of messages. For full citizenship and participatory democracy, critical and cultural literacy have to be part of education and civil society (Yosso, 2002). In the digital era, this means literacy should not just be conceptualised as different types of skills people have to satisfy needs or let them use platforms in the way intended by designers and seen as productive by 'authorities' (Luke, 2012). Learning in this context is more open-ended. Breaking things, anti-normative behaviour, play, interacting with others, and creating content are just as important.

This conceptualisation of digital literacy follows the work of critical media literacy scholars (Jenkins, 2013). Buckingham (2007) defines engagement with ICTs as rooted in a critical understanding of how content is produced. Content creation enables a person to resist political and commercial forces, especially those acting against their interests. This approach defines skills necessary to live in digital societies by looking at whether the person and the collectives she belongs to are able to engage with ICTs in ways that contribute to a fairer and more equal future society. For example, if Ana were to take digital skills training, would her newly acquired information navigation and content creation skills empower her to use ICTs and improve education for young mothers? Would the training make her realise the value of her community and network management skills, or just teach her how to manage privacy settings on social networks? This is important because digital literacy draws on social, cultural, and technical knowledge acquired in other formal and informal contexts. For this reason, it cannot be taught through simplistic one-off courses because digital literacy is embedded in broader life trajectories and social structures.

Skills and literacy in increasingly digital societies is about more than the ability to use a particular device. Digital skills are also more than just intense use of the internet. Frequent use is indeed related to a person's confidence in engaging with the wide variety of resources available online (Livingstone & Helsper, 2010). Nevertheless, this use may not be skilled or effective in achieving beneficial outcomes or adaptability to rapidly-changing digital environments. Therefore, I propose the following detailed definition of digital literacy, based on the definition of digital inclusion given in Chapter 2:

> An individual is digitally literate when they have the knowledge and skills needed to use (or decide not to use) ICTs in ways that help them achieve beneficial, high-quality outcomes for themselves and others now and in the future.

This brings me to how definitions of digital skills and literacy are measured. The challenges with available measures reflect the issues of conceptualisation I hinted at above. At the most basic level, they do not measure skill, but rather use of specific technologies or platforms. In high- and low-diffusion countries alike, the effectiveness of interventions tackling digital inequalities is often measured by looking at the number of people using the internet, online activities undertaken, and the number of people who have attended courses. Looker and Naylor (2010, p. 135) lament that this approach is lacking, especially when it comes to young people: 'Simply because students today appear to be exposed to new technologies does not necessarily denote literacy with ICTs.' Indeed, much of the fascination with 'digital natives' equates use of technology with skilled use of technology (Hargittai, 2010; Selwyn, 2009). There is a correlation between use of technology and skills when they are measured separately, but they are not equal; just because a person is not using ICTs for certain tasks does not mean they are unable to. Similarly, being active on certain platforms does not mean that use of these platforms is of high quality. Ana, for example, uses social media on an almost daily basis. Nevertheless, she struggles with changing settings, is not confident that she can distinguish real from fake news, and does not understand issues around filter bubbles, algorithmic selection, and so on (Ofcom, 2019).

Even when questions are asked about separate skills, measures are often reductive in their assumption of what matters for full participation in digital societies. Many tests, instruments, and policy documents focus on information navigation and interpretation skills. Skills related to interactivity, 'Web 2.0' activities, and critical literacy skills are not always included. In a book chapter for UNESCO, we compared four large surveys that measure digital skills in an internationally comparative context (Global Kids Online, MIL, DigComp and EAVI). It became clear that basic content creation and operational skills measures were often absent, especially for personal, mobile technologies (Livingstone, Burton, et al., 2017). Information navigation skills and social skills – limited to privacy and data protection rather than netiquette – were covered by almost all surveys.

Furthermore, survey questions often ask about use rather than skill and rely on self-reports indicating confidence, rather than skill. This reliance on self-reported use leads to individuals from advantaged backgrounds overrating and their skill levels. A few people are discussing better ways to ask these questions. For example, in the DiSTO project, we avoided contextual items related to specific platforms or activities (Van Deursen,

Helsper, & Eynon, 2016). A problem with platform- or device-based survey items is they are dependent on what type of activity is popular. They are not good indicators of enduring, transferrable skills or different contexts in the digital space.

Understanding which skills are equivalent to grammar in language is indeed difficult. At the moment, there is no agreement beyond broader acceptance of the existence of 'hard' and 'soft' skills. It has proven difficult to incorporate measurements of critical digital literacy in population tests, but they seem important for a digitally-engaged and empowered citizenship. Previous measurements of information skills were individually context-dependent, measured only in relation to particular tasks or digital texts (Livingstone, Burton, et al., 2017). Yet, the training and performance tests these skills require are often conducted in formal education settings and not available to many people (Pagani, Argentin, Gui, & Stanca, 2016). Take Ana. She dropped out of school, but even when she was in school her engagement with ICTs was minimal. Classes restricted her to working with spreadsheets. The only courses available to her are at her local community centre, set in computer rooms with teachers, a context in which she feels uncomfortable.

Another struggle in this field is whether digital skills and literacy can be measured among those who have only limited engagement with ICTs, such as Ana's parents. There is an implicit assumption that only those who use technologies are skilled, but knowledge, skills, and use are not identical. The DiSTO project created scales that were not subject to social desirability or 'confidence' bias (Van Deursen et al., 2016). It also asked questions that someone who has not engaged with a type of activity online could answer. It proved vital, for countering social desirability bias, to allow people to make a distinction between knowing how to do an activity without having actually done it and not knowing at all. Asking how much certain statements apply to them – rather than asking them to rate their own skill level on scales from good to bad – also helped overcome these methodological challenges.

There are still challenges in separately measuring different kinds of skills and literacy, and separating awareness or knowledge, skills, and actions. However, there is high value in separately measuring different skills, and constructing measures that are not subject to bias and target transferrable skills. These types of question permit a more nuanced understanding which allows for more targeted policy making, effective skills training, and accurate evaluations of digital inclusion initiatives. An important part of evaluation is to make explicit what being digitally literate is supposed to lead to, because we should be interested in what these digital skills help us to achieve rather than about the skills themselves.

What are digital skills and literacy for?

What digital skills are for depends on who is being considered as the 'subjects' of concern. Those preoccupied with adults, focus on basic digital skills and social and economic marginalisation. That is, they are concerned with the most disadvantaged individuals in society who could benefit from digital skills. They see the elderly and unemployed as most at risk. For example, Ana's grandma lives on her own, but needs care. She would be 'disadvantaged' because she does not know how to operate a PC, and lacks the basic skills to navigate the internet. She is likely to be missing out on benefits related to managing her pension and accessing health services. Skills training available for such socio-economically disadvantaged groups alleviate fear of computers, increase confidence, and impart basic operational and information navigation skills (Huang, Cotten, & Rikard, 2017; Schumacher & Morahan-Martin, 2001). The unemployed are also of concern. Lower digital skills for them complicates accessing online job opportunities, as well as a lower likelihood of being hired since they do not have skills needed to do many jobs (Chapter 3). While there is an acknowledgement that the lesser-educated often also lack digital skills, there is very little emphasis on how a lack of digital skills makes it hard to study or find information. Many digital skills programmes, including those with younger disadvantaged individuals who are not in education employment or training (NEETs), conduct digital skills training to help people find jobs, rather than further education (Helsper & Smirnova, 2016; Simmons & Thompson, 2011).

The second part of the debate about what skills are for relates to the other end of the spectrum: advanced skills, employment, and formal education. Those concerned with the 'digital skills deficit' mostly refer to the high-end skills that get people into tech or digital jobs. Language here proliferates around coding, digital entrepreneurship, and social innovation. These are considered important because they are needed to get youth into high-tech jobs, become programmers, or work in a STEM career (Robinson et al., 2018). The concern is that women and minority groups are not acquiring the knowledge and skills needed to get into digital careers. Ana's story aligns with this idea of inequalities. She dropped out of school, but even if she had stayed, she would have been unlikely to choose a degree in sciences or computing. She definitely did not enjoy or succeed at the more technical subjects in school, and felt that it was a 'geeky men's thing'.

In summary, concerns about the 'digital skills gap' and inequalities focus on getting more people to work in the tech sector. They are grounded in a market-driven logic of supply and demand in a digital economy, which demands a skilled workforce (Davies et al., 2017). It is considered problematic if many do not have the skills or the confidence to be able to take up these jobs (Martinez-Cantos, 2017). Policy makers and the tech sector are concerned with skills inequalities, so far as they concern market economics. Strikingly, there is hardly any incorporation of critical information literacy and everyday content creation skills in research and interventions with adults, yet these are fundamental to citizenship and participation in digital societies. Programmes emphasise either high-end content creation skills or very basic operational and information navigation skills through formal or institutionalised learning.

The third strand of the debate around what skills are for focuses on the youngest generations. It has its own unique notions of why and which digital skills are important. The inequalities debate is less prominent in this discussion, partly because the myth of the digital native dominates. Within the formal education setting, digital skills are largely thought of as coding, robot design, and programming. The goals of these skills are to get young people into STEM subjects, paving the way to future employment opportunities, mirroring the discourse about young adults (Lyons, Zuchetti, Kass-Hanna, & Cobo, 2019). Nevertheless, research and interventions with the youngest citizens often focuses on risks, staying safe, and critical information literacy skills (Livingstone, Haddon, Görzig, & Ólafsson, 2011). For example, the one thing Ana's son has talked to her about is cyberbullying, which was part of the discussions around recent play at school. He also picked up somewhere that Wikipedia is untrustworthy and should not be used. Contact risks, such as bullying and grooming, which position young people as vulnerable and potential victims, take a prime position in the concerns of parents and teachers. To mitigate these risks, most interventions with children emphasise quite technical skills, such as protecting personal data, blocking strangers, and reporting bad behaviour, rather than socio-emotional and norm-based skills related to appropriate online behaviour.

The EU Kids Online (2019) and Global Kids Online (2019) projects are the most prominent studies contributing to knowledge in this area. These researchers specify the need to look at opportunities and risks as outcomes from digital engagement. Yet, the more detailed analyses and conceptualisations have gravitated towards risks rather than opportunities. There are positive signs of a move towards a more holistic approach that does not stop at protection skills, and reflects an understanding that digital skills are needed for everyday life. This shift privileges social and content creation skills over technical skills and information navigation skills. Recently, more comprehensive social approaches have been incorporated into Ana's son's schoolwork. Classes now discuss awareness and netiquette training of online behaviours, and for the older kids, revenge porn and cyberbullying.

When responding to the question of what digital skills are for, I suggest they should lead to the avoidance of negative outcomes and the facilitation of beneficial outcomes. This means acknowledging that the same activities can carry both benefits and risks. It is resilience, rather than total risk avoidance, that is the most important consequence of digital literacy. Digital resilience is defined as learning from past positive and negative experiences online to avoid negative outcomes and to exploit the benefits from ICT use in the future (Mascheroni & Ólafsson, 2016). Taking risks and having negative experiences are not signs of low levels of literacy, in this context. Instead, it is how much one is able to reduce the harm and increase the benefits of use that denotes literacy (Livingstone & Helsper, 2010). This is a definition that should apply across generations.

Who is most skilled and learns most?

Throughout this chapter, I have argued that digital skills are fundamental to participation in digital societies. The economic and societal consequences of a lack of digital skills are rightly of concern to researchers, policy makers, the third sector, and industry. Yet, their concern is not often underpinned by a nuanced understanding of who lacks which skills, or which skills inequalities impact outcomes of engagement with ICTs. This section will focus on exactly this question: the quantitative and qualitative evidence for the causes and consequences of a lack of digital skills.

Causes of inequalities in digital skills

The lack of cross-national, cross-generational, and longitudinal comparative data about skills challenges our understanding of what factors predict digital skills or subsequent improvements. For this reason, I will have to rely mostly on cohort and population-specific data. Despite shortcomings, I will argue that consistent patterns in the data, backed up by limited panel data, allow for conclusions about what the causes are of inequalities in skill.

Internationally, data collection and quality are not consistent across countries. Questions suffer when asking broadly about use or platforms rather than specific skills (Helsper & Van Deursen, 2018). Nevertheless, these studies do inform our understanding of the link between skills and broad inequalities between regions of the world. The ITU maps visualise differences in digital readiness, including skill-level differences between countries from the Global South and North (ITU, 2018). Breaking general skill levels down shows that developed countries have higher levels of the more basic skills than developing countries (Helsper & Van Deursen, 2018). Differences for more advanced skills, such as programming, are smaller because they are relatively rare. Unpublished analyses of the 2018 ITU data show that many basic activities, such as sending emails with attachments and transferring files between devices, performed by more than half of the population in developed countries, are out of reach of two-thirds of the population of developing countries. These patterns reflect colonial pasts and global flows of capital and labour.

It is not a surprise that these inequalities in digital skills exist, and are strongly related to general education and wealth. The hope is that with improved education and digital skills, these countries can leapfrog and catch up, or even surpass others in GDP growth. The accumulation of evidence consistently defies such a simplistic perspective; opportunities that would allow citizens of these countries to acquire these skills in ways that build on their existing resources and then translate skills into beneficial outcomes are simply not there. It might initially seem that differences in traditional literacy and education provision are to blame. Confusingly, analysis of OECD's Programme for the International Assessment of Adult Competencies (PIAAC) data shows that, among the adult working-age population, the links between traditional literacy, numeracy, and problem solving, and ICT skills at home or work is not strong (Figure 4.2) (OECD, 2019).

Poor infrastructure and a lack of access to personal devices that would allow for informal processes of learning are other common explanations for inequalities between countries. This would mean that once ICTs are widely diffused and accessible, inequalities in skills should disappear. One only has to look at the between- and within-country inequalities in Europe to understand that infrastructure or access levels cannot be the full explanation.

At first glance, Eurostat data show a familiar pattern: the wealthier and more equal Nordic countries have the most skilled citizens (Eurostat, 2019b). The southern and eastern European countries have the fewest citizens with high skill levels (Figure 4.3). However, these patterns do not fully mirror infrastructure and wealth differences. Lithuania, for example, has a very developed infrastructure, but is lower on the list than equally connected countries. Italy has a more developed digital infrastructure and more wealth than Croatia and Latvia, but lags on skills. Researchers continue their struggle to

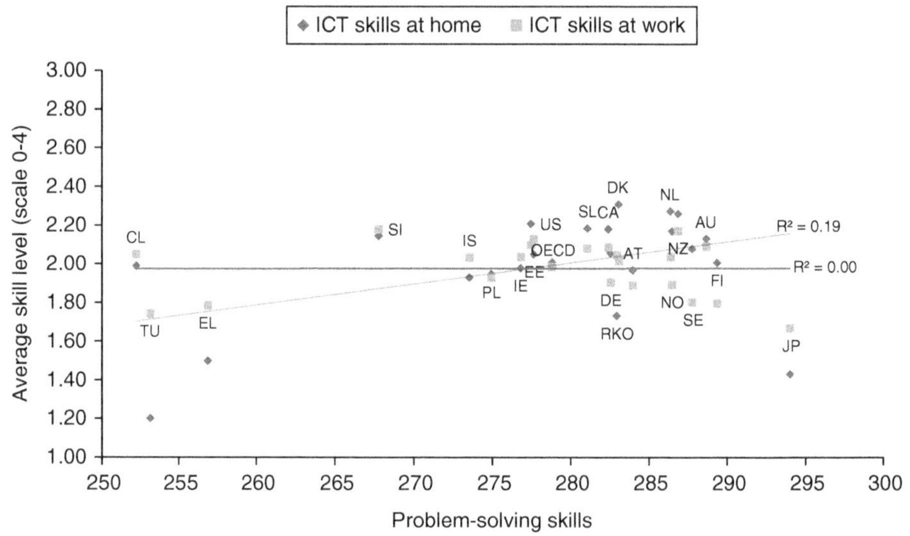

Figure 4.2 Average digital skill levels at home and at work for countries with different levels of problem-solving skills

Source: 2017 PIAAC data (OECD, 2019). Analysis original for this chapter.

Note: The index of use of ICT skills at home/work (derived) ranges from 0 to 4. Problem-solving skills range from 0 to 500.

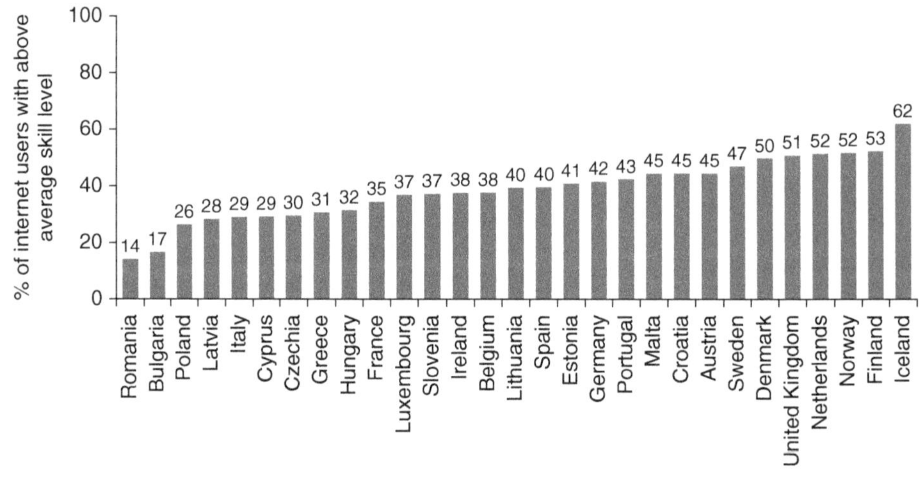

Figure 4.3 Internet users with above average skill levels in European countries

Source: Eurostat (2019b). Analysis original for this chapter.

Base: Adult (19–74 yrs) internet users (used the internet in the last three months).

find country-level explanations for general skill differences based on indicators that are generally used to rank countries in terms of wealth and well-being.

One might expect fewer skill differences between households with children across Europe than between general adult populations, since children are often a motivator to get home access. While there are differences in parental skill patterns, they are not clearly linked to traditional differences in the socio-economic status of a country. For example, even in countries like the Netherlands and Sweden, where there are strong infrastructures for education and low social inequality, only around one-third of parents report high content creation skills (Lupiáñez-Villanueva et al., 2016). Nevertheless, while the correlation between operational and information navigation skills is high (r=.74), the correlation between social and content creation skills (r=.16) is low at the country level. For example, while Swedish parents are likely to have high social skills (83 per cent), there are fewer parents with high levels of information navigation skills (67 per cent) and content creation skills (32 per cent). A more thorough analysis of public policies and education is needed to understand why these countries have these levels of certain skills. Notwithstanding these complicated patterns, most research confirms that inequalities exist between adult populations in advantaged and disadvantaged countries that reflect a historical legacy of inequalities in traditional educational and other opportunities.

This negative picture of the relationship between socio-economic status and digital skills has made policy makers and other stakeholders optimistic about future leapfrogging – if equal access can be provided to all. Their hope is based in a belief that children are digital natives with an innate ability to use and take advantage of technologies. Giving all children, especially disadvantaged children, access to technologies should allow countries that are currently disadvantaged to catch up with more affluent other countries. As described in Chapter 3, this has driven the One Laptop Per Child (OLPC) programmes (Selwyn, 2013). Yet, there is little empirical evidence to support the effectiveness of simple access for leapfrogging. OLPC did not improve children's traditional or digital literacy beyond traditional education, although there were improvements in how to use computers (Ames, 2019; Cristia, Ibarrarán, Cueto, Santiago, & Severin, 2017; Meza-Cordero, 2017). Data from the Global Kids Online project show persistent inequalities in digital skills when children have access and wealth constraints are supposedly overcome. The considerable differences between children from different countries in communication and interaction skills are more surprising. Between a sixth and a third of young people lack the communication and interaction skills needed to safely and effectively manage social digital engagement. This difference might relate to children's exposure to technologies outside the home environment. For example, the OECD report found that 'despite the pervasiveness of information and communication technologies (ICT) in our daily lives, these technologies have not yet been as widely adopted in formal education' (OECD, 2015b, p. 15). The opportunity to learn how to use ICTs in environments where young people spend the most time is unequally distributed between nations and different areas within countries. For example, research in the US and the UK on inequalities in digital skills among schoolteachers shows that teacher subject-specific training and digital literacy are lower in schools in disadvantaged neighbourhoods. Even when ICTs are present in these schools, they are underused in teaching. Lack of expertise combined with missing everyday opportunities to experiment with technologies limits opportunities for learning. This came out strongly in the focus groups with young people not in employment education or training (NEET) (Helsper & Smirnova, 2016): 'P1 I learned by myself … P2 Me too. Pretty much. IV: Nobody was taught in school? P3 I tried to but it was always crap. Everyone would just sit and play games…' (P=participant, IV = interviewer).

Individuals: Traditional factors, confidence and general skills

At the individual level, characteristics linked to traditional inequalities in wealth and health correlate with confidence using ICTs. That is, education, age, and gender of adults are related to internet-related confidence levels. When it comes to basic skills, the results are less clear on gender differences, but household education levels, traditional literacy levels, and age remain strong predictors of digital skills. Analysis of DiSTO survey data from London and Los Angeles consistently shows that level of education among adults strongly predicts overall skill (Helsper, 2021). In these highly-connected cities, about 26 per cent of those with a graduate education have all skills to a high level, while only 10 per cent do not have any skills to a high level. On the opposite end of the spectrum, 23 per cent of those who have only completed secondary school have no high-level skills while 16 per cent have all skills.

Still more interesting patterns emerge when looking at skills where inequalities are explained by individual socio-demographic and socio-economic characteristics. For example, the PIAAC studies show that the association between socio-economic status and digital reading performance is most apparent in critical information navigation and evaluation (OECD, 2019). This difference is explained through inequalities in traditional reading skills, rather than in digital skills differences between those with different educational backgrounds. In other words, it is traditional literacy rather than digital literacy that causes problems in online information navigation.

DiSTO research project data from the Netherlands, the UK, and Latin America, show that gender resurfaces as an explanatory factor when different skills are examined separately. Women are less likely to have more technical skills and content creation skills, but tend to have an advantage in critical information and information navigation skills. Ana seems a good example of this. She had problems in navigating online content, such as when she was trying to find a dentist, and struggled with navigating websites and filling out forms. She knew the orthodontist's website she found was likely to be a scam, but was not able to find better dental care because she lacked other skills. Other research suggests that women have better communication skills, mostly due to higher average levels of general emotional intelligence rather than higher communication skills specifically for digital communication (Correa, Hinsley, & de Zúñiga, 2010).

Age relates to digital skills in unexpected ways. While older people indicate having lower skill and confidence levels, educational background, general health, and experience with ICTs are more important predictors of use than age. That is, there are more similarities between Ana and her parents than between them and other people of the same age.

In discussions around age, it is also important to distinguish between different types of skill. Van Deursen and Van Dijk (2014) counter the universal myth of digital natives. Older people are more digitally literate in critical information seeking and more complex social and communicative skills and younger people have more technical skills. In Ana's household, her son knows how to push buttons and make things work, while Ana better understands how to manage communication and social networks. Nevertheless, her son is at a relative disadvantage to kids at his school whose parents have higher general literacy and skill levels. The experience of Kaya, a classmate of Ana's son, illustrates how important the educational background of parents can be: 'My mum home-schooled me, she is really intelligent. [She] is qualified in music, languages, and psychology. ... What you should do is, if you don't know how to take necessary precautions to prevent [having your profile hacked] in the future, ask your parents ... my mum has a Facebook account. She got it to keep an eye on me. So she gave me independence, but she's also helping me with it.'

One of the main differences between Kaya and Ana's son is the level of education of their mothers and the general availability of expertise in a household. Numerous studies confirm the importance of the childhood home for digital skills and confidence. This confirmation signals how future inequalities in digital skills are established in early life, similar to other inequalities (Camerini, Schulz, & Jeannet, 2018; Jackson et al., 2006). While young people are influenced by the characteristics of their household and association with their parents, the reverse is not necessarily the case with skills. Analyses of the 2013 EU Kids Online data from interviews with a parent and a child dyad in the same household show that highly skilled parents are unlikely to have children with low skill levels, while quite a few skilled children have parents with low skill levels. This suggests that children do not always teach or motivate parents to get skilled, although they do drive parents to get access (Eynon & Helsper, 2015).

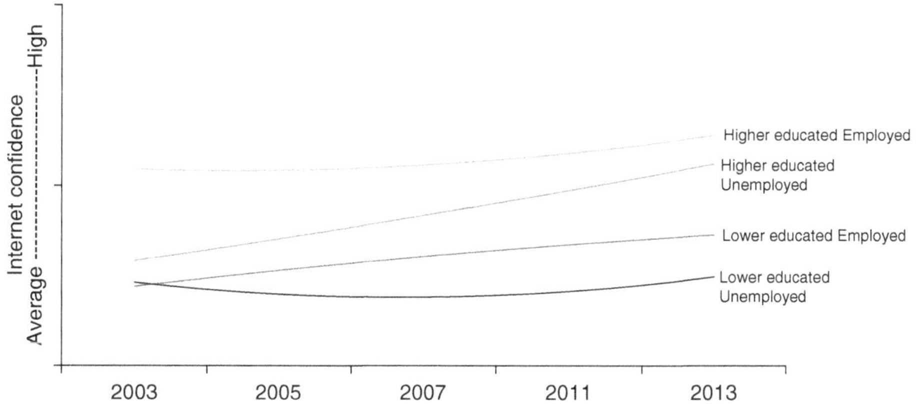

Figure 4.4 Trends in internet confidence by education and employment status

Source: Oxford Internet Survey (OXIS). Adapted from Helsper (2011) and Helsper & Reisdorf (2013).

Base: British Internet users of working age.

Oxford Internet Survey (OxIS) data show internet use confidence levels of employed individuals with lower levels of education have not risen relative to the better educated (Helsper & Eynon, 2013). Speaking to the intersectionality of socio-digital inequalities, the confidence levels of the unemployed with poor education have remained low (Figure 4.4). It is unlikely that skill levels have not changed over the years. It is more likely that levels needed for comfortable and effective use of the internet have risen and that those with higher education have more possibilities to learn new skills. Ana, though she is employed, had bad experiences with formal education at a young age and a life that does not give opportunities to learn informally or formally at work or elsewhere. This puts her at a disadvantage in terms of acquiring new skills or getting formal training (Ignatow & Robinson, 2017). These early life inequalities are related to amplification increasing over time, as societies become increasingly digital and the skills required to navigate, judge, and learn from online sources become more complex.

Consequences of digital (skill) inequalities on learning

Up until now I have discussed how historically lower levels of education might cause lower digital skills levels in certain countries or individuals. This corresponds to the social factors are causes argument, which sees ICTs as resource enhancement technologies (the drivers in Figure 4.1). Then there is the skills and online learning as causes argument, where differences in learning outcomes are explained by digital skill and use levels, making it harder to translate ICT use into beneficial learning (the outcomes in Figure 4.1). This second part is the focus of this section. ICTs such as the internet provide formal educational and informal learning opportunities. In this age of information overload, the answer to anything is at everyone's fingertips as long as they can navigate the 'information super highway'. In principle, anyone can go online and access courses at elite universities. In many studies, the educational value of ICT use is studied from this perspective of formal learning, with less

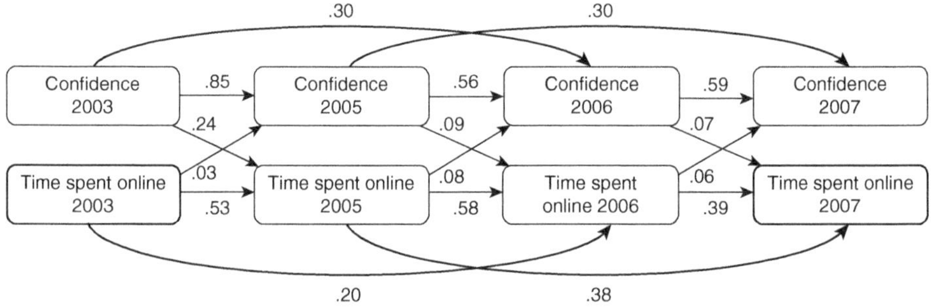

Figure 4.5 Relationships between confidence and time spent online over time

Source: US World Internet Project panel data (Annenberg Center for the Digital Future, 2020). Original analysis for this chapter.

Base: Internet users who completed all waves between 2003 and 2007 (N=355).

Note: No data were collected in 2004.

emphasis on informal learning. Within the 'skills and use as drivers for inequalities in outcomes' discussion, a related debate concerns the directional relationship between skills and use. Those who see digital skills as resources for (or drivers of) use argue that people who have confidence and skill will have better experiences using ICTs, which leads to more use. The 'use as a driver of skill' argument positions ICTs as an experience technology (Dutton & Shepherd, 2006). That is, people learn by acquiring skills and gaining confidence as they use ICTs.

If you want to win a bet on who is a confident internet user now, look at who was confident a few years back (Figure 4.5). Similarly, if you want to predict who uses the internet intensively now, you should look at who was using it intensively in previous years. Yet, time someone spent online will be less useful in a bet on who is a confident user. That is, confidence predicts future use more than use predicts future confidence (see size of coefficients in Figure 4.5). This suggests that internet use is a result of confidence and skill in a reinforcing, 'digitally rich get digitally richer' feedback loop. Interestingly, we can observe a time delay effect observed in traditional educational settings, where high confidence and skill in a given year impacts how confident an individual feels two years later. This suggests that having a head start in confidence in using ICTs has a long-term impact. Inequalities that exist in skills in early years are likely to be exacerbated in inequalities in skills and use in later years.

The Programme for International Student Assessment (PISA) study of trends over time also shows that differences in use are strongly related to students' skills (OECD, 2015b). The PISA study found diminished inequalities in digital reading between young people from different backgrounds – the result of a weakening of the relationship between socio-economic status and digital skills – and not of student experience in reading. Over time, inequalities in digital reading diminished when digital skills increased, but inequalities in traditional reading performance remained strong. The PISA data also contain information on informal learning taking place in students' free time. Inequalities in informal digital learning were larger than those in formal digital learning for school. Advantaged students read online and used the internet to obtain practical information more than disadvantaged students, even in countries where advantaged and disadvantaged students spend similar amounts of time online. In our study with NEETs, we heard repeatedly that less technical skills were not taught, and students figured it out themselves.

Davies, Eynon, and Wilkins (2017) show that disadvantaged young people are locked into patterns of narrow, task-oriented internet usage. They do homework or use the internet to help with family chores while more affluent peers use it more to explore and try things out. Therefore, it seems that learning outcomes are limited to more formal, externally-driven activities for disadvantaged young people. Those who are advantaged get more opportunities for informal learning in addition to those other types of learning. These findings suggest that learning outcomes of use depend on socio-demographic and socio-economic characteristics. Further supporting this relationship, DiSTO data suggest that characteristics related to educational inequalities determine learning outcomes, even in a high skill and low social inequalities country like the Netherlands. These inequalities in outcomes are strongest for formal learning (e.g. getting a degree) and for negative outcomes (e.g. misinformation, failing a course). The economically disadvantaged have more negative and fewer positive outcomes from using the ICTs for learning. Interesting here is that there are no gender differences in positive outcomes, but women are more likely to have negative outcomes from online knowledge acquisition.

DiSTO projects demonstrate that, while demographic and access variables have a direct and beneficial influence on opportunity take-up, being more skilled is important in itself (Van Deursen & Helsper, 2017). Our research with NEETs shows that breadth of skills explains satisfaction with financial, employment, and educational outcomes from using the internet (Helsper & Smirnova, 2016). For economic outcomes, basic and higher-level content creation skills predict getting higher-quality jobs. For the more formal educational outcomes, social digital skills are the strongest predictors of getting a certificate online and finding useful educational materials. Informal learning outcomes are more strongly related to social digital skills. Hence, a broad range of skills – not just technical or information navigation skills – helps translate practical, task-oriented activities into high-quality outcomes.

We find similar results for older and younger individuals (Van Deursen et al., 2017). Content creation skills are related to property, educational, employment, and financial uses of the internet. They mediate the ability to translate use into tangible outcomes. Similarly, results around more informal types of learning related to personal outcomes show that social skills and content creation skills are important to translating use into tangible outcomes. This echoes other research that shows that 'soft' skills lead to cross-domain benefits, even those that do not rely directly on social interactions. These studies suggest that while operational and technical skills are fundamental, they are not enough to translate use into outcomes on their own. Instead, they pave the way for social and content creation skills that do allow this translation to happen.

In our studies with adults, internet use and beneficial outcomes remain directly linked to traditional inequalities such as age, education, and employment (Van Deursen & Helsper, 2015). While skills relate to the quality of the outcomes achieved, achievement of the outcomes is a more direct result of use. Similarly, a young person's level of education and traditional problem-solving skills remain the most important predictor of economic and educational outcomes, independent of the skills that this young person has (Helsper & Smirnova, 2016). In other words, other factors create inequalities in learning outcomes in addition to inequalities in access and skill levels.

To illustrate, let's return to Ana and her desire to further her education so she can find a job and leave the neighbourhood. She browses the internet and finds a list of courses about social work, which interest her. She decides to sign up for the first course on the list. However, the course turns out not to be very good and is more expensive than an offline college course. The degree is also not recognised for the jobs she would apply for. If she had had better information navigation skills, she could find her way to a better course. If she better understood how professional networks work online, she could inquire about the best courses. Of course, if she had continued education, this would have shaped her online search skills and networks. Her education would help her to have less frustrating online and offline experiences. Ana's social and educational background have shaped her digital skills.

In turn, her digital skills have shaped what she was able to achieve online. With her limited skills, she was able to achieve an outcome but not one of quality. In the future, she will probably stick to the more comfortable informal learning she has done before, because she has the social digital skills to navigate her friendship networks and attain more helpful answers.

The relationship between skills and use is a cyclical process where confidence, skills, and literacy are simultaneously consequences and causes of digital engagement and its outcomes. As long as this chicken and egg problem remains unsolved, we will be at a loss to understand which digital skills lead to resilience that will help disadvantaged people survive and prosper in a digital future.

Policy and interventions

Policy making and interventions have come a long way, especially in higher diffusion countries. There is now widespread recognition that inequalities in skills determine inequalities in opportunities to translate internet use into tangible educational or economic outcomes. Disappointingly, interventions are still focused on learning to operate specific software, devices, and platforms rather than to embrace a broader understanding of the skills and literacy needed to navigate the digital world (see Lyons et al., 2019; Martinez-Cantos, 2017, for a critique). The extensive literature on the failure of the OLPC programme is ignored in programmes that provide access through PCs, tablets, or phones without the accompanying skills and literacy training (Helsper, 2018). There is also evidence emerging that a reliance on the mobile phone for digital engagement leads to 'deskilling' (Ofcom, 2016b). That is, whereas those who use a variety of devices (PCs and laptops in particular) show increases in their digital skill levels over time through learning by doing, this increase is much lower or absent for mostly mobile users. Policies and interventions often rely on a techno-optimist principle that cheap and ubiquitous mobile access will help countries and individuals to overcome existing inequalities. The evidence suggests another response is more effective: sustainable future use with beneficial outcomes starts with confidence and skills training, alongside high-quality access provision.

One issue is that policy documents rarely define digital literacy targets, nor how they are to be achieved (Helsper, 2018). It is unclear what beneficial outcomes are expected beyond increased employability. There is even less clarity about which skills are needed to achieve which outcomes of ICT use. This makes evaluating effectiveness implementations extremely difficult. Another problem is that the majority of digital skills training programmes are in formal educational and institutional settings. These courses often fail to meet expectations because they do not take into consideration the political, economic, and social inequalities in which programmes and policies are embedded (Liff & Stewart, 2001; Meneses & Momino, 2010). The relative success of the OLPC project in Uruguay can be attributed to it being introduced in a country with high levels of traditional literacy and a quality public education system (de Melo, Machado, & Miranda, 2017).

I argue here that outcomes of digital literacy training should be defined as diminishing existing inequalities in economic, social, and civic opportunities. It is very unlikely that narrowly-targeted technical and operational skills training will alleviate inequalities. For example, the classes that are currently on offer in Ana's local community centre follow a common pattern. They focus on learning how to use a mouse, which buttons to push for video chat, and which apps can be used for banking. There is little attention paid to how to engage online or manage an online profile. Nor do these courses involve teaching about how to recognise reliable and unreliable sources of information, let alone how search results are different depending on your background.

The big problem is that people with the lowest levels of literacy and least engagement with ICTs are unlikely to take advantage of formal training opportunities. The open, free programmes in public settings such as libraries are taken up by those with higher skill and motivation levels. The courses Ana has access to are limited. But if she lived in the Global South, it would be even less likely that these courses would be available. If they were, it would likely be limited to basic operational skills. The exception there tends to be courses on setting up community websites through NGOs which are concerned about preserving local culture and amplifying the voices of disenfranchised populations. The problem with these efforts is that they often only speak to the community, and do little to create awareness about injustices or inequalities (Chapters 5 and 7).

These formal training initiatives for access provision and technical one-off skills training have led to devices sitting unused in many people's homes. Short-term use was not sustained because of unsafe or inexpert use with negative outcomes and frustrations around the process (Condor, Rojas, & Ccora, 2019; Kraemer et al., 2009). Skills training needs to be embedded in everyday environments with available, long-term support structures in multiple locations (Newholm, Keeling, McGoldrick, Macaulay, & Doherty, 2008). In high-diffusion countries, buddy or digital champion systems have gained popularity. Whether they succeed often depends on the quality of the relationship between the individuals and mentors' levels of expertise. The real trick that makes programmes work is offering informal, multi-sited learning opportunities that are not narrowly focused on technology.

Targeted learning, such as for those working in social care or experiencing homelessness, are key for the most marginalised or disadvantaged groups. We should go to where the people are and avoid one-off formal training (Liff & Stewart, 2001). The literature on education estimates that around 80 per cent of learning is informal. It takes place at work and in other everyday settings (Cross, 2007; Sefton-Green, 2006). Here the Pareto principle pops up again; in companies, 80 per cent of the budget goes to formal training but is estimated to provide only 20 per cent of learning outcomes (Cross, 2007). Since learning is often social in nature, it is important that interventions think of how access and learning are distributed in networks and in the local community.

For adults and disadvantaged youth, promises about an educational digital nirvana are driven by hopes for financial and economic gains. There is comparatively little thought given to how interventions will further education, broader well-being, or self-actualisation. These skills programmes are based on the individualistic, neoliberal paradigm. Digital skills are linked to gaps in the job market or financial gains, situating the individual as an employee or consumer in ways that are reminiscent of factory work and industrialised consumption (Davies et al., 2017; Olssen & Peters, 2005). Even within a neoliberal paradigm, policy emphasises training for work in the IT industries at the expense of the basic skills needed for 'everyday' jobs and intermediaries who help others get online. The fear of a digital skills gap and related inequalities in policy and industry has led to the dominance of certain types of training (Selwyn, 2008). It makes sense for formal education and on-the-job training to be leading when it comes to high-end skills such as programming and coding and systems management. Nevertheless, inequalities at the lower end are harder to tackle because they involve a wider set of skills. Interventions or courses sometimes jump to higher-end training without understanding that people have issues with more basic and diverse skills that impede them acquiring more advanced skills. To overcome inequalities at the advanced level, more complex interventions are needed at the basic digital skills level. Such interventions need to emphasise interactive, critical, and participation skills rather than those purely related to passive consumption.

An interesting distinction has emerged from my work with disadvantaged young people and adults in larger metropolitan areas. How learning is perceived to take place around different types of skill reflects a certain dynamic: more explicit training and development of thinking has gone into the technical and information navigation skills than into the softer skills that allow for full participation. Technical skills are explicitly taught through hands-on teaching, while information navigation and critical digital information literacies are taught through more abstract methods, including advocating for 'common sense' or 'general knowledge' (e.g. Wikipedia is bad, use trusted sources). Social skills were learned through observation, and content creation skills were acquired through trying things out. As a result, softer skills were not part of formal training. Instead, they were the result of trial and error without much feedback.

In work with young people, there is much emphasis on negative outcomes and what parents can do to make sure that children avoid risk. More recently, emphasis has been placed on which digital skills can help young people to avoid harms associated with risky activities. While there is not yet sufficient longitudinal data on these efforts, it seems that parents' and children's skills are a reaction to negative experiences, which lead to resilience (Livingstone, Ólafsson, et al., 2017). This is a conundrum for policy makers, because it can hardly be good policy to expose young people to negative experiences online so that they build stamina in future situations. Yet, this idea might not be as crazy as it sounds. A 'homeopathic' solution might be appropriate – low doses of smaller risks or low levels of harm administered in a controlled safe setting could lead to later resilience. We do know that simply creating awareness of risks does not enable youth to avoid negative experiences. Paradoxically, vulnerable young people are more likely to experience negative outcomes of internet use when they become more skilled (Helsper & Smahel, 2019). The key here is awareness of offline vulnerabilities and reframing digital skills training.

Conclusions

Digital literacy was defined in this chapter as skills and capabilities that allow people to make the most out of their use of ICTs by taking up opportunities and avoiding harms. This chapter showed that digital skills translate ICT access and use into tangible benefits in everyday life. To understand how digital skills allow us to take advantage of the opportunities that are available, and how these are unequally distributed in digital societies, we need to adopt a wider definition of digital literacy. This definition should include functional and critical skills and cover technical-operational and information processing skills, but also social-interactional and content creation and consumption skills. To forge a citizenry ready for a digital future, strategic and critical skills that allow everyone to co-create the digital as well as the social environment are fundamental.

A more robust framing of skills will enable an improved understanding of why inequalities continue to exist, and assist the design of more effective interventions. We must be wary of the type of skills training that just responds to 'deficits' in the current labour market, which slots individuals into gaps, like workers on a digital factory floor. Our digital environment constantly changes and the skills we need in order to participate and be fulfilled now and in the future need to be transferrable to different platforms, devices, and socio-digital environments. A future where virtual reality (VR) and artificial intelligence (AI) are embedded in our everyday life requires a literacy that is adaptable, building on an understanding of how we can remain autonomous and take advantage of the opportunities without suffering further disadvantage (see Conclusion).

Formal training programmes on their own are unlikely to achieve this goal because:

- They are likely to put off disadvantaged people with less positive educational experiences.
- They are often unavailable to people outside formal education or white-collar employment.
- Informal learning drives the development of the kind of literacy that allows individuals to be full citizens in digital societies.

That is, most digital skills acquisition takes place through observation and trying things out. Achieving this requires the right kind of social environment and relevant content, both of which are currently unequally distributed. More structural social change, alongside the development of targeted hard and soft skills and critical digital literacy programmes, is needed to prevent a future rich-get-richer or amplification of inequalities scenario. So far, the meritocratic ideal of a level playing field under conditions of equal opportunities in access and training provision underpinning this chapter's opening quote is not lived up to when it comes to equality of outcomes in socio-economic and personal well-being.

In answer to the first question posed at the beginning of the chapter, the unequal distribution of digital skills means that the abundance of learning opportunities online is not taken up equally by all once they have gained access to ICTs. Those who have been historically disadvantaged in terms of education are less likely to have these skills. They are also less likely to live in environments where opportunities for formal and informal learning of these skills are available. This means, in answer to the second question, that formal and informal learning outcomes are linked to traditional inequalities, because digital literacy is unequally distributed. More worryingly, I have also shown in this chapter that even without differences in skill, those who have been historically disadvantaged face tougher odds. They are less likely to translate ICT use into high-quality educational outcomes and are more likely to have negative experiences with online learning.

In conclusion, digital skills are necessary to survive in the 21st century but will not have the same impact for everyone, barring systemic change. If the right content is not online, or if people's socio-digital ecologies do not stimulate learning, then digital skills are unlikely to lead to positive outcomes in self-actualisation or formal education. The importance of a person's environment and interests will be explored further in the next chapter, which discusses the relationship between civic participation and attitudes towards and discourses around ICTs.

CHAPTER 5

INEQUALITIES IN POWER AND PARTICIPATION IN DIGITAL SOCIETIES

> 'Internet is not water; internet is not air. Internet is very important. However, if we use it as a revolution tool to incite others to kill and burn, it will be shut down not only for a week, but longer than that.'
>
> Ethiopia's Prime Minister Abiy Ahmed's press conference after a *coup d'état* (Shaban, 2019)

In previous chapters, I described economic and educational inequalities of digital engagement that dominate research and policy agendas. Another domain that has received attention is digital civic engagement. This area's history in media and communications research and policy stretches back to before the mass diffusion of the internet; critical media literacy initiatives have tried to unite engaged citizens to fight injustice, stand up for rights, and improve society. In this chapter, I examine the causes and consequences of inequalities in digital civic engagement, defined as institutionalised politics and as informal community engagement. While the bulk of research has focused on formal, political types of digital civic engagement, informal aspects are of rising concern, driven by assertions of 'echo chambers' and 'fake news'. Consequently, the debate around socio-digital inequalities shows a transition from an emphasis on technical skills to critical information literacies and social skills. Accordingly, this chapter covers formal engagement ranging from e-voting and use of e-government services and political organising, to informal participation through local organisations and staying informed.

Concern with civic engagement and ICTs has mirrored techno-optimistic discussions about the alleviation of poverty and inequalities in education discussed in the previous chapters. The list of potential positive outcomes thought to allow the previously disenfranchised to catch up is long. Will direct access to powerful communication tools allow the disadvantaged to speak truth to power and be better informed? Will they be better equipped to participate, organise, and take collective action against injustice? Will they gain access to services without having to struggle through bureaucratic government systems? Evidence shows that the growth of opportunities for digital civic engagement is not a foregone conclusion, and must contend with the amplification of traditional inequalities. To conceptually illustrate these interwoven processes, I return to my Corresponding Fields (CF) model. It connects paths from resource domains with related digital resources (i.e. critical digital literacy and civic digital engagement) which feed back into traditional resources by empowering certain people (Figure 5.1).

To my broader question of what happens to traditional inequalities as societies digitise, I add three sub-questions in this chapter:

- What does civic engagement look like in digital societies?
- Who is most likely to use ICTs for civic engagement?
- Who takes advantage of these types of opportunities to have a real impact on their own and others' everyday lives?

The literature on civic engagement uses different language to discuss inequalities from the one introduced in Chapter 2. 'Mobilisation' refers to how the previously disengaged

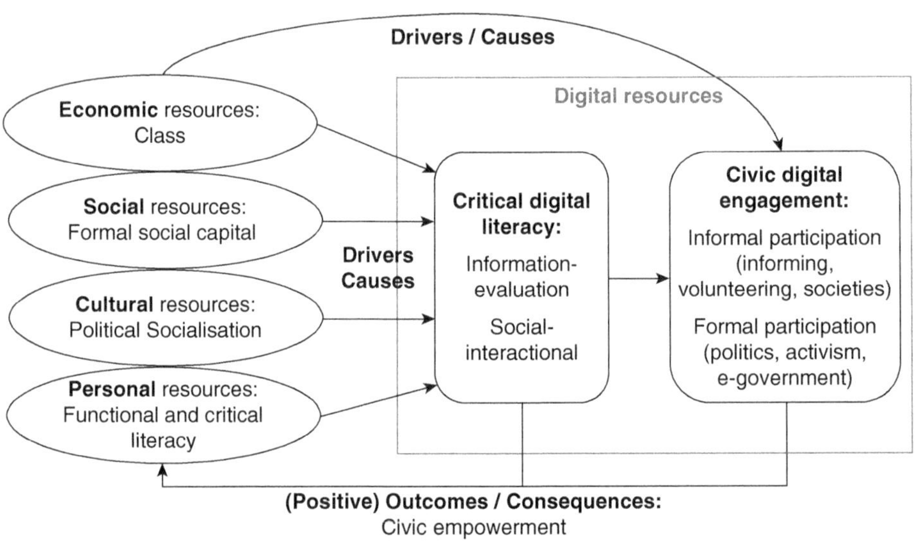

Figure 5.1 Links between traditional and digital inequalities in civic engagement and influence

Class = employment and education. Formal social capital (participation in diverse organised networks).

Being heard different from making a change

are engaging civically online, similar to normalisation and leapfrogging. Nevertheless, the term 'normalisation' in the civic engagement literature refers more to the stratification hypothesis that inequalities are replicated but not necessarily exacerbated online (Sinpeng, 2017). To avoid confusion, I continue to use the digital inequalities language of Chapter 2 which distinguishes between amplification, stratification, normalisation, and leapfrogging processes (see Figure 2.2).

To illustrate how civic engagement in increasingly digital societies reflects these four scenarios, I turn to Priya. As with Ben and Ana in the previous chapters, Priya is a vignette compiled from the experiences of people I have encountered in my research.

Case Study: Priya

Priya lives in Kolkata, India. She is a Vaishya Hindu, married, and 55 years old. Her husband is from a reasonably well-off jewellers' family, and she works as an assistant in one of his shops. She also takes care of their three-bedroom apartment and family affairs. Her cleaner, Kavita, comes in a few times a week to help. Her children – Amir, Pradhi, and Tanya – have studied in the US and the UK, and may not return. Still, she hopes they might marry someone from back home. While socio-economically and by caste she is relatively privileged, she does have a problem with her leg that limits her mobility. This disability means she has not yet visited her children. She is a woman in a country with one of the highest levels of gender inequalities in the world (UNDP, 2019). She supports Modi, India's president, but has never been part of a political organisation.

She has a smartphone and her family has a PC at home. This makes her digitally privileged in a country where only a quarter of the population uses the internet, and a quarter of mobile phone users owns a smartphone (Taylor & Silver, 2019). The PC is reserved for work and serious activities. She is savvy with technology and uses Microsoft Excel to manage her personal and household finances. She uses her phone to communicate with her children using WhatsApp and Facebook. She is also involved in charity work for girls' education in rural India. Because she cannot travel to the schools her family supports, she uses the internet to help at a distance by donating money and giving suggestions. To learn what happens in India and the wider world, she prefers newspapers for news over online sources.

Priya is historically disenfranchised by gender and disability, but is otherwise part of an elite, relatively upper-caste, urban-dwelling, Hindu majority. Her example and other evidence presented in this chapter show that without considering people's political-historical contexts and personal experiences – and associated community norms and expectations – we will not be able to counter civic empowerment inequalities in digital societies. To understand how inequalities might perpetuate or shift, I will start by explaining why inequalities in civic digital engagement are problematic. After that, I address the three above questions about definitions, causes, and consequences of digital inequalities in civic engagement.

Why should we worry about civic engagement in increasingly digital societies?

Digital inequalities research and interventions started with enthusiasm at the beginning of the 21st century. There was initial hope for activism – that repressed and underrepresented groups could use social and other digital media to form global movements. From Occupy Wall Street to the 'Arab Spring', hope seemed to spread like wildfire, accelerated by digital networks. Similarly, optimism initially existed for formal civic engagement: 'Build it and they will come' was a familiar mantra. With e-government and community platforms, people would finally have unfettered access to services and information. Yet, the digital Pareto principle still frustrates; those least likely to engage with ICTs remain heavy users of public services (Nakamura & Chow-White, 2013). Neither does access and interaction with government services and representatives automatically lead to participation and empowerment (Jenkins & Carpentier, 2013; Looker & Naylor, 2010). The flame of enthusiasm for both activist and everyday uses of digital technologies has also been challenged by an awareness of increased state oppression, surveillance, the re-emergence of familiar conflicts, and the rise of populism (Ghodes, 2018).

Policy makers in many high-diffusion, European countries have created policy to digitise all government services, trying to increase their use. Implementation of these policies has not been as successful since many are designed to save costs rather than to increase formal civic engagement and empowerment (Fotopoulou, 2016). There are also signs that governments are scaling back on digital-by-default policies because they underestimated the social and economic costs. Also, those who most need services are not able to take up the opportunities on offer (Macaya, Alves, Meirelles, & Cunha, 2019). In this chapter, I will examine whether digitisation might perpetuate a digital 'underclass' – a group of people who are increasingly civically disadvantaged (Helsper, 2011).

In addition to perpetuating class inequalities, we should examine how unequal digitisation shapes our normative valuation of civic engagement. People who are active, embedded in the community, with the necessary time and resources tend to drive what is collectively considered 'valuable' civic engagement (Byrne, 2005). Political, business, academic, and other elites have resources offline, and have also had the resources to design and participate on public communication platforms online (Carpentier, 2015). These elites have historically been male, part of ethnic majorities, and of higher socio-economic status. Their privileged access to communication platforms empowers them to determine what worthy subjects of discussion are, and who can participate in the shaping of civic life (Byrne, 2008). Despite that this was the case for radio and television, many initially ascribed a unique status to ICTs. Eubanks (2011, p. xv) described this as the 'massive, collective, consensual hallucination about the power of technology, particularly information technology to "level the playing field", create broad based economic and social equality, and nurture transparency and accountability in democratic governance'. Despite early optimism, traditional inequalities in participation are likely to be reproduced even under conditions of equal ICT access and skill distribution.

Confronting power imbalances in technology and media are nothing new. ICTs have been used to strengthen and subvert power relationships, even under repressive conditions (Gerbaudo, 2012). When I started thinking about this chapter, I assumed that we would be looking at a preservation of the status quo (stratification), rather than amplifications of inequalities. The reality is more complex with room for optimism (normalisation) and pessimism (amplification), depending on the socio-digital inequality in civic engagement. This complexity makes it more likely that negative feedback loops will go unnoticed and the positive ones will be emphasised. Therefore, we should worry about civic engagement inequalities in digital societies in particular. In the next section I consider if we need to rethink what inequalities in civic engagement look like.

What does civic disengagement look like in digital societies?

The lack of consensus on what constitutes digital civic engagement reflects debate about inequalities in formal social capital being about social status and hierarchy (Bourdieu, 1986), trust and community engagement (Putnam, 2002), and distributions and flows of information and resources in networks (Coleman, 1990; Portes, 1998). Here, I highlight potential changes in understandings of civic engagement in three areas – critical, active, and more passive digital citizenship – and how they relate to different platforms.

Civic digital skills: Critical literacy and trust in digital societies

The PISA framework (OECD, 2018, p. 29) defines reading literacy as 'understanding, using, evaluating, reflecting on and engaging with texts in order to achieve one's goals, to develop one's knowledge and potential and to participate in society'. This definition links literacy to civic engagement as an outcome in a way that skills literature does not, because in digital civic engagement studies, the critical media literacy tradition remains strong (Buckingham, 2005). The skills-based approach emphasises that we need skills akin to print reading and writing literacies to navigate information overload in a knowledge society. In contrast, the critical media literacy approach emphasises spotting commercial and ideological motives and misrepresentations. Once aware, people can challenge dominant power structures hidden behind algorithms and flashy designs. The former refers to information navigation-type skills, while the latter sparks critical understanding of how and why content is produced (Jenkins & Carpentier, 2013). The third part of the critical media literacy tradition stresses content creation skills and creativity (discussed in Chapter 7).

For the purposes of this chapter, I take civic digital literacy to include the functional and critical information literacy to find, consume, and evaluate content and its producers (Polizzi, 2020). For example, concern about people not being able to distinguish 'fake' from 'real' news is mounting. The assumption embedded in this concern is those who lack critical skills are more gullible to extremist and populist views that would undermine civic processes. Accordingly, in relation to digital skills, critical information literacy often refers to our ability to judge the reliability of information accessed through search engines, news, and social ICT platforms. However, civic engagement and democratic participation traditionally focused more on trust in people and institutions than information. For societies and relationships to function there needs to be trust (Putnam, 2002). Trust in fellow citizens, political institutions, and legal institutions creates societal cohesion and drives volunteering for the common good. Similarly, trust in media is necessary for people to stay informed and take action. Media trust is important because sometimes a lack of civic digital engagement is not a sign of disengagement (i.e. passive non-participation) but an informed decision to distrust certain platforms or services (i.e. active non-participation) (Casemajor, Couture, Delfin, Goerzen, & Delfanti, 2015).

Quandt (2012) suggested that we need to redefine trust now in a networked society. He writes, 'trust in participatory forms of communication on the net is based on some plausible, but probably misleading assumptions; and these assumptions are based on an anthropologically explainable misconception of network trust as being something very similar to personal trust in face-to-face situations' (Quandt, 2012, p. 16). In other words, online we apply our traditional skills in determining trustworthiness to situations where they do not apply. We are judging information and requests through online networks and algorithms as if they were given to us personally from friends. People, he writes, need to be aware that information distributed on networked platforms relies on 'largely unchecked communication of a very peculiar group of self-selected, anonymous persons, which might be filtered and altered by invisible infrastructure providers' and that it should not be 'regarded as being more "authentic" and "real"' (p. 17). Therefore, critical digital information literacy in digital societies should include an understanding of how content is generated and ICT platforms are managed.

The active, selective citizen: Network capital and echo chambers

Digitisation has been thought to shift society from hierarchical, top-down organisational structures to flatter, less hierarchical, and seemingly leaderless mobilisations. Castells (2000) argued that it is easier to organise collective activities in a network society. Networked structures allow for information, discussions, protests, and voting to be rapidly distributed, without the need for existing connections and face-to-face contact subject to hierarchies embedded in traditional Bourdieusian social capital (Bennett & Segerberg, 2012). For example, activist organisations and social movements rely on weak rather than strong ties to recruit new members and engage existing members (Wellman, Boase, & Chen, 2002). The social capital that builds community and drives collective action in these societies allows someone to establish, maintain, and use affective, informal relationships through networks (Cammaerts, 2018; Juris, 2012). This network capital does not rely on membership of formal traditional organisations, as defined by Putnam (2002), and is more reliant on loose networks that can easily form and have fluid memberships (Lovink & Rossiter, 2018).

These networked ideas of capital go against the emphasis in Habermas's public sphere on rational debate and the creation of consensus (Dahlgren, 2002). Instead, networked capital steers us towards affective interpretations of social capital that emphasise participation in the public sphere as creating a sense of connection (Gerbaudo, 2012). Supposedly, in these networked collectives, demonstrating that you are part of something becomes more important than arguments and consensus. This is why these affective, community creation processes have also been blamed for polarisation and an increase of extremist views. People can move in and out of network connections more freely, selecting discussions and relationships that most align with their own views, while avoiding contrary opinions. For this reason, scholars still hotly debate whether the openness of networks might lead to 'echo chambers' (Bruns, 2019). Some scholarship suggests that, in digital societies, our networks might become more homogeneous. Another pessimistic view proposes that digitisation leads to a more passive citizenry, disengaged from real politics and democracy.

The passive, consumer citizen: Slacktivism and low-cost engagement

Derogatory terms like 'slacktivism' and 'clicktivism' describe how people civically engage in ways that do not require a lot of involvement. They 'like' social media posts, sign WhatsApp petitions, flag posts on Weibo, or donate money online (Halupka, 2018; Harlow & Guo, 2014). The argument goes that these easy behaviours are more about warm feelings, substituting for 'real' behaviour change which requires time and effort (Morozov, 2009). People engage in this low-cost digital civic engagement to signal to others that they are virtuous. They consider themselves 'off the hook' in terms of taking real action and grant themselves the 'moral license' to act in un-civic ways (Lane & Dal Cin, 2018; Soyer, Cornelissen, & Karelaia, 2013). Karpf (2010, p. 9) argues that these lower cost, reactive types of civic engagement 'represent a difference-of-degree rather than a difference-in-kind'. He argues that virtue signalling and moral licensing existed before the advent of the internet. Karpf (2010) uses the example of distributing copied petitions to random fax numbers, and questions whether that is so different from forwarding an email or a link through a messaging service.

Nevertheless, there is more evidence that low-cost activities lead to further participation, or engage people who would not have otherwise (Christensen, 2011; Karpf, 2010). Returning to Priya's example, she continues to support her families' involvement in the charity for girls' education and she now also donates to these types of charities online through GiveIndia.org. She also 'likes' news around girls' rights to education, in particular when she comes across a post on Facebook, and has started clicking on information about women's rights. Rather than being a substitution for other forms of civic engagement, her digital engagement is supplementary. She follows the patterns and interests that are common and considered proper among her network of relatives and acquaintances. These potentially new forms of supplementary civic engagement have largely been left by the wayside by socio-digital inequalities scholars.

Civic digital media?

In traditional civic engagement research, the routes to empowerment were seen as membership of political organisations, clubs, voting, and reading newspapers. Where can we find these traditional routes online, particularly through social media? On this question, social media merits special attention, because civic engagement can be linked to Coleman (1990) and Wellman's interpretations of social capital (Wellman et al., 2002). Their network theorisation of civic engagement proposes that those with more extensive, diverse networks are more likely to have access to people in power than those with narrow, homogeneous networks. Therefore, research that investigates how ICT use is related to civic engagement often starts by measuring individuals' online network size and organisational ties (Lin & Erickson, 2008). Social media also helps people to stay informed about social and world affairs through weak ties. That is, social media users are likely to come across novel sources of information on social media that they would not otherwise access (Xenos, Vromen, & Loader, 2014).

Research on social media has thus gravitated to networked approaches to researching how people establish and maintain broad, diverse, information-rich relationships in digital societies. Nevertheless, most research tends to ask people about social media use without specifying a particular platform or type of use. When it is more precise, it focuses on Facebook for everyday civic engagement, or Twitter for political participation. Both the definition of social media without specification and a focus on single platforms are problematic. It is not general ICT use that is important. Rather, what people use ICTs for counts when understanding inequalities. Inequalities in sharing pictures of pets and information about the family might lead to inequalities in personal well-being. Yet, they are less likely to lead to inequalities in civic empowerment, *per se*. This heavy emphasis on social media platforms when it comes to civic engagement also means that there is less data on other types of inequalities in civic digital engagement, such as signing petitions, making donations, or becoming a member of organisations.

Inequalities in civic empowerment are more likely the result of inequalities in the sharing of news stories or opinions about government functioning and politics. Newman, Fletcher, Kalogeropoulos, & Kleis Nielsen (2019) divide countries into four models in terms of news consumption and sharing through ICTs: direct, social media first, reliant on news aggregators and search engines, and 'pick and mix' models where people consume news across platforms. This means that analysis of social media use in civic engagement is more likely to be accurate for 'social media first' countries such as Chile than in 'mainly direct news' countries such as Finland. Even in a country where the majority of internet users is on Facebook, the single-platform approach is problematic. Nearly all of American social media users (87 per cent) visit multiple social media sites, and most (63 per cent) regularly get information about politics and government from traditional news media (analyses of Pew Internet & American Life Project, 2018; Pew Research Center, 2017).

Causes: Explanations of inequalities in civic engagement

As media and technologies change, citizens will continue to participate in and contribute to the communities and societies in which they live. Platforms will come and go, and socio-digital inequalities as a whole are not platform dependent. Therefore, the next section examines evidence of inequalities in critical digital skills and civic engagement between regions and individuals. I start by comparing regions of the world, to understand whether national as well as regional economic, political, and cultural contexts might explain inequalities in civic digital literacy, formal, and informal civic engagement of citizens online. This is followed by an examination of inequalities in digital civic engagement based on individuals' economic, cultural, and social resources.

Socio-political systems and inequalities in critical digital literacy and civic engagement

The democratic model of active citizen discussion and participation is seen as the ideal in the academic literature and efforts by international and intergovernmental organisations (Jenkins & Carpentier, 2013). There is less reliable data on critical, formal, and informal civic engagement in countries that are not as enthusiastic about democratic conventions. This means the data favour understanding social democracies, and comparative conclusions about other political systems can be drawn only cautiously. This section first looks at inequalities between countries and regions in the distribution of the skills needed to engage civically and then at formal and informal civic engagement.

'Civic digital literacy'

To hold governments to account, find trustworthy services, to participate in online discussions, and become members of community or social groups, citizens need critical skills to evaluate information. If these skills are unequally distributed between countries, then it is unlikely that their citizens can equally engage civically. The best predictors of a country's digital information literacies are its levels of print literacy.

As a consequence, digital inequalities in civic engagement are most related to historical differentials in education and critical civic literacy in general (Figure 5.2). There are countries that buck this trend. For example, Brazil has higher levels of digital reading literacy than would be expected based on Brazilians' print literacy. On the other hand, the United Arab Emirates (UAE), Poland, and Shanghai all underperform in digital literacy compared to their levels of print literacy. Notwithstanding, the levels of digital literacy in Brazil, the UAE, and Colombia are still very low, while Poland is somewhere near the average, and Shanghai and Singapore are well above average.

The Reuters Institute defines critical literacy akin to Putnam's definition of social capital: trust in information and institutions (Newman et al., 2019). However, they also found that current political climate is a stronger predictor than historical trust. For example, they

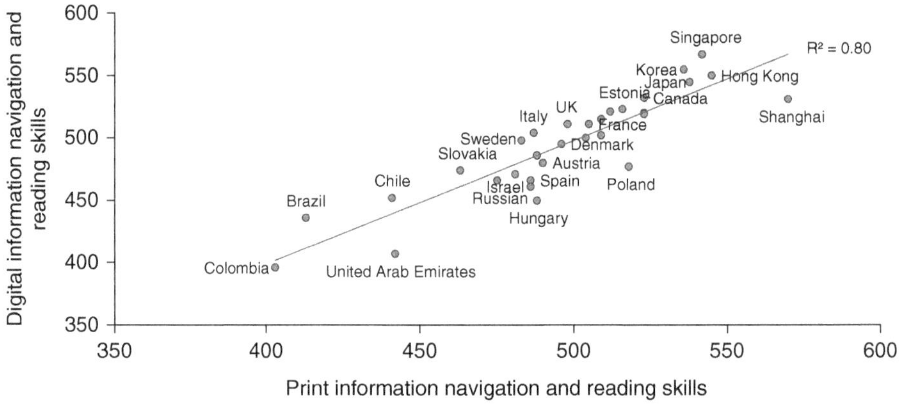

Figure 5.2 Relationship between print and digital reading skills

Source: PISA 2012 (OECD, 2015a) data for 31 regions. Original analysis for this chapter.

Note: PISA measures digital reading literacy (i.e. the ability to read, navigate, and understand online texts) by testing students in a simulated browser environment, with websites, tabs, and hyperlinks. This is a controlled setting in which not only students' reading performance, but also their browsing behaviour, can be observed.

suggested that surges in populism and political scandals make citizens more concerned about distinguishing real and fake news online. Trust in professional, traditional sources of news has gone down, and is not much higher than that accessed through ICTs. Whether the COVID-19 pandemic might turn this trend around remains to be seen. Regardless, countries with traditionally high levels of social capital in the form of trust in institutions will likely continue to have higher levels of trust in online information and news (Newman et al., 2019). For example, the Netherlands has low levels of concern (31 per cent are worried) about what is fake and what is not online, while Brazilians (83 per cent), South Africans (70 per cent), and Mexicans (68 per cent) are sceptical about online news. Indians' trust in WhatsApp and online news sources is as low as in traditional newspapers. Priya would probably have less trust in social media and more trust in traditional newspapers if she were Dutch.

There are also global trends in critically informed news consumption that are cause for optimism. Many people have started checking news sources. For example, 29 per cent say they have decided not to share an article because they doubted its veracity (Newman et al., 2019). However, vetting news sources is not equally distributed. In countries with high levels of concern about fake news, deciding not to share information is more prominent than in countries with low levels of concern. These data suggest that those who most need it are taking more skilled actions. Yet, to what extent this awareness of fake news on various platforms helps a person to make more informed decisions is debatable. Since we do not have data on the extent to which citizens from different countries are exposed to this information, we do not know whether higher levels of literacy in certain countries lead to an increase or decrease in inequalities. If people from countries that are not exposed to propaganda and misinformation do not develop the skills to combat this, while those who are exposed take action but still consume high levels of undetected fake news, then the most optimistic scenario is that normalisation takes place (i.e. the difference between the civically disempowered and the powerful countries is significantly reduced). It is more likely that the status quo is maintained, resulting in stratification. That is, those who are in a position of disadvantage in terms of exposure to content and interactions undermining democracy will need to work to stay as correctly informed as those from countries with more social capital.

Formal civic engagement

'In order to transform the entire ecosystem of public services through the use of information technology, the Government of India has launched the Digital India programme with the vision to transform India into a digitally empowered society and knowledge economy.' (Indian Government, 2020)	'We don't want to give that instrument to the enemy until things settle down. In a week or 10 days, everything will be alright and we will gradually open lines of communication.' (Jammu and Kashmir Governor Satya Pal Malik about the shutdown of communications in Kashmir (Srinagar, 2019))

The initial enthusiasm about citizens of countries with political oppression 'leapfrogging' others hinged on anonymity and networks benefitting those whose freedom of movement and speech were curtailed. Network principles would allow people to organise and subvert powerful regimes without having to go through traditional gatekeepers. This leapfrogging failed for several reasons. Governments are better than citizens at controlling social media and digital communication platforms (Ghodes, 2018). That is, authoritarian governments use hard power (i.e. threats and torture) to control what is published more than less authoritarian governments. The president of Ethiopia, quoted at the beginning of the chapter, dismisses the internet as not important but puts it alongside food and water, indirectly recognising that ICTs provide sustenance to citizen participation. The government of India advocates that citizens need electronic sustenance for empowerment (first quote of this section), but not all citizens are created equally. Kashmiris' digital participation rights were taken away before revoking the region's special autonomous status (second quote).

The difference between authoritarian and democratic regimes' abilities to control ICTs means inequalities between citizens from politically free as compared with those from oppressed countries will increase through direct censorship and self-censorship (Meng, 2012). Citizens with the most opportunities to use ICTs for civic participation come from regions where citizens least need civic empowerment. Those who most need possibilities for participation, such as the citizens of Kashmir, see it increasingly restricted. Governments justify shutdowns as necessary to preserve peace and prevent bloodshed. But the result is the amplification of inequalities. 'Civically poor' regions fall even further behind since alternative, non-digital ways of engaging with those in power are increasingly cut off for many in societies.

There is also evidence of regional inequalities in the use of government services. The *UN eGovernment Survey* (UN Department of Economics and Social Affairs, 2018) shows that

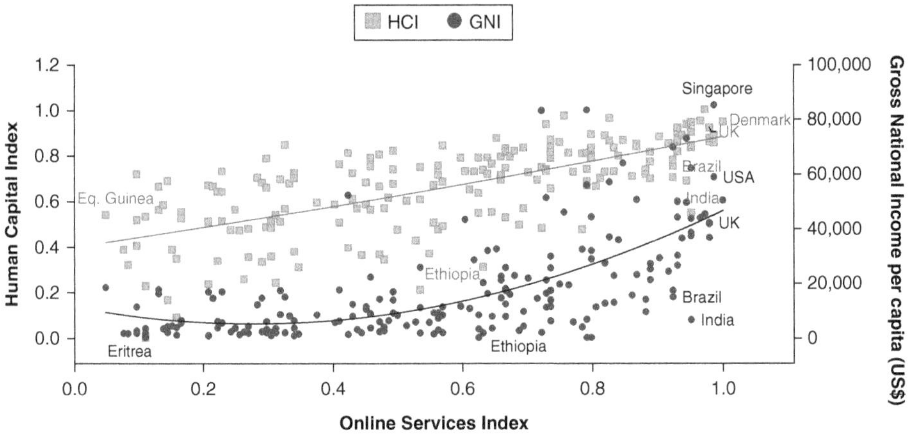

Figure 5.3 Relationship between economic (GNI), education/literacy (HCI), and online government service provision (OSI)

Source: UN eGovernment data (UN Department of Economics and Social Affairs, 2018). Original analysis for this chapter.

Note: Small city states with Gross National Income (GNI) of over US$100,000 excluded from graph for clarity purposes.

countries in the Global South which are consistently, historically disadvantaged in terms of the economy and governance are also least likely to have implemented wide-ranging e-government services, and adoption is low (Rose, 2005). The correlation between the Online Services Index and the Human Capital Index (HCI, r=.68) is stronger than that with Gross National Income (GNI, r=.52), suggesting that inequalities in skills and education are better predictors of inequalities in the use of online services than economic inequalities (UN Department of Economics and Social Affairs, 2018).

In Figure 5.3, low-income African countries with low literacy levels are shown in the bottom-left, while the top-right is made up of European countries, Australia, and Singapore. Interestingly, India is part of the top 20 in terms of the provision of services, and Indian policy is digital-by-default. Yet, this version of 'digital India' still has very low literacy rates and internet use stands at only 40 per cent of the general population. Priya will benefit from being able to access online services to overcome her mobility problems and the public shame she has about her leg. Kavita, her cleaner, who does not know how to read or write, will not. This 'build it and they will come' approach should be questioned. For example, even when everything is forced online, existing patterns of inequalities will likely be exacerbated during the COVID-19 pandemic.

Informal civic engagement

There is evidence for global differences in who consumes news and engages in informal political discussions. Data for informal types of civic engagement somewhat contradict data on more formal political participation. For example, WhatsApp and other private messaging tools have become popular in the Global South, especially in countries with scarce information sources and distrusted public institutions (e.g. Brazil, Malaysia, South

Africa) (Aneez, Neyazi, Kalogeropoulos, & Kleis Nielsen, 2019). Citizens in the Global South are also more likely to implement Wellman's networked capital on these platforms. They exchange information about political issues with 'weak tie' networks beyond family and friends. Priya is typical of the Indian news consumers who go to their smartphone first (68 per cent). Like other Indians of her age, she reads the *Dainik Jagran/Hindustan Jainik* newspaper that her husband brings home (Aneez et al., 2019). Her US-based sons also rely on their smartphones, even though in that country only 23 per cent mostly use their smartphone for news compared to 31 per cent in India.

Informal civic engagement is relatively high in Europe while formal civic engagement is lower online, as with most regions (Eurostat, 2018a). Scandinavian countries are high on both types of participation, but for the rest regional dominance is less obvious. There are relatively few countries where formal engagement is high and informal engagement is low. Only the UK and Turkey clearly have this profile. The Czech Republic stands out for being high in informal engagement but low in formal political engagement. There are a few more countries low on both informal and formal engagement, notably a cluster of the Balkan countries. The lowest in online participation are Belgium and France as well as Ireland. There are few hypotheses about why these European countries fall within certain clusters, although a combination of historical and current political and societal factors could explain this clustering.

To make accurate predictions about which countries are more likely to engage civically, better theories need to be developed and tested beyond Europe. These theories should take into account the complexity and intersectionality of political, social, and cultural histories. Would online civic engagement trends in a region like Europe, which shares a political history and political institutions, be evident on a global scale? To know, we require better theories and research to predict whether there are limiting factors. This is particularly important to prevent entrenchment in countries with a history of civic disengagement.

Disenfranchised groups: Inequalities in civic digital literacy and engagement

After discussing inequalities between countries in digital civic engagement and how they might be explained by national economic and political contexts, this section examines within-country differences in digital civic engagement and skills. Specifically, I explore how these differences might be explained by differences in an individual's economic, social, and cultural resources. The Pareto principle also applies here because individuals who would most benefit from civic engagement are least able to undertake these activities online, even in countries where overall digital civic engagement is high (Nakamura & Chow-White, 2013). Accordingly, this chapter shifts the book towards socio-cultural and social inequalities, and away from dominant socio-economic explanations for access, skills, and related economic and learning inequalities.

Individuals from certain socio-cultural groups have been historically disempowered when it comes to civic engagement. Disempowerment includes being kept from participating in the social organisations that influence decision-makers, and being discouraged to see social and political issues as relevant to disadvantaged groups. For example, women, ethnic minorities, those with health problems, and young people have been disempowered through these processes. The question is whether a pattern of disempowerment is replicated in the digital realm, or if historically-disempowered individuals can use ICTs to inform themselves, speak out, and challenge power in new ways.

Socio-economic inequalities

This section on socio-economic inequalities in civic engagement reviews the evidence for inequalities in trust and how these inequalities relate to online civic engagement. There is a severe lack of evidence on trust, and who is more likely to be part of homogeneous networks and echo chambers online. Nevertheless, research on political activities online suggests that people who have been empowered by socio-economic status continue to benefit digitally. Similarly, when focusing on civic digital literacy, people with higher education levels display greater awareness and a more proactive stance to countering misinformation. Those of higher socio-economic status also report greater overall trust in news and traditional sources of information. Reuters Institute studies conclude that traditional news media and reporting is more aligned with the world-views of elites whose views are already represented in these media outlets (Newman et al., 2019). Too little and too much trust are both problematic, because they can lead to passivity or acceptance of the going norm. Healthy levels of mistrust lead to activism and a desire to improve society (Gil de Zúñiga & Valenzuela, 2011). The right amount of cynicism drives people to hold people in power to account, question the actions of others, and seek out more diverse opinions. In other words, an optimal level of trust is not necessarily the maximum level of trust (Goldfinch, Gauld, & Herbison, 2009).

The same amplification principles observed for regional differences can be applied to differences between individuals from different socio-economic backgrounds. The DiSTO data that I analyse below are from only four locations (Chile, the Netherlands, the UK, and the US). I use caution when generalising these to other contexts, since from the previous section it is clear that country context is important in shaping individuals' digital civic engagement. Civic literacy – in terms of trust in people and institutions on the internet – is much lower among young people not in employment education or training (NEETs), even though they trust information online equally to their more advantaged peers, and have significantly lower levels of trust in others online (Helsper & Smirnova, 2016). On the other hand, scepticism towards general online information is higher among those with higher education. These differences have several explanations. NEETs are less trusting of others online because they have experienced everyday disrespect and lack of empowerment (Helsper & Smirnova, 2016). This distrust of people and institutions leads them to rely on trusted offline networks, even in digital spaces, although the information provided by those individuals might be less diverse and reliable. The information-sceptical, educated elite turn to reputable online information sources, and build on their broad, influential offline and online networks. This amplifies inequalities between them and the civically disadvantaged in terms of staying informed and being connected.

Simultaneous to amplification, there is evidence for normalisation effects. For example, research in Thailand suggests that there is greater equality among political activists online than among people active in traditional politics. There are more individuals of lower socio-economic status politically active on Facebook political party pages than there are active in party politics, in a country where political critique is risky (Sinpeng, 2017). In Thailand, inequalities online are less pronounced than in more traditional forms of political participation. As I discuss later, this normalisation might be due to online politically active citizens being younger.

Dutch DiSTO data help to illustrate socio-economic inequalities in formal and informal civic digital engagement (Van Deursen et al., 2017). At first glance, the Netherlands' socio-economic trends confirm the amplification hypotheses; higher education, income, studying, and employed individuals all have higher levels of civic engagement (Figure 5.4). Yet, education is the only significant direct predictor of civic engagement. In a two-step cumulative process, lower education relates to lower levels of civic digital literacy which then lead to less civic digital engagement. Unlike employment and income, education is also linked directly to inequalities in engagement, independent of literacy (Van Deursen et al., 2017). This suggests – in Bourdieusian fashion – that socio-cultural factors associated with completing graduate education also motivate people to engage civically. Analysing DiSTO data from London and Los Angeles – two highly unequal cities – leads to similar conclusions. Socio-economic inequalities in civic digital literacy are even more pronounced there than general digital skills inequalities (see Chapter 3).

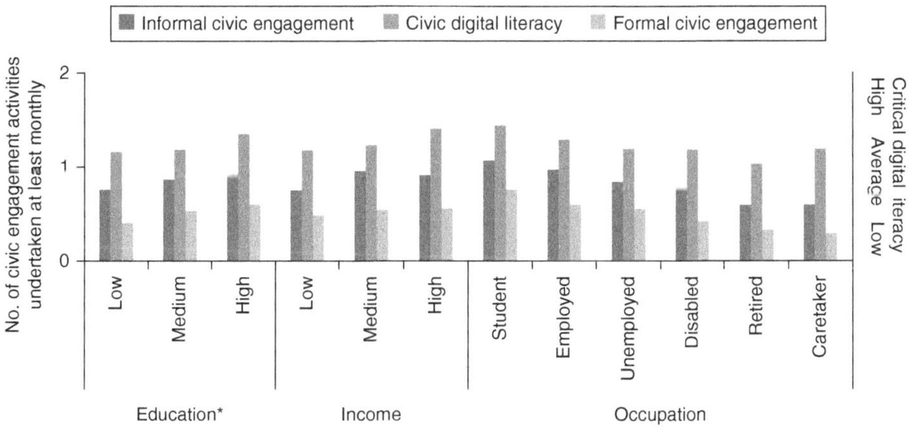

Figure 5.4 Socio-economic inequalities in civic digital literacy and engagement

Source: DiSTO NL 2018 data.

Base: Dutch Internet Users (N=1691). Original analysis for this chapter.

*Differences significant for political civic uses in multi-variate analyses.

Note: Civic digital literacy refers to the ability to find and understand how information is organised online. Informal civic engagement includes finding information about and participating in community and civic activities (from sport and hobby clubs to political discussion). Formal civic engagement includes seeking information about and interacting with government and political parties.

However, not all countries and demographic groups follow this pattern. In Santiago, Chile, digital literacy is higher among the lowest and the highest educated. This might relate to the highly unequal education system, coupled with a lack of services and opportunities for engagement offline. It could be that those with personal resources but without socio-economic resources are pushed to acquire problem-solving skills outside formal education. For these resourceful individuals, the digital world offers opportunities for civic engagement that are out of reach offline.

The younger generations are often 'accused' of being civically disengaged, even when movements such as the climate rebellion protests counter this idea. Some studies find amplification effects when it comes to younger generations, and civic literacies that replicate regional differences. PISA's research shows that lower social status students have lower digital reading skills and engage less digitally with news and information seeking across OECD countries (Drabowicz, 2014; OECD, 2015a). Nevertheless, our research in the UK with NEETs contradicts this (Helsper & Smirnova, 2016). Unexpectedly, young people who have a history of poverty are more likely to use the internet for formal civic engagement. Since this group is most likely to require government services, this trend could be viewed as empowerment. This is good news, suggesting leapfrogging effects. Other socio-economic inequalities in use between disadvantaged youth who are NEET and their more advantaged counterparts are not significant. The trend paints a more pessimistic picture associated with people's negative experiences with institutions and how willing other people are to let them get involved.

Socio-cultural inequalities

Research on socio-cultural inequalities in using ICTs for civic engagement mostly addresses generational and gender inequalities, but some research looks at minority status. Overall, there is evidence for amplification effects with female and older individuals using ICTs in more limited ways (Wei, 2012). Yet, generational inequalities are also an area where socio-cultural amplification claims are most contested. The assumption is often that older individuals are less likely to be interested in using ICTs (Rose, 2005). Especially in countries with stable political and digital infrastructures, younger people are more likely to take up these opportunities and older generations are more likely to stick to what they know offline. Nevertheless, DiSTO research in LA and London suggests that middle-aged adults are the most civically active online. Traditional patterns of more engaged older generations and less civically engaged younger generations might be reversing, especially for lower socio-economic status individuals. Marchi's (2017) research with low-income Latino immigrant families suggests that youth inform themselves with updated and more diverse news than their parents. Their online participation allows them to develop the critical and social skills beneficial for civic engagement. This means a reversal of generational inequalities in civic engagement for low-income families. Even though young disadvantaged youth might be catching up, several authors have cautioned that inequalities between youth based on family background are still unresolved (Oyedemi, 2015; Thorson, Xu, & Edgerly, 2018).

Dutch and Chilean DiSTO data suggest that younger people are indeed more likely to engage in political discussions and activities online than offline (Prevost & Schaffner,

2008; Sinpeng, 2017; Xenos et al., 2014). Nevertheless, different processes among younger than older generations complicate conclusions about generational differences. Hirzalla, van Zoonen, and de Ridder (2011) found that for online political information-gathering, Dutch youth behaviour reflects normalisation, mobilising previously inactive youth. Unfortunately, for older generations the status quo is maintained. Among older adults, ICT use is highly stratified based on local gender, age, marital status, and educational inequalities (Selwyn, Gorard, Furlong, & Madden, 2003).

Notwithstanding, generational inequalities in civic engagement might persist in the digital age, because the critical information literacy necessary for empowered civic engagement is more developed among older generations (Van Deursen & Van Dijk, 2008). Whether generational inequalities persist might also depend on which country is under investigation; in the US and the UK – two demographically-similar countries – the relationship between trust in online sources and proactive action to counter misinformation are related in opposite ways (Newman et al., 2019). In the UK, the older generation is less likely to have started using more reputable sources, while in the US they are almost twice as likely to have done so. In China, people more likely to engage actively in politics online have stronger party identification, associated with lower education levels and older age (Lee, Chen, & Huang, 2014).

Digital civic engagement research also finds gender differences. Men are more frequent users of networked platforms that allow them to gather information (i.e. news, political discussions) – a hallmark of good citizenship. Women with less civic capital were also less likely to have offline civic literacy. There is an intersectional aspect to gender, class, age, and disadvantage which leads to gender inequalities in civic engagement being more pronounced among those of higher socio-economic status in online civic engagement.

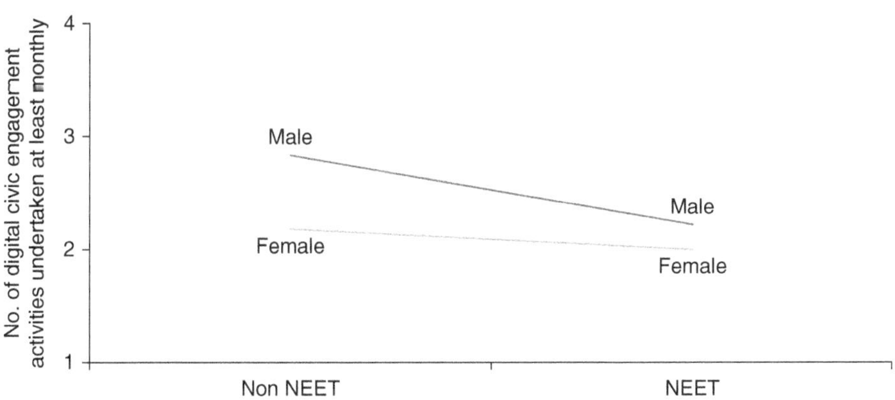

Figure 5.5 Interaction between gender and socio-economic status in digital civic engagement

Source: DiSTO NEETs project data (Helsper & Smirnova, 2016). Original analysis for this chapter.

Base: Young people (16-25) in the UK (N=1026 Non-NEETs and N=318 NEETs).

Note I: Digital civic engagement includes the use of government services, donating or signing petitions for social causes, and coming across political or ideological content.

Note II. NEETs refers to young people not in education, employment, or training.

Additionally, there is little difference in the participation of young women, while there are significant inequalities between young men in privileged and non-privileged positions (Figure 5.5). Since the lower educated are overall less likely to engage, this pattern still leaves young women in disadvantaged positions the least digitally civilly engaged (Helsper & Smirnova, 2016).

Gray, Gainous, and Wagner (2017) compare different countries, finding that this link is stronger in countries where general ICT use is lower. They conclude that for Latin America, 'The potential for the Internet to serve as a social and political equalizing force ... is stymied in part by the gendered digital divide' (Gray, Gainous, & Wagner, 2017, p. 326). Torenli (2006) comes to a similar conclusion for Turkey; non-elite women were similarly unable to engage fully as citizens online due to lower levels of skills and access. Other research looks at active participation in online discussions around social issues, where women are often silenced and bullied. This adoption of 'patriarchal' means of engaging in the public sphere likely amplifies existing gender inequalities in power dynamics, pushing women offline to closed networks for civic engagement (Vochocova, 2018).

Priya's situation demonstrates this effect, where women are pushed to offline resources. India ranks poorly on the UN's Gender Development and Gender Inequality indexes, and is a country where gender inequality has worsened since 1990 (UNDP, 2019). One explanation is that economic prosperity has facilitated the 'enforcement' of more traditional gendered roles. In 2016, around half of the Indian population thought that women should stay at home and take care of domestic responsibilities if their husband earned enough (Naidu, 2016). Norms around binding women to housekeeping are stricter among wealthier, upper-caste households, suggesting that economic growth alone may not alter their influence (Fletcher, Pande, & Troyer Moore, 2017). If Priya's husband earned less, she might have worked more. Despite being an educated woman with an accounting degree, gendered socialisations play out in her life. A few years ago, she was browsing for information about girls' education for the charity and ended up on a news website where she read about sexual violence against Indian women. She made the mistake of bringing this topic up with her husband. He reprimanded her by saying she should not be reading those stories. He reminded her of her responsibility to keep their house in order and to steer away from inciting this kind of behaviour. She never brought it up again.

Priya also remembers a hurtful exchange she had with someone interested in her family's educational charity. The man commented on the website that he did not think that girls should learn about biology, physics, politics, or business. When Priya reacted by saying she studied business and gender equality in education was enshrined in law, the man said her experiences were irrelevant and ignored her arguments. Priya believes in the right to free speech but feels that it often puts people like her in an uncomfortable position online 'if someone's got an opinion, like a political opinion or an opinion about human rights, you can't squash it but there's a way in which they can say it that would perhaps not be off putting to people like me'. She will not mix in discussions about social issues again on public sites.

Ethnicity is a final socio-cultural aspect prominent in civic engagement inequalities research. Ethnic minorities are among the most disempowered groups in society. Around the world, they suffer violent oppression, underrepresentation, and worse education. ICTs give access to knowledge and contacts that are not dependent on official institutions or 'old white boys' networks. They could provide an opportunity for minority ethnic groups to have their voices heard and to organise. Digital inequalities appear to work differently for civic engagement among majority ethnic groups than minority ethnic groups. For example, in the US, moving to online voting may seem worse for people with low-quality connections, such as ethnic minorities. Yet, online voting reduces absentee ballots for ethnic minorities more than for ethnic majorities in the same situation (Prevost & Schaffner, 2008). Others show that high-quality home access predicts formal civic engagement for the white majority in the US, but that mobile-only access is a better predictor of engagement for ethnic minorities (Whitacre, 2017). Studies from South Africa, Australia, and New Zealand show that ethnic background predicts online civic engagement in ways that replicate participatory inequalities, especially for formal politics (Goldfinch et al., 2009; Oyedemi, 2015).

Returning to the comparative DiSTO data, patterns show that Dutch residents born outside Europe are more civically engaged than those born in the Netherlands or the rest of Europe (Helsper, 2021). In Los Angeles and London, ethnicity made no significant difference in explaining the skills necessary for civic engagement, although when it came to civic engagement something interesting happened. In LA there is evidence of amplification: ethnic minorities are less likely to engage civically online. In London these patterns are reversed, suggesting that there, normalisation, if not leapfrogging, might be taking place. In summary, with contradicting forces and regional differences, digitisation has a mixed record on improving ethnic inequalities.

Social inequalities

Finally, there is considerable evidence that people's traditional social capital – in the Putnam sense of having access to trusted community networks and organisations – is the best predictor of the digital equivalent of civic engagement (Skoric, Zhu, Goh, & Pang, 2016). Women, ethnic minorities, younger people, and those with fewer socio-economic resources historically have less access to formal social capital. It is mostly their lack of this social capital, rather than their lack of skills, interest, or economic resources, that drives inequalities in digital civic engagement. This link between social capital and digital engagement might depend on age, gender, and ethnic background. In traditionally disadvantaged groups, people with less formal social capital are more engaged online. In traditionally advantaged groups, the expected rich-get-richer pattern is observed (Nam, 2012).

Research from the Global South and other areas with lower levels of diffusion cautions us against too much optimism. It seems that community engagement is still mostly the preserve of urban elites, who are embedded in networks of power and have abundant time and resources. For example, Mare (2018, p. 90) cautions that while ICTs are reshaping Zimbabwean formal political participation, they have also created 'communication hierarchies and participation inequalities between the [politically] connected (mostly urbanites) and disconnected (especially rural)'. Analyses of Dutch and Chilean DiSTO data confirms that people with more social capital are more likely to have the skills necessary to find and evaluate information and participate in online debates. They are more likely to engage civically online, independent of their socio-economic and socio-cultural background. People who are more open to engaging with others are also more civically active online (Russo & Amna, 2016). While most of their engagement is of the low-cost rather than the involved kind, it mobilises people outside a politically-committed elite (Goldfinch et al., 2009).

In this chapter, I have discussed inequalities in civic digital engagement. Following the CF model, I have not assumed that these inequalities automatically translate to the alleviation or exacerbation of patterns of empowerment. The next and final section of this chapter addresses inequalities in outcomes of digital civic engagement.

Consequences: Inequalities in civic empowerment from digital engagement

Network and information exposure theories propose that inequalities in online networks and uses of ICTs lead to inequalities in civic empowerment outcomes. Nevertheless, there is little research on which people are more likely to benefit. Socio-digital inequalities researchers have unfortunately not been very involved in this discussion. Cammaerts (2018) links this lack of involvement to the dominance of the 'magic bullet' media effects tradition in the area of political action and opinion formation. In this tradition, the impact of media is equal for all. In what follows, I will look at how civic engagement outcomes of ICT use are distributed between different regions in the world, and between individuals who have different ICT uses and skills. I link this back to the previous section, where I described what might explain these differences. The specific outcomes of concern are action-based elements of formal citizenship (e.g. taking political action, participation in organisations or clubs) and subjective evaluations of empowerment (e.g. political efficacy, quality of civic experiences).

Socio-political systems and inequalities in civic empowerment through ICTs

Meta-analyses, generally limited to social media, helpfully review studies about the relationships between ICT use and civic engagement cross-nationally. On the whole, these conclude that informal digital civic engagement leads to formal civic engagement in countries with restrictive press and political freedoms (Boulianne, 2016, 2019; Skoric et al., 2016). There is little research on inequalities resulting from ICT use for other forms of civic literacy and engagement, such as trust in institutions and volunteering, although longitudinal Australian research found that increases or decreases in trust and cohesion cannot be attributed to internet use (Salahuddin, Tisdell, Burton, & Alam, 2016). The World Internet Project collects data on subjective aspects of civic empowerment through ICT use.

The findings support the idea that, in countries where regimes and media are more restrictive, people who use ICTs have higher levels of political efficacy (World Internet Project, 2019). The correlation between a lack of press freedom (Reporters Without Borders, 2019) in a country and internet users' beliefs that the internet is politically empowering is extremely high (r=.84). An internet user in Saudi Arabia (ranked 172 on press freedom) is more likely to have digital political efficacy in relation to internet use than a Swiss citizen (ranked 6). That is, they are more optimistic about their power to make politicians more responsive. Yet, this is by no means true everywhere. People in the US, with a relatively free media and political system (ranked 48), are only slightly more optimistic.

Perhaps even more interesting is to compare users' and non-users' beliefs about political expression and digital engagement. Internet users have more faith than non-users in online and, with the exception of Greece, Egypt, and Lebanon, offline political expression (Figure 5.6). Internet users are especially more likely than non-users to believe that the internet offers political freedom. The largest differences in perceptions of political freedom can be found in the US. In 2018, only 44 per cent of internet non-users believed that the internet should allow people to criticise their government online, while 74 per cent of internet users believed this. The smallest difference for this same indicator is in Greece where, surprisingly, internet non-users and internet users have similarly high levels of confidence in online freedom of expression.

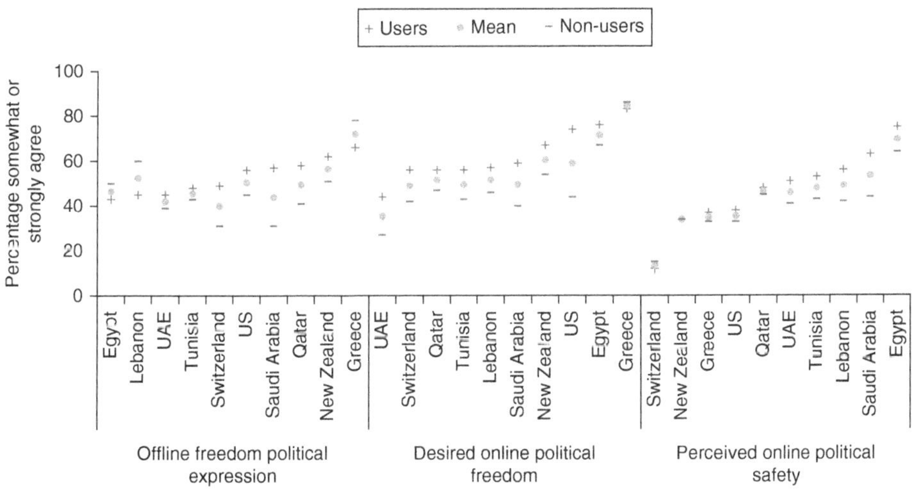

Figure 5.6 Differences in beliefs about offline and online political efficacy between internet users and non-users

Source: World Internet Project Report (World Internet Project, 2018). Original analysis for this chapter.

Base: Internet users and non-users in each country.

Note I: Countries ordered from smallest to largest difference between users and non-users.

Note II: Offline political freedom refers to 'feeling comfortable saying whatever you want to say about politics'; Desired online political freedom refers to believing that 'people should be free to criticise their government on the internet'; Perceived online political safety refers to feeling that it is 'safe to say whatever you think about politics' on the internet.

Interestingly, when fewer internet non-users in a country believe there is offline political freedom of expression, more internet users believe that the internet empowers them politically (r=-.41). What internet users in a country think about offline political freedom of expression is an inadequate predictor of opinions on online empowerment (r=-.09). Between countries with similar levels of conviction in political freedom of expression offline among internet users, there are large differences in internet users' beliefs about online freedom of expression. For example, in the UAE, 51 per cent of internet users believe that the internet empowers them politically, while in Lebanon only 37 per cent of internet users believe this. In both countries, 45 per cent of internet users (and respectively, 39 per cent and 60 per cent of non-users) think there is offline freedom of political expression. There are also large inequalities between countries in terms of perception of online political safety (Figure 5.6). Only 14 per cent of internet non-users in Switzerland and 75 per cent of internet users in Egypt believe that expressing political opinions online is safe. Differences between internet users and non-users are relatively small in all countries, except for Saudi Arabia and Lebanon. Of course, we must remember that what the Swiss consider unsafe is uncomparable to what Egyptians think is unsafe.

India ranks 140 on the Reporters Without Borders (2019) press freedom index, but Priya has not noticed this bias much, and does not necessarily think it is that bad. Her daughter has told her that abroad, people talk of the Hindu nationalist politics of Prime Minister Modi as being anti-Muslim and anti-Christian. Priya assumes that the news she reads and hears is favourable to the prime minister, but also thinks that that is surely the case everywhere! She is convinced it is safe to express your political opinion online in India – after all, it is a democracy. She joins half of the internet users in her country who feel the internet is safe for political expression. If you are inciting people to hatred or violence, she thinks that it is justified for people to be curtailed online. In more private discussions on WhatsApp, she is concerned about expressing political views because it might damage her reputation and not because she fears political persecution. Besides the inappropriateness of expressing political views as a Hindu woman, another reason why Priya hesitates to engage in online discussions is the violence of online discourse in India. Becky, the American mother of a friend of Amir, does not really understand the part about not daring to speak out but understands Priya's concern around violence: 'As this year has gone on with various political events and the, kind of, awfulness of the debate online and that, I have really stopped engaging in any kind of political debates, on Twitter particularly.'

If we asked Priya's cleaner, Kavita, we would get a very different answer. Unbeknown to Priya, Kavita has Kashmiri relatives. They only use WhatsApp, and they left her a voice message before the communications blackout. They said they would stop contacting her on other unencrypted platforms, because they felt it was unsafe. With the blackout, even that contact was lost. The result is that in various ways disenfranchised voices are leaving or are silenced in public and private civic spaces. ICT use amplifies ideological homogeny among middle-class youth and families in India and elsewhere (Banaji, 2017).

In countries where offline freedom of expression is low, internet users are far more optimistic about the civic and political outcomes of ICT use. They are more likely to translate ICT use into political participation and active citizen engagement. In these same countries, there are large inequalities between the beliefs of internet users and non-users. I, therefore, conclude that those who are online and empowered by ICT use come from an elite embedded within the dominant ideologies and power structures. Empowerment among the disenfranchised is limited, even if they use ICTs for civic engagement (Banaji & Moreno-Almeida, 2019). As a result, inequalities in civic empowerment will likely increase within countries where there is less political freedom.

Disenfranchised groups: Inequalities in civic empowerment through ICT Use

This section discusses the little we know about individual inequalities in outcomes of formal and low-cost uses of networked ICTs. Before that brief overview, I return to Boulianne (2016) and Skoric et al.'s (2016) meta-analyses. They show that it is unlikely that ICT use by itself leads to civic empowerment. Rather, high social status in combination with specific types of social media use lead to empowerment. This does not mean that social media should be dismissed as a predictor in the study of or interventions around inequalities in civic empowerment. Boulianne (2019) concludes that social media use is comparable to education in terms of how well it predicts civic empowerment, and is a better predictor than education and social status for civic action among youth. This might be because young people are new to politics and have less clearly demarcated political ideas. They and others in the same situation might be more susceptible to these socio-digital, rather than traditional drivers of civic action (Xenos et al., 2014). For these individuals, literate digital media use could be more empowering than for those with more established politics, ideas, and identities. There is still not enough data to draw conclusions about activist and formal types of civic empowerment through ICT use.

Inequalities in empowerment outcomes from formal civic engagement

There is also little research on who is and is not likely to attain quality outcomes from the use of e-government services. Naturally, if you are in no need of government support you are unlikely to achieve that as an outcome ICT use (Ebbers, Jansen, & van Deursen, 2016). For example, people with health problems are more likely to make appointments and use government health services than those who are healthy. Thus, while the Pareto principle applies to access to ICTs and literacy, it should not apply to the already-online individuals obtaining benefits from these services. However, high-quality outcomes are not about just achieving a goal, such as finding a benefit or contacting a politician, but about finding the right one and having positive interactions with these representatives and the platforms providing the services.

DiSTO analyses show that young people who need government services the most, such as NEETs and the less-educated, are less likely than more advantaged users of these services to achieve positive outcomes from this engagement (Helsper & Smirnova, 2016). This is partly explained by lower digital skills levels preventing them from turning ICT use into civic empowerment. They also do not trust the institutions behind the digital platforms to have their best interests at heart, and take dissatisfying interactions personally (see Chapter 3). Paradoxically, disadvantaged youth are positive about what ICTs can do for society, but pessimistic about benefitting personally. The tendency for disadvantaged individuals to be pessimistic about personal empowerment but optimistic about digital engagement might seem contradictory. Nevertheless, it is based in realism: for people not like them, ICTs can indeed be empowering. For example, Kavita's son worries about Modi's Hindu nationalism and the associated hate he encounters online, but is also 'really into the idea of a web-based democracy. [...] The more that people are enabled to make informed political decisions, impartially informed political decisions, then the better our politics will be.'

When comparing civic outcomes among adults in Chile and the Netherlands in 2018, a positive picture emerges of normalisation, and even leapfrogging for particular groups. Patterns around age were in favour of young people achieving more benefits in both countries. In Chile, gender inequalities were reversed (women and lower educated individuals were more likely to achieve civic outcomes), while in the Netherlands gender differences were insignificant. In the Netherlands, a different type of leapfrogging occurred for those who needed it most. The disabled and unemployed had more positive outcomes from interacting with civic organisations online. However, before they use ICTs for civic engagement, they will have suffered disadvantages that limit their digital civic engagement. The road to empowerment for disadvantaged individuals is full of obstacles that their advantaged peers do not encounter. Traditional inequalities are linked sequentially, rather than directly to civic empowerment inequalities; the disadvantaged are more likely to encounter compounded digital barriers to civic empowerment in terms of access (Chapter 3), skills (Chapter 4), and norms around digital civic engagement (Van Deursen & Helsper, 2017; Van Deursen et al., 2017). The disadvantaged who jump through those hoops will take advantage of the available opportunities perhaps even more so than their advantaged peers. More work is needed on inequalities in the quality of outcomes to discover whether these patterns of normalisation and leapfrogging are found in countries with different political and socio-cultural environments.

Networked inequalities in outcomes of low-cost digital engagement

At the very beginning of this chapter, I mentioned that researchers and political activists look down on 'slacktivism'. We do not really know who engages in this low-cost civic engagement, but there is evidence for positive outcomes. People who engage in informal, low-cost ways are more likely to participate in voting, and be members of political parties and community organisations. They are more knowledgeable about societal issues and more likely to feel engaged with them (Christensen, 2011). Still, who benefits from civic digital engagement strongly depends on how someone uses ICTs to mobilise their relationships (Gerbaudo, 2012). If there is no quick reaction from others, no matter how initially motivated a person is, digital engagement peters out. Similarly, people using high-level social digital skills in combination with information navigation skills are better at translating their use of ICTs into civic engagement than others (Hargittai & Shaw, 2013). This is true for everyday activities such as volunteering and more formal political actions such as getting the attention of government representatives.

Yet, network principles mean that even if you are not central to a political network and have influential friends, you can still make changes in other networks. Social change might happen if an active group of individuals appeals to what Barberá et al. (2015) calls the 'critical periphery'. The critical periphery consists of people who are not very politically active, but willing to click on and like media that interest them. Even if it does not lead to further civic action by that person, their low-cost engagement can make a cause visible to others, creating momentum and pushing collective action. For example, Priya's liking of a girls' rights news item did not lead to her voting differently or going to a protest. It did, however, create a discussion among her sons about women's rights in India, thematically linking it to the US #MeToo movement. More studies are needed to test the hypothesis that lower-cost digital engagement is important to indirectly empowering the disenfranchised.

The higher up one goes on the ladder of involvement and political action, empowerment is increasingly unequally distributed according to traditional types of socio-cultural inequality (Slavina & Brym, 2019). In all countries, a majority ethnic, higher social status male is more likely to turn civic engagement into real empowerment. This sequential disadvantage occurs because these individuals are less likely to have a social status and position where online mobilisation can be turned into actual action, even if they have the same level of skill and are using these platforms to the same level. Even if Priya was motivated and courageous enough to overcome the social norms against participating in protests, she would have a much harder time getting other people to join her in campaigns. Her online and offline networks consist mostly of family members and women her age who have husbands with similar views. Even younger women in India would have a harder time making real change unless they could get a Hindu male with extensive connections and close to the centres of power in Delhi to take up their cause. It would be slightly easier for her daughter, an Indian immigrant in the UK, and easier for Becky an American middle-class woman. A combination of inadequate cultural and social capital means that Priya is less likely to turn ICT use into the empowering civic engagement that goes beyond interaction with services and individuals (Carpentier, 2015). In rapidly digitising societies, inequalities researchers and activists are 'still dealing with the "old" issues of power and resistance, and structure and ownership' (Weimann, Weiss-Blatt, Mengistu, Tregerman, & Oren, 2014, p. 804). They should be aware of how the networked nature of ICTs can accelerate empowerment effects for some and limit them for others (DiMaggio & Garip, 2012).

Conclusions and recommendations

Equal opportunities to access and engage in the processes that shape society produce high levels of well-being. In digital societies, this means access to platforms, relevant content, and engagement with people who hold resources. ICTs' accessibility and non-hierarchical structures have led to optimism that digitisation will allow everyone to become civically engaged, and those who most need it will be newly empowered. Nevertheless, the extent to which digital opportunities translate into tangible, empowering outcomes for all citizens is 'driven by the equality of power relations in all decision making processes in society' (Jenkins & Carpentier, 2013, p. 261). How digital literacy and engagement with government, civic causes, community organisations, and political discussions translate into influence depends on our societal positions. Inequalities expressed in everyday social contexts are key to shaping inequalities in digital civic engagement. In the language of my CF model, if social inequalities restrict content and interactions, access and skills do not necessarily lead to empowering outcomes from ICT use.

This chapter calls socio-digital inequalities researchers and stakeholders to contribute more to this debate. By focusing on critiquing digital-by-default policies and the digitisation of government services, inequalities in non-traditional and newer forms of civic engagement have gone understudied. This chapter highlights how existing data are insufficient to draw conclusions about informal types of engagement. For example, we know little about inequalities in online community engagement, petition signing, and who is likely to end up in polarising environments. Similarly, we know little about who is subject to implicit silencing by restricting certain topics or activities. Specifically, inequalities in the following newer aspects deserve more attention:

- Critical digital literacy: the ability to select and understand where information comes from, who to trust, how to contribute to debates, and how to ensure you are listened to.
- Networked activism: inequalities in digital participation in institutional politics, organised collectives, activism, sharing ideas, and connecting to unknown others.
- Low-cost engagement: inequalities in content and actions constituting 'mere' clicking, liking, or browsing.

There remain puzzling contradictions in the data and relationships between critical digital literacy, engagement with ICTs, and empowerment outcomes. Optimal levels of trust in information and institutions develops in response to everyday political realities online and offline. Trust is based on past experiences with media and fellow citizens. It is deployed when and where needed by those who have been able to acquire these skills. Citizens in politically stable countries with historically strong public services and trust in institutions have a lesser need for critical digital literacy. They engage with digital public services no matter their levels of digital literacy. In countries with less political freedom, it seems encouraging that internet users believe more strongly in the power of ICTs to influence those in power. Yet, closer analysis shows that those who are able to use ICTs for political or civic purposes are part of the already-empowered elite supporting the regime. In countries which have more press and political freedom, those active on social media and other civic platforms are more likely to be counter-establishment.

At the beginning of this chapter, I asked: Who is most likely to use ICTs for civic engagement? And who takes advantage of these types of opportunities to have a real impact on their own and others' everyday lives? The answers reveal sequential and compound processes. We see amplification (i.e. worsening) of inequalities in terms of literacy, stratification (i.e. persistence) of inequalities in terms of use, and normalisation (i.e. diminishing) or even leapfrogging (i.e. reversal) in terms of outcomes. Digitisation increases civic engagement among some of the traditionally disempowered and reinforces existing inequalities among others.

Education is the one factor that consistently predicts civic digital literacy and civic engagement. For this reason, digital and traditional literacies that help people to navigate political systems go hand in hand. Even in countries with high levels of social capital – where there is trust in institutions and less need for critical civic literacy – civic literacy is disproportionately acquired by elites and cements power among the historically privileged. Critical digital literacy training, which provides individuals with the cognitive tools to spot injustices, will allow the literate to give voice to those who have been historically disempowered on public platforms only if they orient towards these politics (Polizzi, 2020).

Strong links to social inequality means that there are many obstacles – access, skills, and socio-cultural norms around civic engagement and ICT use – to attaining equal civic empowerment. Sequentiality is a real problem: those who traditionally have lower social status are less likely to have quality access and the literacy needed to fully digitally engage, and they are less likely to use ICTs in ways that influence political decisions. But civic digital engagement is not all doom and gloom. There is evidence for greater equality in online civic engagement among the disadvantaged. For example, historically disenfranchised youth are more active online than they are offline. It is not clear if this will last, because their generation may revert to stratification patterns observable in older generations once their opinions and identities become stabilised. There is also evidence for reversing traditional inequalities in civic engagement (e.g. based on gender or disability) in terms of digital civic engagement translating into everyday civic engagement.

Nevertheless, the most disadvantaged are still a long way away from catching up with their advantaged peers in terms of the quality of these outcomes. The largest issue is with the unequal distribution of symbolic power – the power to shape what can be talked about (Chapter 1). That is, if disadvantaged people manage to translate their ICT use into civic engagement, their socio-economic and socio-cultural background makes it more likely for them to be ignored or silenced.

Compoundness (or intersectionality) in inequalities is also important for understanding how inequalities in civic engagement will play out in future digital societies. The example of Priya and the people she knows illustrates how gender, caste, and religion come together in India to push her away from engaging civically. The silencing of certain voices and topics of discussion – and the limits of the networks that the disadvantaged have to influence others – remain in place offline and online.

Being realistically optimistic, I conclude that the end result is stratification. Yet, historically more equal, democratic societies have a higher chance to convert this into normalisation through equal opportunities to use ICTs for civic empowerment. Soft power actions, such as cutting off digital engagement for some, as in this chapter's examples of Ethiopia and India, become very problematic in combination with populism and authoritarianism. They will increase inequalities in civic engagement considerably where situations are already dire.

This chapter has examined how people's relationships and norms play an important role in shaping how digital opportunities translate into equality of civic empowerment. These relationships go beyond the more formal organised relationships and public engagement that are considered among civic engagement scholars. The next chapter will, therefore, take a deeper dive into inequalities in informal, intimate relating and connecting in increasingly digital societies.

PART III

THE FUTURE: NEW FRONTIERS OF SOCIO-DIGITAL INEQUALITIES

CHAPTER 6

INEQUALITIES IN LONELINESS AND CONNECTION IN DIGITAL SOCIETIES

'Thanks to social media, the pandemics of the future could be psychological.'

(Thomas, 2018)

Introduction

So far, this book has discussed the inequalities that have received most attention and concern from socio-digital inequalities researchers, policy makers and practitioners. These systematic inequalities in ICT access and infrastructure, skills, and use are worrying, because they exacerbate socio-economic inequalities and historic trends of disengagement and disempowerment. In this chapter, I consider inequalities in a basic human need: loving interpersonal relationships. Without these, we have shorter, less happy, and unhealthier lives. I focus on informal interactions and social and well-being aspects of ICT use. These are the kinds of relationships that scholars of network sociology, such as Wellman et al. (2002) and Granovetter (1983), refer to as social capital.

Platforms and applications that provide opportunities for interpersonal communication and relationships are widespread across the globe. They are often the first to be taken up by late adopters and laggards in Rogers' (1995) diffusion process. On a ladder of increased engagement with ICTs, social uses are 'the lowest rung on the ladder' – the entry-level activity after information seeking (Blank & Groselj, 2014). ICTs are now indispensable for the majority of us when managing our social and emotional lives.

These are relatively new, unexplored frontiers for socio-digital inequalities researchers. New frontiers carry excitement as well as a fear of the unknown, especially when it comes to topics central to everyone's lives. Excitement about social uses of ICTs was apparent around the world with the COVID-19 pandemic. When many were forced to keep physical distance, ICTs were seen as a saviour that would bring people together. Nevertheless, as illustrated by the quote at the start of this chapter, negative well-being outcomes of digital engagement – loneliness, alienation, and bullying – have been prominent in public discourse. As a result, the next two chapters will move to the informal, private sphere and include a more extensive discussion of the negative consequences of ICT use. I argue that we should not confuse the pervasiveness of social uses of ICTs with equality. We urgently need to find better answers to the following two questions:

- Does the widespread diffusion of digital communication tools mean that all individuals engage equally in the social use of ICTs?
- Who is most likely to improve their social and psychological well-being through everyday online interactions?

As in previous chapters, I examine inequalities between people from different socio-economic and socio-cultural backgrounds and different social resources. Here, I add an additional layer: personal, psychological resources. I will also examine whether how and who we interact with online has unequal consequences for the social and psychological well-being of people from different backgrounds (Figure 6.1).

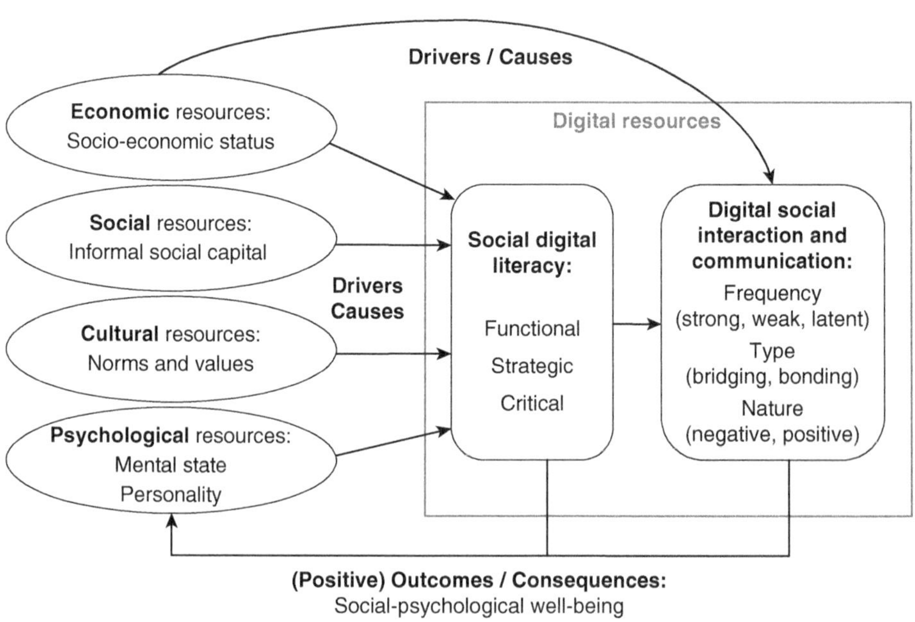

Figure 6.1 The links between social uses of ICTs and inequalities in well-being

Sociologists study inequalities by looking at relationships between socio-cultural characteristics, norms, and social uses of ICTs. They tend to emphasise more positive outcomes of social media use, such as increasing the frequency of our interactions and expanding bridging and/or bonding ties. A flaw in this research is that it discusses inequalities in quantitative terms of social or cultural resources obtained through digital engagement, neglecting to examine well-being or the quality of the outcomes of this use. Psychologists working in this field, on the other hand, hone in on negative social well-being resulting from digital engagement but do not distinguish between individuals from different backgrounds. They 'technologise', hypothesising universal effects of ICT use on well-being. In this chapter, I combine these sociological and psychological frameworks to understand which digital interactions will amplify or ameliorate social-psychological vulnerabilities.

Carol will accompany this chapter. Her story illustrates the links between who we know, who we are, how we use ICTs to maintain our relationships, and how we feel about ourselves and the people we interact with. She is a composition, a vignette, of the people who have shared these experiences in the various research projects I was involved in.

Case Study: Carol

Carol is a 17-year-old living in Vila Mariana in Sao Paolo (Brazil). She moved there from Manaus, a city in the Amazon region, when she was 10 years old. Her mum and dad are strict, middle-class parents to her and her much younger brother, Fabio. Her father is an engineer working in transport and her mother works as a teacher in a private primary school. Carol, unlike her brother, has a strong regional accent accompanied by a slight lisp and does not consider herself to be particularly pretty. She does not have a lot of friends at her current school. Nevertheless, she definitely does not want to go back to Manaus, even though her cousin, Fabricio, whom she is close to, still lives there. She is doing well at school and will probably pass the vestibular (university entry exam) with grades high enough to enter one of the top public universities. She is trying to decide what she wants to study, and likes law.

Carol is also into Alt Rock music, likes watching crime series and telenovelas, and reads science fiction novels on her tablet. Carol is digitally well connected; has a smartphone, a laptop, access to PCs at school, and to a tablet and a games console at home. She has Facebook and Instagram accounts, and of course WhatsApp. Here's how she feels about social media: 'Some people have over 300 friends. I don't because I don't know a lot of people. I don't really go on Facebook and stuff like that, but lately I was using Instagram.'

Throughout the chapter, I will use data from a wide variety of countries. Nevertheless, as the chapter progresses, and we move from social uses to social outcomes and from socio-cultural to social-psychological inequalities, cross-national comparative research becomes scarce. We already saw this happen for inequalities in informal civic engagement. As a consequence, Carol's story is based on experiences and interactions in countries and cultures that are different from the one in which she lives. While these are applicable and relevant to her situation, more research is definitely needed in countries outside the EU, the US, and China.

Before delving into understanding inequalities in well-being, I will explain why we should care about socio-digital inequalities in what are often considered 'private' matters. I will follow this with a description of which skills, uses, and outcomes, research and policy making should focus on. Most importantly, I dedicate the rest of the chapter to examining the evidence to understand whether differences in the social use of ICTs perpetuate or disrupt existing inequalities.

Why should we care about inequalities in the social use of ICTs?

It is not that researchers do not care about the consequences of social uses of ICTs. In fact, there are numerous studies and policies discussing ICT and social-psychological well-being outcomes. Nevertheless, compared to the prolific work on inequalities in access, skills, and economic, education, and civic engagement, there is much less attention paid to systematic differences in social digital engagement. There seems to be an assumption that all of us are equally vulnerable to the negative outcomes, and equally capable of taking up opportunities for interaction. This might be because digitally-mediated communication has the lowest barrier to entry of all ICT uses. Almost everyone who is online uses them to connect with others, especially now that smartphones and social media have become commonplace.

Eurostat (2019b) data show that the most common type of digital engagement in Europe is sending or receiving emails (86 per cent of internet users). Instant messaging (77 per cent) and online social networking (65 per cent) are also among the most popular activities. In Brazil, where Carol lives, social uses of ICTs are the most popular activity: 75 per cent of Brazilians use social media and 90 per cent send messages through apps and platforms (CGI.br, 2019). Social media use has been particularly stable in Brazil.

Considering the global reach of social ICT use, and social media platforms in particular, it is surprising that we know little about people's experiences and inequalities in using them. There is work on inequalities in terms of who is underrepresented, harassed, and discriminated in content made by unknown others (Chapter 7), but there is no extensive body of research on adults about systematic inequalities in the quality of interpersonal interactions with known others online. Similarly, we know little about who is most marginalised by the positive and negative outcomes of these interactions. The problem is that data are often inaccessible to researchers because they are a carefully-guarded commercial property (LSE Commission on Truth Trust and Technology, 2019). When big data on negative interactions are available, they are not coupled with a wide range of indicators of traditional inequality, such as gender, socio-economic status, and ethnicity. Data on positive interactions are rarely available because social media companies do not want to share this valuable information. Unavailable data make it hard to examine the causes of inequalities in social uses of ICTs, or in the consequences this has for our relationships and well-being. Considering how important our relationships are for healthy, well-functioning societies as a whole, this needs to be remedied.

The scarcity of research on these inequalities does not mean that there are no frameworks to think about inequalities in socio-digital well-being. The amplification hypothesis is that people with high-quality, diverse networks and greater social psychological well-being are more likely to have the skills to use ICTs for social purposes. They are more likely to achieve positive social outcomes and avoid negative ones. The leapfrogging hypothesis is that people compensate for a lack of interpersonal relationships by using ICTs to connect with people they could not otherwise engage with. There is some research on this for children and young people, but less for adults. Researchers also rarely couple leapfrogging to systematic socio-cultural and socio-economic inequalities. I will examine the evidence for these inequalities later in this chapter. First, I will explain how social interaction and well-being might look different in digital societies.

What are social-psychological capital and well-being in digital societies?

Technologies are tools; they allow us to satisfy the fundamental human needs to love and be loved. These needs have always been there, but what constitutes social resources and well-being might need to be revisited, because digitisation could bring a change in communication and the nature of relationships. Here, I will briefly review what literacy, 'social' media, the social use of ICTs, and social-psychological well-being means in this increasingly digital world.

Social-digital literacy

Interacting and communicating with others is perceived as easy online, supposedly because sending a text message or sharing a photo requires relatively few technical skills. Communication and social skills required in digital societies are not seen as something you can learn – you are 'born into' them. Carol figures that 'it's not rocket science!' Since social media use is so widespread and accessible, it seems logical to assume that the social use of ICTs depends on personal interest. From this perspective, differences in use are based purely on individual preference, not on systematic inequalities in skills or resources. But this simplicity is deceptive. A fuller understanding of social digital literacy is most definitely needed to progress in increasingly digital societies (Van Dijk & Van Deursen, 2014). These skills include:

- Functional skills: being able to read, understand, and produce written and visual language used for interactions on different online platforms.
- Strategic literacy: understanding how to connect and who to connect with or reject in order to establish and maintain beneficial relationships, while avoiding unsafe situations.
- 'Netiquette': understanding what accepted norms of interaction are in different digital environments and how to act on this knowledge.

Much of the literature places too much emphasis on functional and strategic safeguarding skills that require technical know-how, not socio-emotional digital literacy. There is little data on netiquette and strategic networking skills. Measures targeting these concepts are still in their infancy (Van Deursen et al., 2016). However social digital literacy is defined, some platforms might be more likely to help people in applying those skills and making connections. In the next section, I define the characteristics of ICTs used for social, relating purposes.

What are social digital media?

So far, I have consciously not used the term 'social media'. Instead, I use the slightly more cumbersome term 'social use of ICTs' because managing our social lives and interactions with others takes place on a variety of platforms, including those not normally defined as 'social media'. Researchers are often blinded by size when researching and talking about the social uses of ICTs. Large platforms such as Facebook, Weibo, and Instagram dominate research and policy agendas. Because these platforms have more 'citizens' than any single country on the planet, we assume that everyone is on them. Consequently, we ignore inequalities in access to and uses of these platforms. Additionally, because they dominate in user numbers, we overlook their role in broader communicative digital ecologies where individuals use platforms for communication with different people in various contexts (Madianou & Miller, 2012).

Social uses of ICTs include text messages, phone calls, in-game chat, dating sites, and social media on larger platforms. Carol, for example, posts occasionally on Facebook to keep her uncle and aunt in Manaus up to date with what she is doing. Her classmates and friends from primary school are also on Facebook, but she does not really interact with them. While she has an Instagram account, she does not post there. She has made friends around the world on Alt Rock fan sites. While Instagram is likely to be included in social media research, the fan sites would not – I want to include them here. I will include platforms that primarily facilitate existing relationships or connecting with friends (e.g. Facebook, Weibo, WhatsApp) and those that are more open and give access to unknown others (e.g. chat boards, Twitter) and supposedly do not rely as much on offline networks and identities (Amichai-Hamburger, Kaplan, & Dorpatcheon, 2008).

I critique the dominant perspective in interpersonal, mediated communication that social media equates to social interaction. Often, activities on social media are less about social interaction than mass self-communication. Castells (2013, p. xiv) coined this term and uses it to refer to a 'process of interactive communication that can potentially reach a mass audience, but in which the production of the message is self-generated, the retrieval of messages is self-directed, and the reception and remixing of content from electronic communication networks is self-selected'. That is, these platforms are used to broadcast material related to the presentation of self, as well as being used for the maintenance and development of relationships. For this reason, I will not include video-sharing platforms such as YouTube, Flicker, and TikTok in the analyses in this chapter, because they are used more to broadcast and reach a mass audience than for interpersonal or group relationships.

Instagram has developed into a similar platform, but I include it here. The next chapter will focus on the broadcast, audience, and content creation aspects of ICT use, and how it relates to cultural symbolic capital. This chapter focuses on inequalities in the development and maintenance of closer, personal relationships with family, friends, and colleagues.

In summary, I define 'social use of ICTs' by how they are used – establishing and maintaining relationships – rather than relying on affordances. This emphasises the outcomes of ICT use, rather than their intended design or potential of their use.

Digital social resources

For the purposes of this chapter, I distinguish concepts based on objective, quantitative aspects of the social use of ICTs (e.g. number of contacts) from those based on subjective, qualitative aspects (e.g. how we feel about these relationships). Scholars researching social capital in digital societies distinguish between bonding and bridging ties and between strong and weak ties. In practice, they quantify qualitative aspects of network approaches to studying digital social resources (Boase & Wellman, 2006; Lin & Erickson, 2008). As a result, research on digital relationships often counts the frequency of interactions or externally labels a certain type of connection, rather than asking the person what a given relationship means to them.

In addition to applying existing concepts in digital settings, work has been done to redefine what social resources look like in digital societies. Haythornthwaite (2002, p. 389) suggested the existence of latent ties – relationships 'for which a connection is available technically but that has not yet been activated by social interaction'. She argues that latent ties are important for facilitating connections with weak ties. These ties, presumably, were not available before the advent of digital technologies. In Carol's case, Magda, the friend of one of her Facebook contacts, would be a latent tie. Magda commented on one of the videos her friend posted mentioning an old Nirvana concert. Carol saw this and then decided to send Magda a contact request indicating that she was into the same music. She has not yet responded, so remains a latent tie. Magda would convert into a weak tie if she accepts Carol's contact request, and perhaps later, convert into a strong tie if they establish a close relationship.

Reyes-Acosta (2016, p. 56) identified liquid ties – 'social ties, which become highly relevant in one instance and lose significance in the next' – as a new digital phenomenon. She questioned the traditional idea that ties can be easily identified as either strong or weak, bridging or bonding. She argued that how they are defined depends on the meaning and needs of the person at a certain point in time, thus their character is not stable. A relationship that simmers in the background as a contact on social media might have started out as a latent tie, activated as a weak tie when needed, and even become a strong tie, disappearing again to the background as part of a sphere of anonymous connections. For example, @Altlover was a generic person Carol followed on Instagram until she remembered them because she wanted tickets to an Alt Rock gig. After Joao told her he had no more tickets, he disappeared into the Instaverse, losing meaning as an individual to Carol. There is some inequalities research on differences in bridging, bonding, weak, and strong-tie connections depending on socio-economic and socio-cultural background, but no research in relation to inequalities.

Social capital refers to the people we interact with. Another set of social resources that is important in this domain is how we feel about relating and interacting. Three levels exist here: the macro level between individualistic and collectivist countries; the meso level between positive, constructive and negative, authoritarian family or friendship dynamics; and the individual level between dispositional, personality-based and situational, circumstances-based loneliness (Valkenburg, Schouten, & Peter, 2005). These three levels of resources have all been linked to how people react to opportunities for social resource-building through ICTs. None of these is explicitly linked to or incorporated into the digital inequalities literature. However, I will include them in this chapter because they might better predict inequalities in the social use of ICTs. At the very least, they should be combined with explanations of socio-digital inequalities based on socio-economic and socio-cultural resources.

Digital (social) well-being and moral panics

Moral panics followed the introduction of the telephone, radio, and television (Joinson, 2003). As new media come onto the scene, people worry they will negatively impact their well-being and how we interact with others. This worry follows cyclical processes. When early adopters are taking ICTs up there are utopian visions of bright egalitarian futures. As they get taken up by Rogers' early and late majorities, these fears turn into dystopian visions of alienation and impoverished human interactions. In the second decade of the 21st century, many countries find themselves in a phase of mass adoption of the social uses of ICTs. The popular press writes little about potentially positive outcomes and emphasises negative outcomes in academic research (Przybylski & Bowes, 2017). When I looked for a positive headline to start this chapter, they were almost impossible to find. Similarly, in designing the theatre play 'Cookies' about cyberbullying, it was difficult to get young people to reflect on their everyday experiences, rather than parrot the extreme negative experiences that news media often focus on (e.g. suicides following cyberbullying) (Helsper, 2020). I do not deny that mediated experiences with terrible outcomes occur, nor do I argue that they should not be reported. Nevertheless, a one-sided emphasis on the extreme makes us blind to more prevailing micro-aggressions: smaller everyday acts of harassment, bullying, and silencing. It also makes us forget that these are lived alongside positive interactions which broaden horizons and open us up to interactions that cross borders to provide support and connection (Baym, 2015).

Different academic disciplines look slightly differently at negative well-being outcomes. Psychologists emphasise outcomes of ICT use in relation to emotions and physiological processes (e.g. depression), social-psychologists look at outcomes related to our interactions with others (e.g. loneliness), and sociologists examine feelings of alienation and exclusion from networks and society. One heated debate has coalesced around addiction, and whether traditional forms of well-being need to be rethought in the digital age. The American Psychiatric Association decided not to include internet addiction, but included internet gaming addiction in their *DSM V* manual. Their description of internet gaming addiction specifically refers to negative well-being outcomes; persistent internet gaming must lead to significant impairment or distress (American Psychiatric Association, 2017). In the broader literature on internet addictions, on which this recommendation is based, outcomes are described as akin to those of substance abuse (Kardefelt-Winther, 2017). Later in this chapter I will discuss the evidence for inequalities in these negative outcomes from social and other uses of ICTs.

For digital social well-being, it is important to distinguish between risks (online experiences) and harms (actual negative outcomes of internet use) (Global Kids Online, 2020). Risky behaviours that might lead to harm are classified as conduct, contact, and content risks. The contact risks relevant for this chapter include cyberbullying, meeting strangers you got to know online in person, and exchanging sexual messages (Byrne, Kardefelt-Winther, Livingstone, & Stoilova, 2016). Harm of these acts is measured by asking how upset young children are when these experiences are negative. The distinction between risk and experienced harm is important. Inequalities in negative well-being outcomes can only be studied through the latter. Buchi, Festic, and Latzer (2018) advocate for distinguishing between psychological and social aspects of subjective well-being. They adapt the existing definition of social psychological well-being to the digital world as follows: digital belongingness (social well-being) is 'an individual's perception and feeling of being part of the information society' (Buchi et al., 2018, p. 3693).

In summary, when looking at digital psychological and social well-being, we must consider affective, emotional outcomes, as well as quantitative measures like the breadth or diversity of online social networks.

Causes of inequality in digital inequalities in social engagement

As I wrote at the beginning of the chapter, techno-determinist, generalist discourses are commonplace. 'Magic bullet' effects theories abound about ICT use connecting everyone and making us narcissistic and behaving anti-socially, thus creating the psychological pandemics referred to in the quote introducing this chapter. There is very little discussion of who might benefit more and suffer less from social uses of ICTs. Here I will compile research from different sources to draw conclusions. I will start with evidence for systematic differences in social skills and use between regions and countries, then move to consider differences between individuals from different socio-demographic, social resource, and social-psychological well-being backgrounds.

Communication cultures? Regional inequalities in social uses of icts

International databases with comparable datasets include only generic social ICT use and are restricted to certain countries. A combination of World Internet Project (2018) and Eurostat (2019b) data shows that emailing remains an important means of communication in many countries but that there are considerable differences between countries (Figure 6.2). Those who have sent or received emails range from over 90 per cent of internet users in 13 of the 28 European countries to less than 50 per cent in Turkey and Kosovo. Countries in the north of Europe, followed by eastern and southern European countries, use email most. Beyond Europe, the spread is considerable between North African (Egypt 66 per cent, Tunisia 77 per cent) and Anglo-Saxon countries (New Zealand 98 per cent, the US 96 per cent). But emailing is still more popular in those than in many Southern European countries.

There is more variation in email use than for engagement with social networking, and the ranking of countries is very different for the two types of social ICT use. In Europe, on average, 64 per cent of the population uses the internet to engage in social networking, which hides large disparities between countries (Figure 6.3) (Eurostat, 2019b). More than four out of five individuals in Iceland (91 per cent), Denmark (82 per cent), and Norway (79 per cent) are active on social networking sites. Less than half of France (42 per cent), Italy, and Bosnia Herzegovina (46 per cent) is engaged in the same way. If we just look at internet users between 25 and 65 years old, then France (45 per cent), Switzerland (55 per cent), and Germany (55 per cent) have citizens least connected on social media, while Iceland (94 per cent) and Norway (86 per cent) remain high social media users. Romania (85 per cent), with very low levels of internet use in general, rises to the top three. Combining these data, lower social media use is not fully explained by the level of internet use in a country in general. Nor can the socio-demographic make-up of a country, such as age differences in the population, explain these differences.

Comparing Figures 6.3 and 6.2 and the statistics on data sharing on social ICT platforms, a few things stand out. First, countries at the bottom of email use – Turkey, Romania, and Malta – are at the top of social networking use. Second, there is less clear replication of traditional

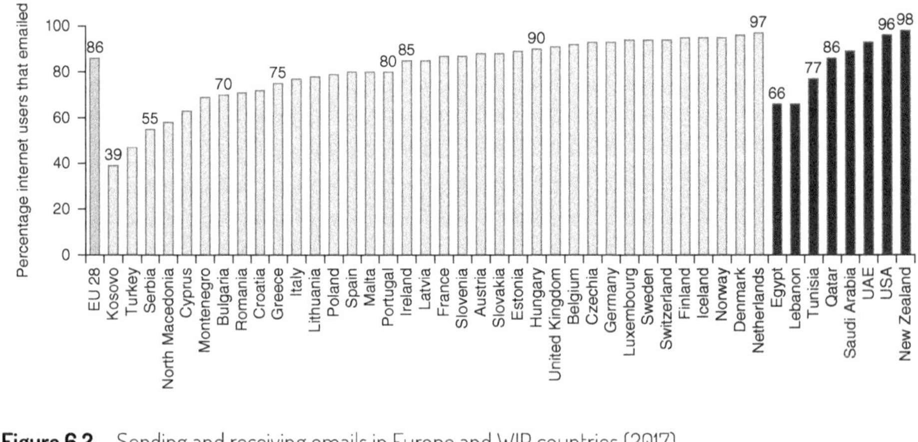

Figure 6.2 Sending and receiving emails in Europe and WIP countries (2017)

Light bars: Eurostat (2019b) online data code: isoc_ci_ac_i. 2017 data refer to sending or receiving emails. Base: Internet users 24-65 years old.

Dark bars: Derived from World Internet Project (2018). 2017 data refer to checking email at least monthly. Base: Internet users 24-65 years old.

Note: The World Internet Project used a slightly different question but the differences between countries included in both databases were within the error range. The data from Eurostat were used for EU countries.

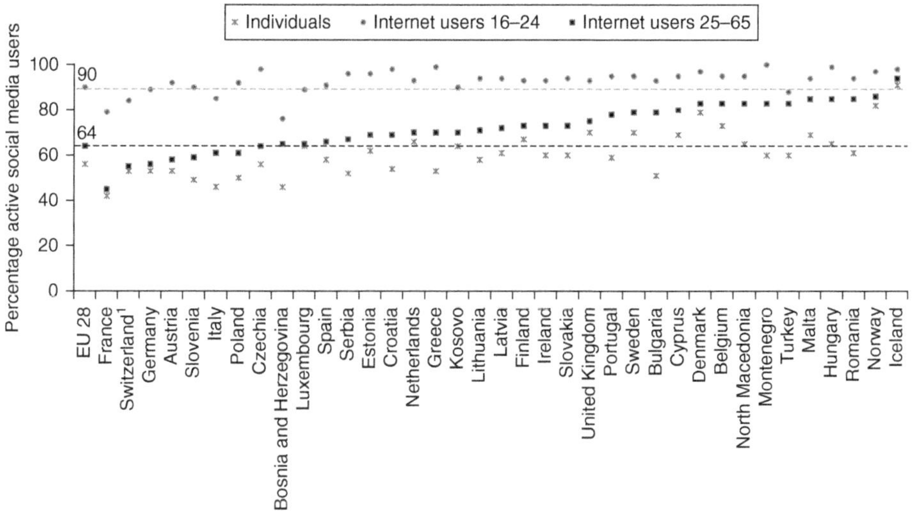

Figure 6.3 Individuals who use the internet to participate in social networking

[1] Data for 2017 instead of 2018 data.

Source: Eurostat (2019b) online data code: isoc_ci_ac_i. Original analysis for this chapter.

Base: Individuals who have used the internet in the last three months.

Note: Active social media use includes participating in social networks (creating user profile, posting messages or other contributions to Facebook, Twitter).

Line = European 28 country average.

patterns of socio-economic inequalities in the use of social media than in the use of email. The richer countries have higher percentages of email use (r=.58, p<.01 with GDP) but levels of social media use do not differ significantly. To predict email use in a country, we could use the wealth of the country, but this is not a good predictor of social media use. Third, other Eurostat data show that while social uses of ICTs are common, creating a safer environment when interacting with others – a crucial digital social skill – is not widespread.

Further analyses highlight disparities in how European internet users manage access to their personal information online (Eurostat, 2019b). More than one quarter (28 per cent) of EU-28 internet users do not provide personal information over the internet. By country, this ranges from just 8 per cent in Luxembourg to half or more in Bulgaria, Portugal, and Romania. This means that over 70 per cent of EU-28 internet users provide personal information online. Many of them undertake different actions to control access to this personal information. Almost two-fifths (40 per cent) limit access to their profile or content on social networking sites. More than one-third (37 per cent) of internet users read privacy policy statements before providing personal information, while just under one-third (31 per cent) restrict access to their geographical location. In other words, whether citizens of different regions are savvy depends on the types of literacy under investigation and the questions asked in research projects.

If national wealth is not as relevant, what might be a good explanation for these variations in the social use of ICTs? Providing a clear answer is difficult, because we do not have good global data on the social uses of ICTs to link it to relevant indicators. Within a region like Europe, there is not enough variation on these indicators to be able to make statistical predictions. That is, European countries are too similar in their orientation towards giving family or bonding ties preference (i.e. collectivism), and emphasising the rights of the individual (i.e. individualism), even though they differ considerably in how connected they are on social media. This is not just the case for differences between countries within a region, there were significant differences in social media take-up between different states in the US (Pick, Sarkar, & Rosales, 2015) which were hard to explain based on socio-economic or socio-cultural characteristics.

Cross-national comparisons between two countries on how young people use social media suggest that there are more similarities than differences between countries (Keipi, Rasanen, Oksanen, Hawdon, & Nasi, 2018; Schroeder, 2010). Yet, Buchi, Just, and Latzer (2016) compared five countries and found that questions about the social use of ICTs were understood differently between countries. This confusion suggests that ICTs mean different things to different people. As a result, they could only compare three English-speaking countries that share socio-political systems, histories, and languages – New Zealand, the US, and the UK. Most of the differences were explained by individual socio-demographic characteristics and not where people lived. They did find differences between countries in the way gender influenced the social use of ICTs. Others suggest that the relationship between social uses of ICTs and social resources is stronger in individualistic countries than collectivistic countries (Jackson & Wang, 2013; Liu, Ainsworth, & Baumeister, 2016). Considering the scarceness of detailed data on social media use, more research is needed to understand what the exact drivers are for these differences in relation to the social use of ICTs.

How Carol's social use of ICTs relates to her being from Brazil is, therefore, mostly speculation at this point. We do not know whether she is more likely to stick to interacting with family and close friends because of who she is as a person, or because she comes from a collectivist country (Hofstede, 2015). Differences between countries can probably be found in the way in which inequalities within countries in the social use of ICTs play out, rather than resulting from country differences in use. That is, we have found that digital inequalities of a specific kind (e.g. differences in use between men and women in uses of ICTs) within a country are partially explained by corresponding inequalities at a national level (Helsper & Galacz, 2009). In other words, Carol's use of social media is very different from a young woman's in Sweden, and her use differs from Alexandre, the young man who lives next door to her. Alexandre's social use does not differ as much from male and female Swedes. This could be because he and Carol live in a country in which gender inequality and stereotyping are very high, and that this gendered inequality is reflected in digital engagement (Brazil is 79th on the Human Development Report index) (UNDP, 2019).

Social isolation and alienation? Inequalities in social skills uses of icts

This takes me to explaining how inequalities in skilled, social use of ICTs between individuals depend on their background, including the local culture where a person lives or grows up.

Socio-economic and socio-cultural explanations for inequalities in social digital skills

Traditional patterns of inequality can be observed in the ability to manage social interactions online. The Pareto principle rears its ugly head again here. Rainie and Wellman (2012) argue that people with the largest need to acquire bridging capital (e.g. the unemployed) are at risk of losing more in digital societies because they are less likely to build large and diverse networks online (Ellison, Steinfield, & Lampe, 2011). There are no global data on socio-emotional digital skills. The ITU's new ICT Development Index (IDI) (ITU, 2017a; see also Chapter 4) will include a few questions related to privacy protection and the use of social platforms, but does not really cover the socio-critical skills referred to earlier. In my research, I find that patterns of inequality in skills might counter patterns of traditional inequality in socio-economic terms, but reflect socio-cultural inequalities based on stereotypes or life circumstances.

Traditional socio-economic inequalities are reflected in social digital skills, but socio-cultural differences do not play out in the same way as other digital inequalities (Helsper, 2021). Ethnic minorities have higher levels of skills in managing interactions. Since we do not really have data on why this might be, I must speculate again. In the literature on bonding and cohesiveness of communities, ethnic minorities often have more cohesive communities. They are warier of social interactions in societies where they have lower status. This might explain their heightened awareness and ability to deal with privacy and network management.

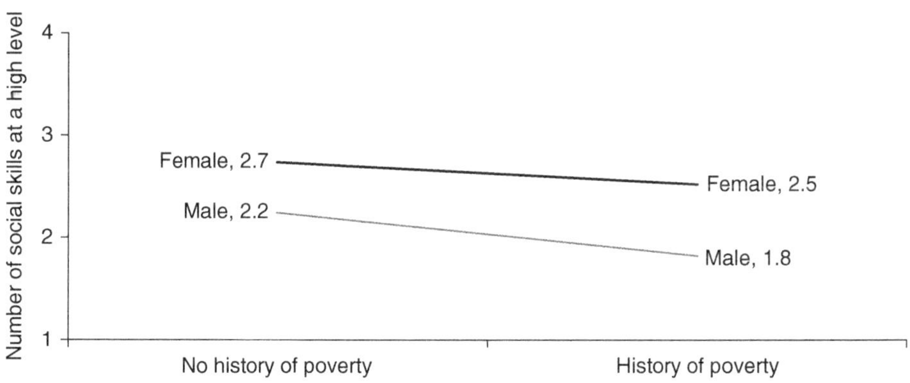

Figure 6.4 Social digital skills of young people (UK) by gender and history of poverty

Source: DiSTO NEETs study (Helsper & Smirnova, 2016).

Base: Internet using young people (16–26 year olds) in the UK with an overrepresentation of NEETs (N=318 NEETs; N=1026 non NEETs).

Note: Social skills include definitely knowing which information you should and should not share online; how to remove people from your contact lists; being careful to make your comments and behaviours appropriate to the situation you are in online; knowing how to report negative content relating to you or a group to which you belong

Socio-economic inequalities are reflected in social skills (Figure 6.4). That is, young people with a history of poverty have lower levels of skills in managing online interactions. There is, however, a socio-cultural catch – the real difference is between women with no history of poverty and men with a history of poverty. This reflects gendered socio-economic role distributions in who has traditionally taken responsibility for relationship management. The gender gap is significantly larger for those with histories of poverty than for those without. In Carol's case, this plays out in the age difference between her and her brother being smaller than that between her cousin Fabricio and his sister, Carla. For example, Fabricio unintentionally upset his parents with the messages he posts on the family WhatsApp – something Carla and Carol would never do. Carla told Fabricio 'what you put on has to be tailored to friends, family, work, college. It has to be tailored to everyone, so that it can't have a backlash in the future.'

Socio-economic and socio-cultural explanations of inequalities in social uses of ICTs

In the next two sections, I will examine how socio-economic and socio-cultural resources relate to inequalities in the social uses of ICTs to add depth to our understanding of psychological resources. As is the case for research on inequalities between regions and countries, research on differences between individuals is largely descriptive. That is, researchers focus on describing differences between individuals from different socio-economic or socio-cultural backgrounds without having a clear theorisation around why these differences might exist. Theorisation is most developed around gender. Explanations refer to stereotypical ideas that women are better at communicating than men, and are assigned responsibility to manage intimate and family relationships. This has led to the hypothesis that women are more frequent users of social media than men, which relies on stereotypes without testing for differences in skills. There is also research on how differences in heterogeneity and homogeneity of networks for different ethnicities are replicated in online spaces. Other research describes differences in the social use of ICTs between individuals from different socio-economic backgrounds. Consistently, age is an important predictor of the uptake of social uses of ICTs. Older people are less likely to engage with social media, but there is no clear explanation about why this might be the case, except that they are late adopters (Feng, Zhang, & Lin, 2019).

There is much vagueness in the definition and an accompanying inconsistency in the measurement of types of social media uses (Feng et al., 2019). In Feng et al.'s meta-analysis of 71 articles on adoption, they concluded that 'the effects of age, income level, gender (female), and urban residence were unambiguous, but the rest of the effects are less clear across the literature' (Feng et al., 2019, p. 11). Contradictions occur even when just looking at the adoption of social media. For example, ethnicity, marital status, and employment status did not have uniform effects on social media adoption across a variety of countries. That it is important to distinguish access (simple use) and engagement (different types of use) is shown by Pearce and Rice (2017). They found that the inequalities in general use between elites and non-elites are greater than inequalities in specific activities.

Income and education are often included in studies about differences in the social uses of ICTs, but the reason why there are differences between these groups is not always theorised. L. Robinson (2018) theorised the effects of household income on the social use of ICTs by teenagers in the US based on a hierarchy of needs approach. Poorer students without fixed internet at home use social media in more limited ways, because when online they have to focus on more pressing issues, such as homework. These needs often conflict with interest or attitudes. Less well-off youngsters are more enthusiastic about the informal communication features, while their better-off counterparts are more critical and more driven by practical aspects, building contacts and managing their social lives and activities through use of these platforms (Correa, 2016; Micheli, 2016).

Socio-cultural factors take centre stage in research explaining differences in the social uses of ICTs (Blank, 2016; Straus Jacob, 2016; Vera-Sanso et al., 2014). In addition to age, the two socio-cultural characteristics that these studies include are gender and ethnicity. Gender is where studies find differences, even in countries where gender inequalities in access and skills have diminished (Van Deursen, Van Dijk, & Ten Klooster, 2015). These relationships are often the reverse of other digital inequalities; women are found to use ICTs more for social purposes (Buchi et al., 2016). This confirms historical patterns of inequality, since stereotypically women have been assigned roles that emphasise communication and relationship maintenance (Hofstra, Corten, van Tubergen, & Ellison, 2017). Life course studies suggests that use becomes more gendered as people move into roles, such as becoming parents, that are more gendered. In other words, gender shapes ICT use depending on the particular point of life you are in (Helsper, 2010). Gendered aspects become more important as women get married or become mothers. They are tasked with bonding capital while men are 'in charge of' or free to do bridging, thus reinforcing socio-cultural inequalities and economic inequalities (Thiessen & Looker, 2010). This is another expression of how gendered use depends on the gender norms and inequalities of the communities in which we live (Buchi et al., 2016; Jackson & Wang, 2013).

The research on ethnicity is also inconsistent (Feng et al., 2019) and limited, concerned mostly with the diversity and types of contacts people have. Research shows that segregation is a real problem online, and individuals who belong to a majority ethnic group have personal networks that are more homogeneous (boyd, 2012; Hofstra et al., 2017). This reflects what we know about offline networks: people tend to hang out with people like them, and this is the same in digital spaces. Those who have the power to decide who they want to be with are more likely to select people who are like them, thereby consolidating their position of advantage. This area of research is also dominated by US scholars, who place race-related inequalities and injustices high on the policy agenda. Mesch's (2012) Israeli study looks at a different context. He finds that in multicultural societies, ethnic minority groups are more motivated by improving work-related contacts (i.e. bridging ties). The ethnic majority was more driven by maintaining existing family and friendship relationships (i.e. bonding ties). This echoes Dutch and US results described in Chapter 5: people from outside Europe and from mixed ethnic backgrounds were most civically engaged.

Social-psychological resources and inequalities in social uses of ICTs

Based on her socio-demographic profile, we would predict that Carol uses social ICTs to build up bonding and bridging ties. She is a young woman from a middle-class family with good educational prospects. The problem is that our predictions would be wrong. She has Facebook and Instagram accounts but, in comparison with peers, she is not active on social media at all. She logs in on Instagram every once in a while, but does not post much. Carol uses Facebook similarly, mostly to browse posts by family. She uses WhatsApp because it is required for the organisation of her social life: her parents use it to check where she is and the school sends messages on it about homework and holidays. Whenever there is a birthday party, she is added to a group where they organise gifts and arrival times. She is not on Twitter, Snapchat, or the other social platforms that she has heard about. Her lack of engagement has more to do with her social-psychological resources than with her socio-economic or socio-cultural resources. This is what I will explore here.

It is difficult to look at social resources in isolation from other forms of disadvantage. Money and education provide access to friends and contacts. In turn, friends and contacts enable access to money-making and educational opportunities (Chapter 1). Here I discuss inequalities in social-psychological resources as drivers for inequalities in the social uses of ICTs, fully aware that they are also related to other domains of resources in ways that compound disadvantage (Helsper, 2012). Luckily, there actually is longitudinal panel research that allows us to understand what comes first, social-psychological resources or social uses of ICTs. Research in this area shows that while the socially rich stay socially rich as societies become more digital, the socially 'poorer' are able to get richer in different ways.

There are two hypotheses about how social-psychological resources and the social use of ICTs are related. They might seem contradictory, but can co-exist once we distinguish different types of platforms and social-psychological resources. The two hypotheses are the rich-get-richer and the social compensation hypotheses. The rich-get-richer hypothesis is a staple of socio-digital inequalities research and needs little further explanation. The social compensation hypothesis has more in common with the normalisation hypothesis (Chapter 2). It postulates that individuals who go online to compensate for an offline deficit with social interactions use ICTs to compensate. In the process, they become intense social users (Valkenburg, Koutamanis, & Vossen, 2017).

There is evidence to support the social compensation hypothesis. Several researchers have found that people with fewer social skills or are naturally shy are more likely to engage in social activities online than offline. These activities include online dating (Poley & Luo, 2012) and interacting with friends from school (Desjarlais & Willoughby, 2010). Valkenburg et al. (2005) found that shy young people who were uncomfortable with offline interactions engaged in more experimental, open communication online. Similarly, people driven by a desire to have more friendships were more likely to talk about personal things to relative strangers online. This self-disclosure led to them forming more friendships. Carol's cousin, Fabricio, WhatsApp'd her to talk about his desire to leave the small town near Manaus, and told her that social media was his saviour: 'I'm so isolated where

I'm living ... all I've got to do is go on social media. I'm linked to my phone and without it I get panicky.'

This is a very consistent finding. Nowland, Necka, and Cacioppo (2018) also found that situationally lonely people use ICTs to reach out to strangers. They concluded that, when the Internet of Things connects us, people with fewer social resources will be more inclined to use it to connect with strangers.

Carol does not have Fabricio's social compensation motive, she is dispositionally 'lonely'. She is not shy but does not like engaging with people she does not know. She has occasional contact with the Alt Rock fans but will not take it beyond getting information from them. She realises that by not going online and sharing things about herself, she might isolate herself from her peers. However, she prefers that over social overload online (Joinson, 2003).

There is more research validating the rich-get-richer hypothesis than the compensation hypothesis, suggesting an amplification of inequalities based on social-psychological resources. For example, Valkenburg et al.'s (2017) work shows that social self-esteem consistently influences social media use in subsequent years, while the reverse is not the case. This amplification effect is further confirmed by research that shows that people lacking self-esteem are more likely to use ICTs for negative social reasons (Valkenburg et al., 2017), for example, because they are afraid of being left behind and are less likely to post positive messages. Being exposed to the lives of others increases their feelings of exclusion and lack of self-worth, rather than improving it (Buglass, Binder, Betts, & Underwood, 2017; Homero, Trevor, Brigitte, & James, 2017). For Carol, this means that her lack of self-esteem – partly due to her lisp – pushes her to find recognition from strangers online, but her negative experiences mean she is reluctant to follow up.

Similarly, research shows that those with more bridging capital – through larger, more diverse networks – are more likely to engage on social networks (Lee, 2009). Yet, this has to be put into the context of the media ecologies in which people live. While extroverted, highly socially resourced users are more likely to engage with social uses of ICTs, they are less likely to depend on them for information and social feedback (Chen, Lee, Straubhaar, & Spence, 2014). They have a wider range of media at their disposal to achieve these goals. Back to Carol one more time. If she had more friends or was interested in social interaction, she would have been more likely to be active online. On the other hand, she would have depended less on it for her feelings of self-worth and for feeling connected to other people. Simply put, this is why the research on the social use of ICTs can seem contradictory – there are opposing forces at work.

To research and understand these opposing forces, more research should look at how different types of social-psychological resources relate to different social uses of ICTs. Consider how Amichai-Hamburger et al. (2008) showed that extroverted users – generally understood to be highly socially resourced – are more likely to take advantage of nostalgia-based platforms. These platforms allow you to connect with people you already know – Facebook and WhatsApp are typical examples. Amichai-Hamburger et al. used the term 'social service platforms' to describe platforms for social connection popular with introverts. These do not depend on previous knowledge of the other, or linkage to offline identities. They pointed out that non-nostalgic platforms are disappearing, and most existing platforms and new platforms rely on existing networks, favouring extroverts. It is the combination of social resources and the types of platform that are available that allows for both the social compensation hypothesis and the rich-get-richer hypothesis to be true.

Let me return to the importance of considering norms and cultural contexts. Jackson and Wang (2013) show that personal characteristics predict social uses of ICTs more strongly in individualistic than in collectivistic cultures. Their explanation is that individualistic cultures emphasise the uniqueness of a person, and collectivistic cultures stress the importance of family and friends. If Carol lived in the UK, the fact that she was a relatively introverted young woman would impact her social use of ICTs more than in her collectively-oriented Brazil. Living in the UK might have made her more likely to be active on Instagram, since she would have placed greater importance on fostering new, broader friendships and other bridging relationships than on maintaining good relationships with her family via WhatsApp. For now, she makes sure that: 'The only people on my Facebook and WhatsApp are people that I know, have gone to school with, people that I've been with, people that I talk to all the time, stuff like that.'

Now I should get to the crux of the matter. Inequalities research is not just about online behaviour, but about everyday consequences. Maintaining relationships and making new friends online is irrelevant if these activities do not positively impact our feelings or opportunities in life. If these relationships do not provide support and are not loving, then the result is likely to be more loneliness and isolation.

Consequences of inequalities in social digital engagement

The cause-and-effect issue is a significant problem when it comes to social uses of ICTs. With socio-demographics, the sequential nature is salient because gender and age do not change due to ICT use. Previous chapters have shown that poverty, class, and education levels of the household shape ICT use more than they are determined by them. Nevertheless, when it comes to social resources like relationships and personal well-being, it is more difficult to separate cause from effect. In the case of cyberbullying, we see that those who come from dysfunctional home environments and are bullied offline are also bullied online. They are caught in an amplifying cycle of negative interaction with potentially severe outcomes (Gorzig, Milosevic, & Staksrud, 2017; Totura et al., 2009). Similarly, people who are outgoing and confident post more positive things about themselves, and receive more positive feedback. Accordingly, they will feel more confident and happier about their relationships – a feedback loop of positive well-being (Valkenburg et al., 2017). Beyond these effects, there are a few things that we can say about the differential consequences of social ICT use for people from different backgrounds and skills levels.

Collateral benefits of social digital skills

In the papers that we wrote on the collateral benefits of internet use in the Netherlands, two things stood out: the importance of social digital skills to achieving a wide range of outcomes, and the benefits of using ICTs for social purposes (Van Deursen & Helsper, 2017). Social uses of ICTs benefit all domains of everyday life (i.e. economic, personal, cultural, and social), and social digital literacy relates to the quality of outcomes in all domains. In other words, people who engage frequently with ICTs in social ways not only establish relationships, they also find jobs, improve their health, and find information. They do not achieve this degree of multi-domain outcomes if they do not engage through social media and other communicative and interactional platforms. When people additionally have higher social digital literacy, they are more satisfied with the jobs and information they obtain through use of ICTs.

Figures 6.5a and 6.5b illustrate that social skills and uses of ICTs have increased since the original Dutch and UK DiSTO studies in 2015. The level of social digital skills that an individual has (Figure 6.5a) and their level of engagement with social aspects of ICTs (Figure 6.5b) are significantly related to satisfaction levels with economic, learning, civic, social, and well-being outcomes. For a high-diffusion and high social ICT use country like the Netherlands, it seems that all engagements with ICTs rely heavily on interaction with others, be it organisations or individuals. Excelling at this communicative or social aspect of digital engagement is important, even when the activities are not explicitly oriented towards interaction. The vital question is who is more likely to achieve high-quality social outcomes and avoid negative ones?

Who benefits and who suffers from the social use of icts?

This section relies on correlational data from the DiSTO and the EU Kids Online projects, because they have the most detail on negative outcomes, and allow me to look at all the

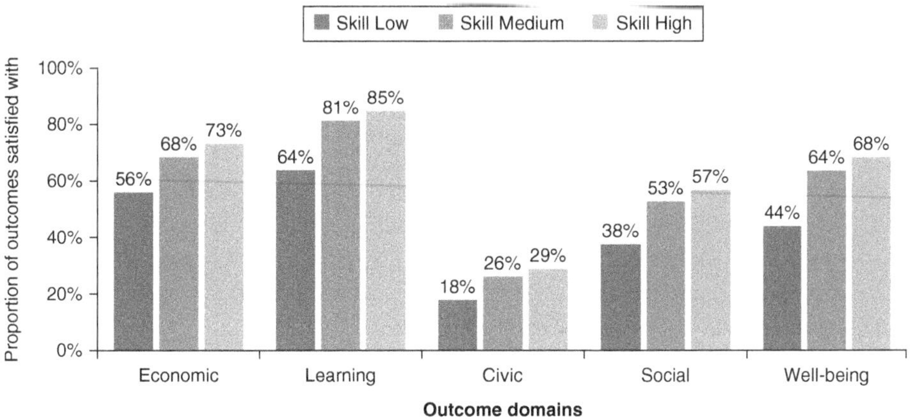

Figure 6.5a Inequalities in high-quality outcomes across domains based on social digital skills

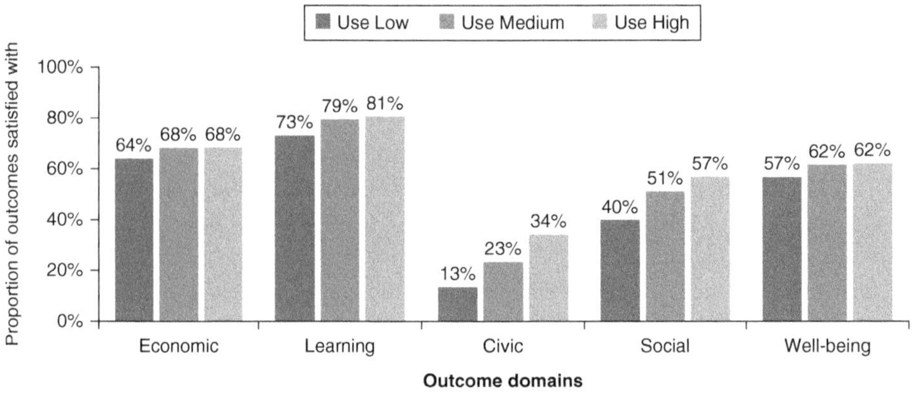

Figure 6.5b Inequalities in high-quality outcomes across domains based on social use of ICTs

Source: Figures 6.5a and 6.5b: DiSTO NL 2018 data. Original analysis for this chapter.

Base: Dutch internet users (N=1691). Weighted data.

processes captured in Figure 6.1. I will also refer to longitudinal data from the US and Northern Europe. These data have more detail on potential causality, but less on social resources and well-being outcomes. This means that the data in this section do not represent the Global South, and more work needs to be done – particularly large-scale research with adults – to validate the conclusions that follow.

The few longitudinal, panel studies that exist suggest that people who are more socially vulnerable and seek refuge in digital spaces are less likely to have positive experiences there (Valkenburg et al., 2017). While objectively they might seem to be well-off, subjectively they are worse off. In other words, when they take risky opportunities, they are more likely to be harmed in the process than their less vulnerable peers. I will explore this pattern for the two types of outcome that are most discussed in relation to the social uses of ICTs: social resources and well-being.

Social inequalities in opportunities through (new) connections

Optimism about social ICT use is driven by the idea that they can give people access to weak, latent, or liquid ties. These bridging ties facilitate access to novel resources which helps to overcome an existing situation of disadvantage (Abbas & Mesch, 2018). In our paper on compound and sequential disadvantage, we found that, even after controlling for skills and use, there were inequalities in the positive social outcomes achieved between individuals from different socio-economic backgrounds (Van Deursen et al., 2017). Socio-cultural characteristics (age and gender) had an impact mostly because they were related to different patterns of use and skill levels. Inequalities in the satisfaction with the outcomes persist in the 2018 data. Patterns of traditional inequality are replicated in the social outcomes achieved. Those with more socio-economic resources are more satisfied with the relationships they have built using ICTs. There is a difference between those with different work statuses for satisfaction with bonding and bridging relationships, which reflect socio-cultural processes. People who participate less in the public sphere, who are not working, and are more bound to the home are less satisfied with the bridging ties that they maintain through ICT use. Satisfaction with bonding relationships was higher, although the unemployed were not as happy with the relationships they maintained with family, friends, and other people similar to them.

Further analyses show more differences by age than by gender. Younger generations are more satisfied with bridging interactions online. The youngest and the oldest are most satisfied with the bonding interactions they have with family and friends online. Carol, a student with educated, middle-class parents, falls in a group who should be relatively happy with her online interactions, but she is not. Her socio-economic and socio-cultural characteristics are not an explanation for why she might not be achieving positive social outcomes.

Social isolation leads to multiple health, emotional, and other problems (Leigh-Hunt et al., 2017). This is true for a lack of engagement with social uses of ICT as well. Therefore, to understand why Carol is dissatisfied with the relationships she maintains online, we must look at social isolation and social resources. From US research we know that use of nostalgia sites can be beneficial for connecting to bridging ties for those with lower self-esteem and who lack everyday social support (Rains & Tsetsi, 2017; Steinfield, Ellison, & Lampe, 2008). That is, they go online to seek larger, heterogeneous networks that potentially give access to new resources, more so than users with high self-esteem and other forms of social support.

The skill to translate potential connections into positive outcomes is fundamental. Research shows that internet users with fewer skills need more traditional social resources to achieve positive outcomes than those with higher skill levels (Chen et al., 2014). For example, Carol's social support is limited, because her parents are authoritarian and do not engage much with her. She has few friends at school, and she is not part of any hobby or sports clubs. She would benefit from the contacts of family and friends that she has on Facebook and Instagram. Yet, she does not use these contacts to ask for information about things she is interested in. This potential for connection is thus not translated into positive social outcomes. She added contacts on Instagram to have more friends, without interacting with them or their posts. Remember, she is unlikely to engage socially because she does not wish to make connections. Even when she does engage socially, she is unlikely to take advantage of the connections that she could build.

Further analyses of the Dutch DiSTO data show that people with bridging capital are more likely to have positive weak tie outcomes (e.g. becoming part of hobby clubs). People with more bonding capital (e.g. stronger family relationships) are more likely to have positive strong tie outcomes. Carol has neither bridging nor bonding capital, and is at risk of falling further into social isolation. At least Carol has a family who is not about to kick her out on the street; however strict they are, they will keep her dry and safe. People who are socially and digitally vulnerable often see their isolation and loneliness amplified online. COVID-19 lockdowns might turn out to be accelerators of these effects of digitisation, leading to especially dire circumstances for the socially vulnerable. The Cybershelter project similarly shows that people experiencing long-term homelessness have very unstable access and use, and cannot maintain contact with family or friends who are not homeless. They are more likely to rely on and become embedded in networks of others experiencing homelessness than those who are able to use ICTs socially. As a consequence, transitioning out of homelessness is difficult for them.

Well-being inequalities from social ICT use

So far I have discussed how inequalities function in relation to the positive social outcomes of ICT use. Research on negative interactions among young people might give us some hints at inequalities in negative outcomes among adults. It shows that children from traditionally-disadvantaged groups are more likely to be treated negatively by their peers. This type of negative interaction can vary widely. For example, ethnic minority and LGBT youth experience more cyberbullying, while girls are more likely to receive unwanted sexual messages (d'Haenens & Ogan, 2013; Totura et al., 2009). Resilience in light of negative interactions – how people cope with them – is important to consider. The first thing to note is that subjectively negative outcomes are not as common, even when people are confronted with what might appear to be harmful interactions, such as bullying or discussions related to well-being; 70 per cent of people do not have negative experiences after having been in those types of situations.

The 30 per cent who experience negative well-being outcomes of use is not randomly distributed (Figure 6.6). Differences based on education, income, and gender are not

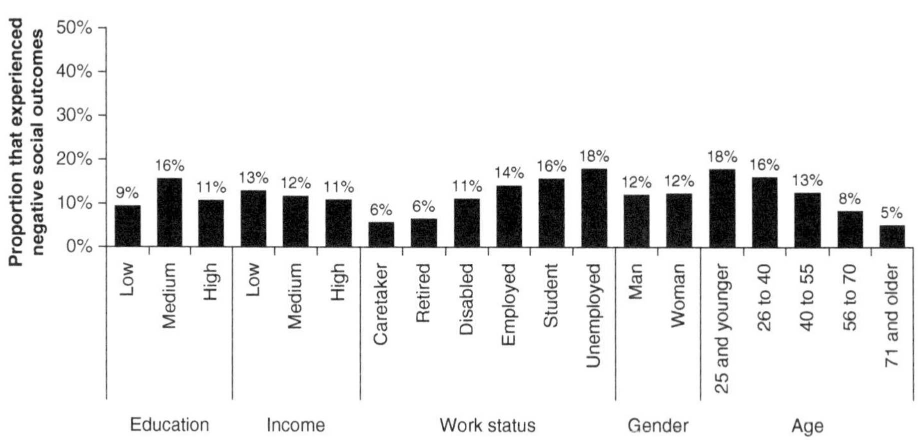

Figure 6.6 Inequalities in negative social outcomes based on socio-economic and socio-cultural background

Source: DiSTO NL 2018. Original analysis for this chapter.

Base: Dutch internet users (N=1691). Weighted data.

Note: Negative social outcomes include being hurt by bullying or harassing messages and receiving advice that negatively influenced health

significant. The unemployed, students, and young people experience slightly more negative outcomes when they find themselves in potentially harmful situations; on average, one in six experiences results in negative social outcomes, as compared to one in 20 for carers and retired persons. Older users also experience fewer socially negative outcomes. I hypothesise that older internet users and those who are inactive in public life are more selective in online social interactions; they interact less and in ways that do not expand their social circle. As a result of their interactions with only close others, they are less likely to be bullied or perceive online interactions as negative.

The simultaneous processes of rich-get-richer (for extroverts and those with greater social capital on 'nostalgia' sites) and social compensation (for those who are circumstantially lonely on 'connection' sites) are how social inequalities are normalised in the social use of ICTs. However, I also hinted at a negative side to coping with risky or negative experiences. The socially confident are more likely to post positive things about themselves. The social use of ICTs is favourable to positive self-presentation, which in turn receives more positive reactions from others. As a result, it is the social-psychological 'rich' who receive a boost in social self-esteem, not the socially 'poor', who are less likely to post this content and lack social support networks to fall back on (Helsper, 2020; Valkenburg et al., 2017). For example, Carla, Carol's much more confident cousin, told her to lighten up and to 'never ever put anything negative on Facebook, there's no need to wash my dirty laundry in public'.

Several studies suggest that the emotionally and socially vulnerable are locked in vicious cycles. They are caught between needing solace online to compensate for negative offline relationships, and being rejected, which subsequently increases feelings of isolation and a need for social recognition, which drives them back online (Nowland et al., 2018; Weidman

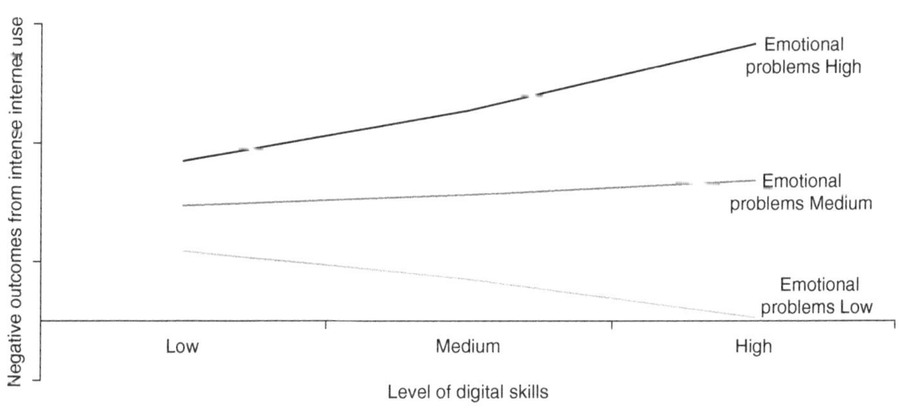

Figure 6.7 Inequalities in negative outcomes by levels of digital skills and emotional vulnerability

Source: EU Kids Online. Adapted from Helsper & Smahel (2019).

Base: European internet using 11-16 year olds (N=18,709)

Note: Emotional problems refers to anger management issues, being anxious, depressed fearful, and having concentration problems. Negative outcomes refers to having conflicts with family and friends, having negative psychological and physical well-being because of internet use.

et al., 2012). That is, those who are socially vulnerable are likely to be more at risk of ending up in an addiction-like, negative spiral of social uses of ICTs.

I will end this chapter by reflecting on the work we did that shows children with emotional problems and high levels of digital skills are most at risk of negative outcomes from intense use (Figure 6.7). The least at risk do not have emotional problems and have high levels of digital skills (Helsper & Smahel, 2019). This means that higher engagement and literacy creates problems for the vulnerable while benefitting people who are social-psychologically stronger. This is why Carol is not engaging socially through ICTs now – her classmates think she is weird because she does not like Reggaeton. She is bullied because of her lisp and accent, and because she is not a Paulista, having grown up in Manaus. This bullying turned into nasty messages on WhatsApp groups and 'jokey' comments on Facebook. Her lack of confidence drove her to Instagram, where she followed and liked posts by people whom she thought were cool and did not know her offline. Nevertheless, they did not like her back, and when she posted stories, she got no likes, or received comments that were similar to the negative ones from classmates. She does not have a social support network to fall back on, but luckily, she did not get caught up in the negative spiral like so many in her situation. Instead, she withdrew from social uses of ICTs. While withdrawing has stopped the bullying somewhat, she is now an outcast at school. Limiting her social media use has not changed the fact that she is depressed and has considered running away.

This leads me to the last important point about the cyclical nature of offline and online socio-psychological vulnerability. As ICTs become increasingly embedded in our interactions and increasingly indispensable in connecting with others, our feelings about how we feel accepted and comfortable in digital spaces become more related to how we feel about ourselves outside them. This puts policy makers and practitioners in a paradox: digital inclusion is important for social benefits, but teaching vulnerable people digital skills and getting them engaged puts them at higher risk than their more advantaged peers.

Conclusions: Implications for policy and practice

In this chapter, I have examined inequalities in uses of ICTs related to the maintenance and formation of everyday interpersonal relationships. These relationships and social uses of ICTs are seen as private issues, resulting in inequalities not being given the same priority on the public policy agenda or in interventions as inequalities with 'real' societal consequences (i.e. employment, education, and civic participation). This is a grave oversight, since inequalities of this type of social capital have broader implications than the digital inequalities discussed previously. In increasingly digital societies, people with higher levels of social digital literacy are able to manage and understand how interactions work online. This means they benefit in a broad range of domains, not just in interpersonal relationships. People who are better at managing interactions on ICTs are able to save money, learn more, get better jobs, and engage more online. All these processes have a broader positive societal impact beyond just building individual social resources.

The implication is that policy making and interventions should start to layer social, everyday relationships around an understanding of socio-digital inequalities and what is needed to ameliorate them.

I have two critiques of existing research on social uses and outcomes: quantification and technolisation critiques. Quantification refers to a tendency to count the number of 'ties' we have online or how many different people there are in our networks as indicating our level of social digital resources. The real inequalities, however, lie in the quality of connections. The tendency to use big data to count who is in a network and how distant they are from each person does not get at this. Existing and frequent interactions between two people also do not mean that they are positive. Technolisation entails a techno-determinist fixation on the technological features of platforms and what they were designed for. We cannot look at a platform and decide that it is a social medium or draw conclusions about the social benefits achieved from using ICTs. We must look at what a person actually does on these platforms, as on other platforms that were not necessarily designed for communication.

Therefore, to understand whether someone is socially included in digital societies, we should go beyond measuring whether they are on Facebook, Weibo, Instagram, or Twitter. People might not be using these platforms to connect with others. Since most research still looks at the use of platforms rather than what is done on them, we remain far away from understanding inequalities in the consequences of this use. To understand where and for whom these inequalities might be ameliorated, we need to examine the quality of outcomes in terms of socio-psychological well-being rather than use. More research is definitely needed on who feels supported and loved, and who feels isolated and hated online, for example. This qualitative subjective aspect of use should accompany and enrich the more quantitative strand of research. Besides these conceptual and measurement issues, one further data-related problem complicates research into inequalities. Unfortunately, the majority of these studies come from the US, Europe, and China. There is a lack of research on adults related to negative social outcomes, as well as a lack of data from the Global South.

Let's return to the question I posed at the beginning of the chapter: Does the widespread diffusion of digital communication tools mean that all individuals engage equally in the social use of ICTs? For social uses of ICTs and our ability to manage our interactions online, inequalities reflect normative and cultural power dynamics, rather than socio-economic inequalities between groups of different socio-cultural backgrounds. Those who come from traditionally disadvantaged backgrounds find themselves able to take advantage of their social resources in digital spaces. This optimistic scenario would suggest normalisation or even leapfrogging effects for close relationships, if they did not replicate traditional normative patterns of responsibilities and relationships. These groups are more confined to the family and strong community relationships, while the traditionally advantaged extend their social use of ICTs outside their closed circles. There is a relationship between wealth, education, and how much you engage socially with ICTs to expand bridging social capital. My conclusion is that stereotypical patterns based on expectations about who has caring, socio-emotional, and relationship-building roles in different domains are replicated online.

These patterns are more pronounced in contexts where gender and other inequalities are larger. This suggests a stratification of socio-cultural inequalities.

However, neither socio-economic nor socio-cultural background are satisfactory explanations in answering the question: Who has the highest quality outcomes of everyday online interactions? To respond to this question, I introduced social-psychological resources in this chapter, alongside socio-economic and socio-cultural resources, as being vital to understanding socio-digital inequalities. In social-psychological resources, normalisation can be observed through contrasting social compensation and rich-get-richer processes. Social-psychologically vulnerable individuals seek refuge in an online world of others that seems more accepting and welcoming than the more hostile world they live in offline. There is room for optimism here, because ICTs are used to socially compensate for offline deficits. Simultaneously, confident people with many diverse contacts use a diversity of platforms to consolidate their existing capital. Sadly, the experiences that the social-psychologically vulnerable have on these platforms are less positive than those of their confident peers. Social-psychologically vulnerable people are also more likely to be bullied online and are less likely to be satisfied with the quality of bridging relationships. This is worrying, because those relationships offer a way out of their negative online situation. This catches them in a vicious cycle whereby traditional vulnerability leads to a greater dependence on digitally-mediated interactions for support. Yet, the ensuing negative experiences lead to lower feelings of self-worth, pushing the person to seek recognition and validation in the only place available to them – the digital world. Pandemics of the future are indeed likely to be psychological, but, as with medical pandemics, they are likely to hit the socially vulnerable much harder.

These conclusions have implications for policy and practice. First and foremost, they mean that solutions to break the rich-get-richer cycle must be social and normative, rather than individual and technical. That is, giving everyone equal access and teaching everyone technical digital skills will exacerbate existing patterns of social vulnerability and exclusion. Instead of one-size-fits-all interventions around social media and their use, policy makers and practitioners must remember the paradox discussed in this chapter: the same intervention can have a positive effect for people in positions of advantage and negative effects for those in positions of disadvantage. We need to grow awareness about the likelihood of negative experiences for socio-psychologically vulnerable individuals among businesses, educators, and third-sector initiatives that work with digital inclusion. There is evidence that teaching vulnerable people only technical skills might place them at greater risk of social-psychological harm from ICT use.

Programmes need to help disadvantaged people to build resilience to avoid negative experiences and to facilitate coping strategies. At the same time, these interventions should recognise the benefits of escaping toxic offline environments by finding support online. Perhaps even more urgently, there needs to be an awareness among people in positions of advantage that every interaction they have online has an impact on how others feel, and that they have an active role to play in creating a better digital future. This requires a multi-stakeholder approach:

- Those who work with disadvantaged individuals should design policies and interventions that take into account that they are more vulnerable than others to negative outcomes.
- Platforms should monitor and intervene when interactions go haywire and use the tools and algorithms to personalise interactions in ways that limit exposure to negative outcomes and increase positive feedback and interactions.
- Privileged users who interact in ways that recreate existing patterns of inequalities by ignoring, excluding, or mistreating others should be made aware of the consequences of their actions.

Integrating socio-emotional digital skills and positive engagement into education and learning programmes at school, work, and at home will help create a digital society where everyone has an equal chance of being loved and supported. The elephant in the room is that the best way to deal with the issues around online interactions raised in moral-panicky headlines is to tackle social and emotional problems offline. If there is less vulnerability and fewer abusive relationships in general, there will also be less of it in the socio-digital world. I will explore this further in the next chapter on content consumption, promotion, and production, which focuses on socio-cultural inequalities: who gets to shape the digital spaces we interact in, and how does this affect what they look like and who is comfortable in them.

CHAPTER 7

INEQUALITIES IN CONTENT CREATION AND CONSUMPTION IN DIGITAL SOCIETIES

> 'In the future everyone will be famous for fifteen people. ... We now have a democratic technology, a technology which can help us all to produce and consume the new, "unpopular", ... each perfectly customised to our elective cults.'
>
> (Artist, Momus, 1991)

There is one more area of potential socio-digital inequalities left to tackle in this book, inequalities in how we express ourselves, share our passions, and unwind. This is a major part of our social and digital lives. There is an ocean of digital content online shared and created by millions. On YouTube alone, around 500 hours of video are uploaded every minute, watched by two billion viewers who log in every day (Wojcicki, 2020). With audiences like that within easy reach, it seems as though anyone can be a superstar as long as they produce attractive enough content. There is power in consumption as well as production of content. With clicks, likes, browsing, and forwarding, we determine what is most likely to be seen by the next person to come along. The techno-optimist 'power to the prosumer' discourse promises to democratise access to and production of diverse types of content.

In this chapter, I will touch on the world of professional content creation (e.g. programming, web design, and media streaming). However, since more questions remain unanswered about inequalities in everyday content creation by 'amateurs', this chapter will mostly be about inequalities in production, promotion, and consumption of User Generated Content (UGC). I do this by addressing the following two questions:

- Who is most likely to produce what kinds of digital content?
- What type of content, produced by whom, is most likely to be consumed and valued?

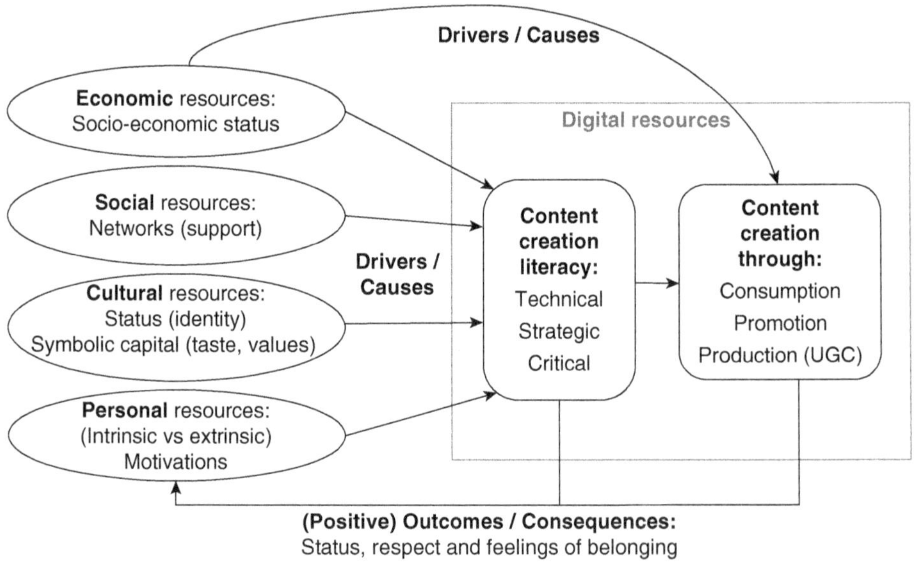

Figure 7.1 The links between inequalities in digital content creation and societal status and belonging

Often, differences in content creation and consumption are ascribed to differences in personal taste and interest, as if these are disconnected from historic patterns of inequality. Yet, when content produced by certain people is more ubiquitous and liked, the digital world represents their norms, values, and tastes (i.e. their symbolic capital), meaning inequalities are reproduced. Due to inequalities in the content produced and what can be consumed, some will feel that they are not represented and respected, and that their experiences are supressed, ignored, and devalued (Figure 7.1).

I address the idea that socio-economic and socio-cultural status inequalities in content creation lead to the domination of particular world-views by posing the question:

- Do inequalities in the production, consumption, and valuation of digital content relate to inequalities in who is respected and our sense of belonging in digital societies?

In this chapter, I unpack issues such as racism, sexism, and homophobia. I examine what is put up online, which content is consumed, and how we react to content put up by groups with different status in society. In terms of outcomes of these processes, I examine how they relate to the cultural resources of people from historically-discriminated regions and groups, such as ethnic, religious, and LGBTQ minorities, in positive (e.g. respect and a sense of belonging) and negative (i.e. discrimination and digital segregation) ways. In asking who gets to decide what is trendy, fashionable, or refined, whose tastes people follow and value, this chapter is about symbolic power (Chapter 1).

JunWen – the vignette for this chapter – illustrates the consequences of socio-cultural inequalities, combined with inequalities in digital content consumption and creation. Like Ben, Ana, Priya, and Carol from previous chapters, his story compiles the experiences of people who I came across through my research. While there is little research on China, where he is from, I assume that the processes of discrimination, silencing, and segregating, are present in all societies.

Case Study: JunWen

JunWen lives in Jiayuguan in the Gansu province. He was born there to an ethnically Tu Monguor family. His Tu heritage shows in his features, which have traces of his Mongol ancestors. He is 28 years old, lives on his own, and has a job as an administrator at Jiuquan Steel. He studied maths and philosophy in Shanghai at Fudan University. After finishing his studies, he returned home to take care of his severely ill mother and got a job. JunWen's mother died three years later, and his dad died a long time ago. He stayed, living in his late parents' apartment. He never told them he is gay. It would have devastated his parents to know there would be no one to take care of him like he had for his mother, and the family line would end with him. He never had a serious relationship, although in Shanghai he connected with an LGBTQ organisation and he visits their website every once in a while.

JunWen is an avid gamer and has an Xbox. He also has a smart TV, an android phone, and a laptop, and he is on Weibo, QQ, and WeChat of course. But his real passion is in mixing music. He has a DJ deck. He describes his relation to technology as follows: 'The positive side is that it allows someone to start to explore tentatively, in a world that is full of discrimination, to get to know people that are like me bit by bit, earn the trust, get the trust.'

Using JunWen's story to narrate data collected through various studies allows me to paint a picture of everyday content creation inequalities, which is the least-explored area in socio-digital inequalities research. I tackle the definitional problem of UGC first, before discussing in more detail why we should care about inequalities in what might be considered frivolous leisure issues. To finish, I examine what the socio-economic and socio-cultural causes and consequences of content creation inequalities might be.

What are we creating online?

There is relative agreement on the skills needed to create content, but most definitions focus on high-level technical skills, such as programming, and exclude basic and critical literacy. In comparison, there is a lack of definitional clarity about online content creation, which makes comparisons between different studies and meta-analyses of inequalities nearly impossible (Brake, 2014; Lutz, Hoffmann, & Meckel, 2014).

Digital content creation literacy

Certain skills are needed to produce digital content, from simple form uploading to advanced website creation. At the most fundamental level, content creation skills involve having the knowledge and ability to produce content in different formats and share them online (Van Deursen et al., 2016). Integrating multimedia and producing more professional-looking end products would indicate high skill levels. This common interpretation of content creation literacy is technical. However, digital content creation also involves strategic decision-making about when and where to upload content, and whom to share it with. In other words, UGC is based on a critical understanding of how content is distributed, promoted, and valued online. This includes comprehending how the data we generate through consumption are used by governments and companies (Polizzi, 2020). People who are able to manipulate digital media to be presented with desired content and who are able to attract the desired audiences to their digital creations have high levels of creative literacy (Buckingham, 2005).

Content creation literacy also involves understanding which contributions people are supposed to make within particular spaces to be accepted and valued. The valuation of content as 'high quality' is a normative decision. What one person considers a digital Van Gogh, another person considers rubbish. The content you and others appreciate depends on who you are and where you come from (Hollingshead, 1996). Bourdieu (1990) and others have argued that those with symbolic capital – whose possessions, tastes, and values are recognised and legitimised by others – determine what sophistication and beauty is, rather than the inherent qualities of the work itself (Chapter 1).

Amateur and professional content

Here, I am mostly interested in User Generated Content (UGC), content that amateur, ordinary users have created without an explicit commercial goal. The distinction between ordinary and professional users – and between commercial and non-commercial content – is not always easy to make. On platforms like YouTube, Instagram, QQ, and Douban, celebrities and artists mingle with 'everyday' users who can be sophisticated content creators (Keen, 2011). To help understand the differences between these users, Blank (2013) differentiates between skilled, social and entertainment, and political content. Blank's skilled content refers to the creation of content intended to be consumed by broader audiences not known to the person, more akin to broadcast content. Social and entertainment content is then shared with peers, and we expect reactions and interactions. UGC should also include online multiplayer gaming. Gaming is a globally top-grossing form of entertainment, requiring the creation of characters, objects and spaces, and other representations of the self and the world we want to live in.

Active and passive content creation

Besides distinguishing between more professional and amateur content, we can differentiate between voluntary and non-voluntary content creation (Lutz & Hoffmann, 2017). I prefer the terms 'active' and 'passive' content creation for clarity. Active content creation or production refers to anything that a person creates, uploads, and shares themselves. There are two forms of passive content creation: low-involvement and non-voluntary data creation. Low-involvement creation refers to non-original content creation through forwarding, liking, and rating or promoting material created by others (OECD, 2007, calls this recycling). Non-voluntary content creation refers to data production through consumption (e.g. cookies, clicks, browsing histories) (van Dijck, 2009). Even seemingly passive consumers looking for entertainment make decisions about what they are going to watch and how they are going to react (Bolin, 2012; Livingstone, 2003). Subsequently, seemingly passive forms of digital consumption, such as watching, lurking, or liking, often translate into active forms of contributing.

Positive and negative content creation outcomes

There is a tendency to assume that high levels of content creation and literacy are always positive for society, and especially for marginalised groups (Literat, 2016). Yet, what might give some people a voice and a sense of belonging might alienate others. As with the skills and engagement types discussed in previous chapters, the outcomes of higher engagement might not always be positive for society. This leads us to normative questions about what is positive and constructive, and what is negative and destructive. Sometimes not consuming content is as powerful in creating digital spaces as actively producing it. To disentangle what reduces inequalities, we need to include conscious non-participation and refusal in content creation because these actions allow people to avoid persecution or surveillance (Gangadharan, 2017; Lutz & Hoffmann, 2017). I am interested in how inequalities are perpetuated through our active or passive content creation and (non-)participation; negative outcomes include discrimination and positive outcomes include a sense of power and belonging for all.

Why should we care about inequalities in content creation?

The production, consumption, and valuation of UGC might seem trivial. We are, after all, talking about homemade videos, quickly snapped selfies, and forwarded memes. Yet, I make the case that inequalities herein are potentially more consequential than the ones discussed in earlier chapters. The content we create keeps on existing even when we are no longer in the world. Active and passive processes place certain types of content centre stage, shaping others' experiences of digital societies. It is impossible to use connected ICTs without leaving a trace (Micheli, Lutz, & Buchi, 2018). More attention should be paid to inequalities in passive forms because they contribute the majority of digital content. In an algorithm-based world, these passive behaviours make things visible and accessible to others. That is, they shape and create digital spaces and make it more likely that content becomes part of others' digital universes (McIlwain, 2017). Whoever enters into that space next will start acting in and interacting with what we left behind. Even when we are not connected or decide not to participate, our thoughts and behaviours are not represented.

The design of technologies and algorithms that drive the digital world are thus based on data that do not include people like us. Content creation is not just about opportunities and risks for us as individuals; it is also about the world we create for the people who will be coming after we are long gone.

While I am more interested in the consumption and production of everyday UGC, I acknowledge that there are significant inequalities in professional production. Research highlights pervasive gender, ethnic, and class inequalities in programming and the digital creative industries (Banks, 2017; Conor, Gill, & Taylor, 2015; Marwick, 2015; Pinnock, 2019). The creation of this infrastructure is not only socio-culturally but also geographically concentrated (e.g. white men in Silicon Valley). In JunWen's China, the tech and cultural industries are geographically concentrated in urban centres on the East Coast (Keane, 2016; Xin & Mossig, 2017; Yu, 2018). Scholars have commented that behaviours in digital environments, including the infrastructure that supports it, has values embedded in it (Eubanks, 2011). Lessig (2005) describes code as architecture, with roads that lead to certain places and not others, and with buildings and spaces that are designed for certain uses and users and not others. The idea that designers embed value in their creations is nothing new; it has always been a 'formalized practice ... it links technology directly to culture ... a set of socially accepted practices and values' (Franklin, 2004, p. 15).

What is new is that digital content is constantly co-created through active and passive use, and that mechanisms that filter and organise content are more hidden than in the creative industries. These processes influence who is valued as producers. For example, pervasive sexism in game design culminated in Gamergate, which saw female designers 'doxed' (i.e. their contact details were published), threatened with rape, and morally shamed (Mortensen, 2018). This event reflects a long history of white, male domination in Western culture industries and eventually ushered in digital activism, such as #OscarsSoWhite and the #MeToo campaigns around harassment (Chattoo, 2018; Molina-Guzman, 2016).

Inequalities in everyday content creation is a new frontier for inequalities research. Before, if you doodled, wrote a diary, or snapped a picture, your actions would not impact others. No one would find your creation, unless you became a professional artist, writer, or photographer. In a connected world, even if no one looks at your private pictures or reads your personal blog, it influences which photos are seen and which blogs are read in the future through algorithmic learning. I am not saying that everyone should create digital content; there are many circumstances in which this would not be a good idea (Lutz & Hoffmann, 2017). Nevertheless, it is a problem if who produces most of the content or who becomes famous comes from an advantaged background, since we are motivated to create in 'our own image'. Indeed, this is actively encouraged in up and coming app and tech developers (Dash, 2016).

A lot of the 'advice' on how to create attractive content assumes a pure meritocracy – a level playing field where you will succeed if you are lucky to have talent and can dedicate time and effort. If you do not, you either did not want it or did not try hard enough. We should be wary of the idea that people freely 'choose' to be or not be creative based on their own interests or talents. Content creation – online and offline – is about the representation of ideologies, norms, values, and lifestyles, or embodied cultural capital learned through socialisation (Chapter 1). What we produce and consume tells us whose values count. If only certain people create content, the world is represented in ways that reflect how they see the world. In relation to socio-digital inequalities, we should ask whether the same privileged people who have always determined value get to continue to determine what should be put on a pedestal in digital societies.

Causes of inequalities in online content creation

To understand whether existing class and cultural inequalities are being overturned (leapfrogging), diminished (normalisation), maintained (stratification), or exacerbated (amplification), we need earlier data on how they were unequally distributed. There is research on the culture industries and how these have been sexist, racist, classist, and ableist. Yet, there is very little on inequalities in who produced more everyday artefacts, such as holiday snaps and diaries. There is more research on who consumed different types of traditional media. The research shows that socio-economic inequalities are related to different patterns of consumption, creating hierarchies based on symbolic power (Savage, 2015). This is an opportunity for socio-digital inequalities research to inform traditional inequalities research, since online there are more data on who does and does not create everyday content. Assuming that what we find can be applied to the offline world, we can start discussing class in relation to everyday digital creativity.

For a long time, active digital content creation was the exception rather than the norm. The widely cited '1 per cent rule' (or the 90–9–1 rule) suggests that on any given platform 1 per cent of users will create content, 10 per cent will interact with it, and the rest will just view it (Hargittai & Walejko, 2008; Whittaker, Terveen, Hill, & Cherny, 1998). There has since been much critique of this 'rule'. New divisions of consumptive and creative labour have been bandied around that were slightly less pessimistic. The separation between active and passive creators is tenuous anyway; people are data providers most of the time, become content creators for short periods, and then become passive consumers and promotors again (Bozkurt, Honeychurch, Singh, & Koutropoulos, 2017; Ewing, 2008). In this section, I will examine who creates content online, and whether there are inequalities in consumption depending on the different socio-economic, socio-cultural, and socio-psychological backgrounds people come from.

Where do people have digital content creation literacy?

There is a dearth of data on strategic and critical content creation skills in different regions of the world. As a result, it is hard to say much about inequalities in digital content creation. Among the skills the ITU (2017b) measures, many can be considered content creation skills, but most are computer skills rather than connected ICT skills. None is related to everyday content creation (Helsper & Van Deursen, 2018).

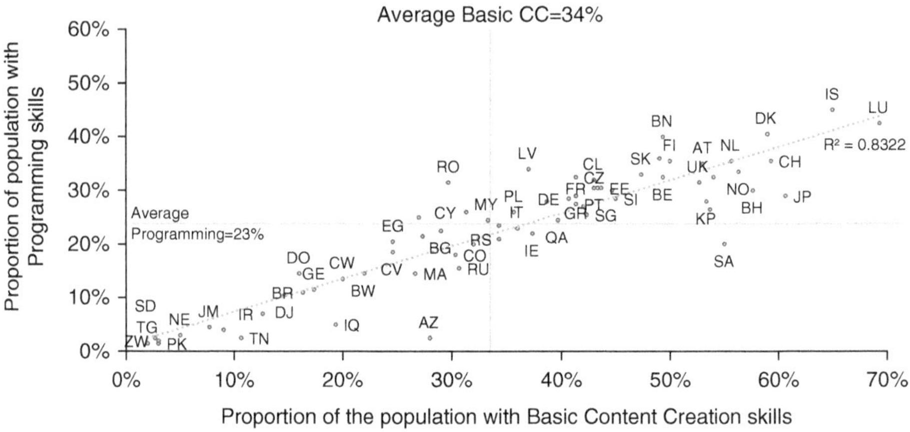

Figure 7.2 Regional inequalities in basic technical and programming-based content creation skills

Source: Data from ITU World Telecommunication/Indicators Database (with permission). Original analysis for this chapter (Helsper & Van Deursen, 2018).

Base: Internet users in each country. Countries excluded which had less than two data points on programming.

Note I: ISO country codes used (International Standards Organisation, 2020).

Note II: Basic content creation skills include: Creating electronic presentations with presentation software; Transferring files between a computer and other devices; Copying or moving a file or folder; Using copy and paste tools to duplicate or move information within a document. Programming consists of: Writing a computer program using a specialised programming language; Using basic arithmetic formulas in a spreadsheet.

European countries have well-distributed basic and programming skills, especially the Nordic and Eastern European countries (Helsper & Van Deursen, 2018). However, some of the Asian powerhouses, such as Japan and Singapore, enjoy a higher diffusion of programming skills too. Romania scores high on programming skills, although not on the basic skills. At the other end of the spectrum lie countries from the Global South and poorer middle-eastern countries. The overall picture these literacy patterns paint is a replication of colonial and socio-economic inequalities (Figure 7.2). Nevertheless, data are missing on countries, such as the US, India, and China, where high-end digital and non-digital content producers are concentrated. This lack of data makes it difficult to discern whether inequalities in digital content creation literacy replicate existing geographical inequalities in the creative industries worldwide.

Where and what content is produced and consumed?

There have always been centres of production of popular entertainment content in the world. The question is whether they are reflected in the digital realm. It is clear that the digital professional and infrastructure markets are dominated by a few US-based players. Much has been written about the 'Big Five' companies located in California's Silicon Valley. Together, they were valued at US$5.5 trillion in 2020 (Kostin, 2020; McChesney, 2013). While Tencent and Sina dominate content creation platforms in China, they are not global companies. There is considerable software creation in China and the Asian tech powerhouses (Singapore, Korea). But within these regions, app creation is still restricted to large economically thriving cities with low participation from emerging markets (Pon, 2016).

Inequalities are found also in lower-level content creation: domain name registrations, Wikipedia entries, and mapping locations come mostly from major world cities. At a national level, they come from the US, followed by Western Europe, with very little presence from countries in the Global South (Graham & Zook, 2011; Zook, 2005). That is, most of the content about the Global South is produced by people living in the Global North. This is similar to how maps and geography books were created in colonial times (Graham & Zook, 2011). In 2020, there were 9.6 billion visits a month to the English language site (one-third from the US), and 23 billion to all wikis (one-fifth from the US) (Wikipedia, 2020). Logically, people are more likely to be intensive consumers if there is more content in their language, making more references to familiar situations (Straubhaar, Castro, Duarte, & Spence, 2019; Taneja & Webster, 2016). If there is little 'culturally-proximate' content in your own language, you will have to make do with what is available.

Consumption and production inequalities in Europe partly overlap with socio-economic inequalities in Europe, but not with where the traditional powerhouses in cultural production are located. The patterns on UGC production are more surprising and hard to explain through historical analysis; they are not typical patterns in terms of socio-digital inequalities at the regional level in Europe (Figure 7.3).

The Nordic countries are not in the highest UGC production group, but in the highest consumption group. In addition, countries that are relatively high in production and low

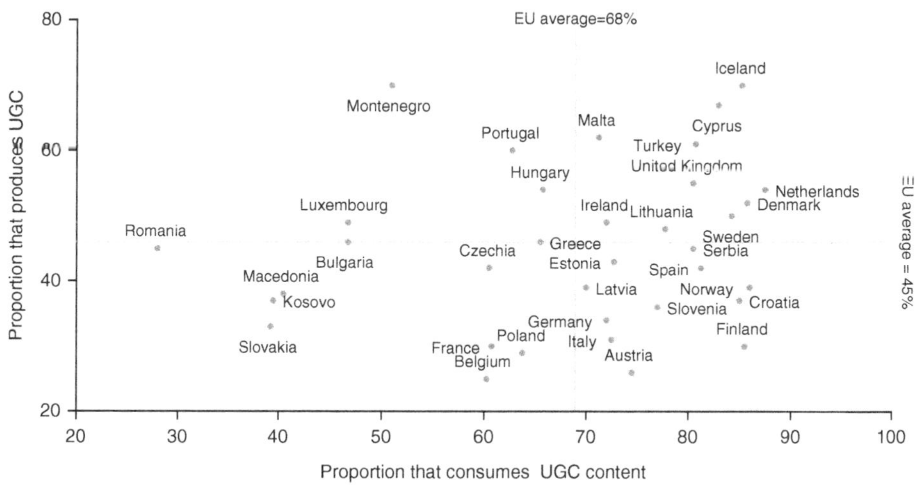

Figure 7.3 Inequalities in User Generated Content (UGC) production and consumption in Europe

Source: Eurostat data (2019b). Online data code: isoc_ci_ac_i. Original analysis for this chapter.

Base: All internet users.

Note: Consumption of UGC content consists of watching video content from sharing services and watching internet streamed TV or videos. UGC production refers to uploading self-created content to any website to be shared.

in consumption, such as Montenegro and Portugal, are not historically strong producers of content and do not have strong economies. France and Germany – wealthy, big producers of professional offline broadcast content – are relatively low on UGC production. Traditional socio-economic inequalities or cultural industries do not seem to drive these differences in everyday content creation.

Inequalities in consumption, promotion, and production

There is some research on inequalities between people from different class, generation, gender, and ethnic backgrounds in content creation. This research focuses on influencers and inequalities in the IT sector, rather than on everyday content production and consumption. Besides this, there is a lack of data from the Global South. We cannot draw firm conclusions about where JunWen's creation of profile pictures and in-game avatars or the production and rating of his amateur music tracks stands in terms of representing inequalities.

With these caveats in mind, I next discuss what we know about the links between economic, cultural, and social-psychological inequalities in content creation literacies of various kinds.

Inequalities in content creation skills and motivation

The literature on content creation skills is problematically focused on technical, high-end content creation skills. This interest is steered by a preoccupation with entrepreneurship and start-ups in policy making (Chapter 4). As a result, we know little about differences in everyday content creation skills. Our research on the collateral benefits of internet use, which incorporates a broader spectrum of content creation skills, shows that content creation skills relate to a variety of uses (Van Deursen & Helsper, 2017).

There is a discourse of choice in relation to everyday content creation – everyone can do it, if they want to. After all, how difficult could it be to make and upload a selfie, like a post, or create a funny GIF? Surely this comes naturally to all of us? JunWen agrees with Carol from Chapter 6 that 'it's not rocket science'. Yet, the research shows that these actions are not that simple. Original content creation takes time, energy, and a particular skill-set. Access to ICTs does not make a content creator. Learning by doing, receiving feedback, and trying again are all necessary for improvements in our creative abilities. The opportunity to build this literacy depends on an intersection of socio-economic and socio-cultural resources that stimulate creativity, and the privileged have more control over their time and autonomy (Schradie, 2011; Wright, 2005). If you have extensive caring duties, have three jobs in order to be able to pay the rent, a boss who is constantly looking over your (digital) shoulder, or share a small room with family members, you do not have time or the ability to try many different things out, let alone have hobbies that allow you to contribute in creative ways to society and build cultural capital.

How easy it is to create things depends on the device or platform you are using (Chapter 3). High-quality, ubiquitous access leads to people creating and sharing their creations, independent of skill level. Since access is still linked to socio-economic inequalities, there are class constraints on content creation. People without ubiquitous, high-quality access need to be shrewd with their use. They tend to do only the 'minimum necessary', which often excludes content creation that requires wider bandwidth, more time, and more devices (Robinson, 2009). Thiessen and Looker (2008) make the case that people who are wed to traditional culture are least likely to be online. This means that people who are the most motivated to contribute certain types of content are least likely to learn these skills by trial and error on personally owned devices. Ofcom's (2019) research in the UK shows that entertainment and leisure activities gained most in popularity. Yet, activities allowing people to build content creation skills did not grow at similar rates. This means that passive use of platforms or instrumental use of ICTs for very specific practical goals does not lead to broader skill take-up.

JunWen is a good example of the importance of access, exposure, and resources. Talking about the sophisticated software he uses to make his electronic music mixes, he says: 'It's a music recording program. Some people might struggle with that but I've been using it for years.' He experimented with electronic music even before he got online, which helped him to acquire the skills. Without his MacBook, it would have been even harder to do what he wants to do with his music; only having a phone would have made it impossible to do what he wants to do with his music. However, it was not only skills and access that led him to develop his musical interests and confidence. It helped that JunWen's parents had not only the economic but also the cultural resources that allowed him to experiment with music when he was young. Alongside more traditional academic subjects, such as maths, they considered music to be part of a proper education.

Several projects based on the Technology Acceptance Model (TAM) and Uses and Gratifications (U&G) framework have shown that extrinsic and intrinsic motivations are important drivers of how we use ICTs (Teo, Lim, & Lai, 1999; Venkatesh & Sykes, 2013). This research often ignores that motivations are not equally distributed; they are shaped by gendered and class-based socialisation patterns, as well as the unequally-distributed availability of leisure time (Bagozzi, 2007). Correa (2010) found that differences between men and women in content creation can be explained by inequalities in their digital self-efficacy and intrinsic motivation; both are lower among women. Even though women thought that creating content could be generally useful (extrinsic motivation), they did not think it was 'for them', nor something they were good at. This combination of believing something is important but not feeling competent to undertake it makes people anxious and less likely to participate. They are more likely to sit back and consume what others have produced. In other words, there are enduring reasons why inequalities in digital creative skills cannot be resolved by putting everyone on a one-off content creation class.

In the studies with adults that use the DiSTO measures for content creation skills, education and gender are good predictors. What we see is that how gender and education intersect depends on location. While people with lower levels of education consistently had lower content creation skills, the gender effect remains unclear. In Europe, men have more content creation skills than women, across lower and higher education groups

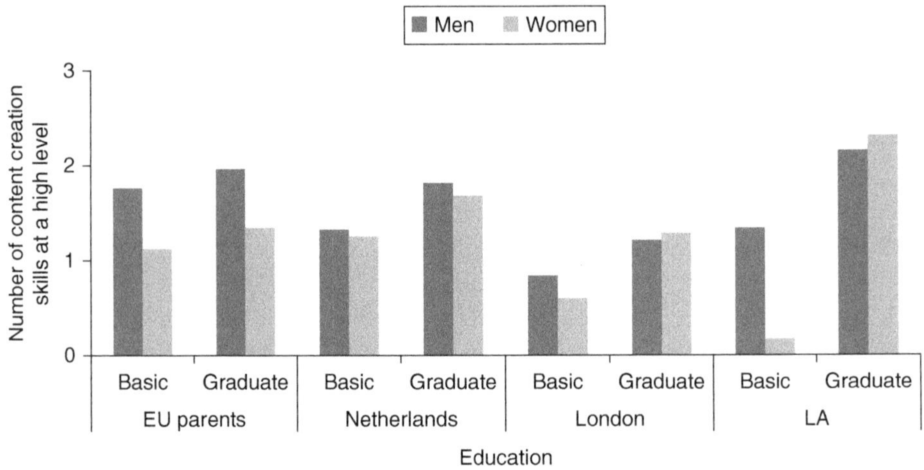

Figure 7.4 Intersections between education and gender in content creation skills

Source: Marketing to Kids (European parents), Original analyses of Disto NL (Netherlands), and DiSTO Networked Inequalities (London & LA) studies.

Base: Internet users.

Note: Everyday content creation skills include: Definitely being able to create something new from video or music that you found online; Edit or make basic changes to online content that others have created; Design a website.

(Figure 7.4). Yet, in the metropolitan digital hubs of London and Los Angeles, there are significant gender inequalities in content creation skills among lower-educated populations, but none or even reversed inequalities in higher educated populations. Generation is also a significant predictor across these high-diffusion countries, with older individuals having fewer content creation skills. In the DiSTO studies that examine content creation skills of young people, education level is not a significant predictor of skills; gender and social status are. Young women, girls, and people not in education, employment, or training (NEETs) had the fewest high-level content creation skills (Helsper & Smirnova, 2016; Net Children Go Mobile, 2020). In all studies, those who have more ubiquitous access, higher general self-confidence, and higher social digital skills also have higher content creation skills.

The learning of skills and the decision to create are restricted by a person's socio-economic and socio-cultural circumstances. In Chapter 5, we saw how critical digital information skills are strongly correlated with traditional print literacy and problem-solving abilities. For content creation skills, traditional inequalities not seen for other types of digital skill, such as those based on gender, re-emerge (Van Deursen et al., 2017). Class, gender, and generation intersect to determine which types of content and activities are considered proper, and should be learned by individuals from different backgrounds (Hoffmann, Lutz, & Meckel, 2015; Selwyn, 2005). These socio-cultural factors drive individuals' self-efficacy and concerns around sharing certain types of content. In turn, these concerns influence whether we create content and what content we create.

Inequalities in passive content creation: Data provision through consumption

There are not much data on passive content creation. We know little about who is more likely to look at, like, forward, or rank content that others have produced (van Dijck, 2009). A lack of data on inequalities in consumption and data generation is especially problematic if 90 per cent of internet users on sharing platforms are 'lurkers', providing data to algorithms which shape what content will be presented to future users (Kushner, 2016).

In the literature on consumption, the use of ICTs for entertainment-related activities is not considered resource enhancing, although the creation of this content might be. It writes in a dismissive tone, leading some to conclude that people from traditionally disadvantaged backgrounds are less likely to engage in 'capital-enhancing' activities (Dutton & Blank, 2015; Zillien & Hargittai, 2009). Notwithstanding, entertainment is often crucial for emotional well-being and helps people to feel connected to the rest of the world. For example, for homeless youth alleviating boredom through entertainment, non-instrumental social media use is important for their well-being. This use improves their health and economic opportunities, even though it is not directly related to things that outsiders consider 'resource enhancing', such as finding information (Rice & Barman-Adhikari, 2014).

Sharing platforms such as YouTube and YouKu offer ways of circumventing the critics, studios, and agents who control what appears on our screens. For example, intense users drive the popularity of content for niche global audiences that would not have been picked up by 'wealthy majority rules' advertising models (Jenkins, Clinton, Purushotma, Robison, & Weigel, 2006; Keen, 2011). There is evidence that hyperlinks connect content from a more diverse range of sources than for networks and connections in the traditional media industries (McIlwain, 2017). Nevertheless, segregation remains an issue online. People consume content and congregate in digital spaces based on their racial and ethnic backgrounds. Individual preferences are aligned with their socio-economic and socio-cultural backgrounds.

Analyses of the DiSTO databases confirm that cultural uses are unequally distributed. The general patterns indicate an amplification of existing inequalities, especially those based on socio-cultural backgrounds related to class, gender, and age-based socialisations about what is 'appropriate' consumption. In European DiSTO studies with young people, ethnicity is not important in cultural uses or entertainment, contradicting the studies done in the US. Nevertheless, those individuals who feel more embedded in and respected by the community they live in are more culturally engaged online. It is this social – rather than a more individualistic – sense of self-esteem that drives engagement with cultural content. This subsequently provides data feeding the algorithms determining what others will see and where they will go in the digital space.

Inequalities in the control we have over who uses the data we create is influenced by the same factors that determine offline forms of autonomy: gender, social class, ethnicity, and education (Gangadharan, 2017; Litt & Hargittai, 2014). In interventions and policy, it is incorporated as a technical skill to prevent malicious data gathering and to combat fraud, identity theft, reputation damage, and undesired data sharing. But in the academic literature, it is about inequality of privacy more than awareness of who shares our information or the ability to use the technical tools to restrict access to our personal information. Those who are in positions of disadvantage have far less control over whether they share data and use ICTs or not. They often do not own or have autonomy over the devices they use and are more likely to be monitored when they use (shared) devices. They often access connected ICTs in monitored public spaces or need to give gatekeepers personal information to log in and use services (Gangadharan, 2017; Robinson & Gran, 2018).

There are other power dynamics at play as well. Disempowered people who depend on others for resources might feel they cannot refuse a request by someone with more power. They feel they must like or engage with something that is created by a person in power. An everyday example for JunWen is his interactions with a former professor he is connected to on Weibo: 'She's posting pictures. Yes, I like them because I have to because she's my teacher.' Similarly, when a boss asks an employee to contribute to or rate something they have created, it will be much harder to refuse than when this request is made the other way around. Studies about inequalities in who feels they can deny such requests are urgently needed. Worrying about privacy is a luxury, because only those with power can decide when to share what with whom.

Inequalities in content creation through production

Active content creation skills are also subject to traditional inequalities: white, middle-class, male users are more prolific producers of online content (Lutz et al., 2014). In addition, they were part of the early adopters, meaning that they have a far larger back catalogue of material online. Consequently, their tastes and needs are overrepresented (Servon, 2002). Content production being in the hands of just a few individuals with strong economic and social capital is nothing new. Media literacy scholars make a convincing argument that, to correct this trend, we should provide digital creative skills training to those who do not dominate the culture industries or have cultural capital (Kendall, 2011). As more diverse content becomes available, the idea is that more people will consume it, which in turn incentivises the production of similar content (Viard & Economides, 2015). Yet, teaching individual skills is only the first hurdle to overcoming invisibility and disenfranchisement, since systematic, structural inequalities underlie inequalities in content creation (Jenkins et al., 2006). Let's explore which socio-economic, socio-cultural, and personal characteristics are most likely to make someone an active online content creator.

On popular, public sharing platforms, content created is likely to come from socio-economically privileged groups aligning with their interests (Brake, 2014; Schradie, 2012). However, when we distinguish different types of active content creation, inequalities emerge that seem to counter traditional socio-economic inequalities. For example, Blank (2013) shows that people with lower levels of education are more likely to create content to connect with friends and family or entertain themselves. He also finds that single, lower-income youth with high levels of technical skills are more likely to produce skilled, broadcast content (Blank, 2013). These 'disenfranchised' have much in common with young hipsters who dropped out of school to try their hand in the start-up entrepreneur world: a middle-class, white, male cohort in the US (Marwick, 2015).

Socio-economic stratification in the consumption of entertainment content might lead to the segregation of online content spaces with diverse audiences and producers of content produced by the privileged, juxtaposed with narrow and homogeneous audiences for content produced by the disadvantaged. The Indaco and Manovich (2016) study on who uploads pictures on Instagram in New York City shows that there is more uploading in rich than in poor neighbourhoods. Rather than stratification, in this case there is amplification of inequalities. People from poorer areas share images from the wealthy areas they worked in during the day, while, in contrast, poorer areas only get contributions from residents. Why is this emblematic of inequalities? As the environments and lifestyles of the better-off get more visibility, they become the norm for those who follow Instagram accounts. This makes the less privileged more hesitant to post online. JunWen hints at this when he comments: 'I don't see the point, some people put everything, like every step they do. I don't know. If I have good things to share, then maybe. But not like every day and everything.' He feels that his experiences and ideas are not of value to others.

At the moment, the evidence on the relationship between socio-economic status and digital content production is too contradictory to draw conclusions about the replication of these inequalities in digital societies. Since content creation represents people and ideas, inequalities between people from different socio-cultural backgrounds might be more relevant than socio-economic inequalities. Gender is an important factor in shaping active content creation. Women are less likely to create content directed at a broader audience, and prefer more private or restricted channels (Schradie, 2015). On more public, broad-audience channels, they are likely to produce stereotypically feminine content. For example, on YouTube in the UK, the most popular female vloggers are beauty vloggers. There is more diversity among popular male vloggers, who reach a wider audience with a notable absence of stereotypically feminine content (Bishop, 2018). Another site where inequalities in public content creation has been studied is Wikipedia. Only around 133,000 of 39 million registered users (0.003 per cent) actively contribute monthly to the English site (Wikipedia, 2020). This select group of contributors, from an already select group of registered users, is mostly male and higher-educated (Hargittai & Shaw, 2015). These gender and class inequalities are also present for more professional content creation. Studies in the Netherlands and Belgium show that men dominate online journalism and use a broader range of platforms to reach out to audiences (De Vuyst, 2017).

Nevertheless, the question of whether there is amplification of content creation inequalities cannot really be answered with cohort data. Rather than taking a one-moment snapshot and seeing whether there are inequalities, we need to understand whether these inequalities have increased or decreased over time. This is where Bechmann's (2019) unique longitudinal study is valuable. It shows that while there are still inequalities between men and women in posting content online, the size of these differences has diminished over time – a sign of normalisation. Similarly, the relationship between gender and content creation often disappears when differences in skills and experience between men and women are taken into account (Blank, 2013).

Inequalities based on age are one of the most consistent findings. Older individuals are less likely to produce everyday material and content requiring higher-level content creation skills (Brake, 2014; Dutton & Blank, 2015; Schradie, 2011). Interestingly, the normalisation pattern seen for gender was not there for age in Bechmann's (2019) study. Even with high skills and ICT experience, older individuals were less likely to create content. This means that the current generation of young active posters will probably show patterns of content creation similar to that of their parents as they grow older.

Research projects at the beginning of the 21st century found that younger ethnic minorities were more likely to use interactive sharing platforms, especially for entertainment news, than the white majority in the US (Correa, 2010; Hargittai & Litt, 2011). A 'white flight' drove those users to leave loose network sharing platforms to dominating close network-based platforms such as Facebook (boyd, 2012). More research is needed to understand patterns of segregation in UGC, and develop explanations for them. Disadvantaged people, such as ethnic minorities, are more likely to share and evaluate others' posts, because cultural socialisation processes steer them into preferring reciprocal, communal processes of communication. On the other hand, they are often more concerned about privacy due to historical abuse of such data (Robinson & Gran, 2018; Yao, Rice, & Wallis, 2007). Women and people from certain ethnic minority groups might have a greater drive to share, but keep it restricted to an inner circle because of concerns about negative reactions. Others have no choice but to use more public forums – where they cannot control their privacy through technical means – to connect with others like them (Correa & Jeong, 2011; Petronio, 2002). Inequalities in self-censorship and privacy norms and options means that certain actions and reactions are published only in restricted communities, creating underrepresentation in public forums and popular content (Litt & Hargittai, 2014).

There is some evidence for segregation around sexual orientation. For good reasons, LGBTQ individuals tend to contribute with material and discussions to private spaces for their community. General public spaces, where users generate content and comment on it, are generally heteronormative and even homophobic (Miles, 2018; Pulos, 2013). More politically-engaged people with stronger networks of support are more likely to contribute on public forums (McInroy, 2016). There are many LGBTQ-oriented spaces online, but they are closed-off through sign posting, moderation, or registration requirements. These echo chambers create safe spaces away from the abuse that they often encounter in other public spaces.

JunWen has been raised with Confucian values, emphasising communal values over individualistic ones. But he also knows he can be discriminated against for being gay. As a result, he has strict reciprocal rules for himself posting on Weibo: 'I mainly login to check up on my cousins, what are they doing. The ones that aren't writing to me. I don't write, I did a little bit but then it's like revealing myself and I don't know if I should.' He is worried that even normal interactions could reveal something about his sexual identity that would get him in trouble with his extended family. He dislikes platforms such as Weibo and WeChat because he feels he cannot be himself. 'It really started to grate on me, the way some people were flashing their wonderful lives in front of me. So I unfollowed a lot of them and then realised I self-sensor a bit more, also on the gaming chats. And then the LGBT centre site is where I'm my truest online-self – if anyone is really a true online person.' He is more private and cautious about interactions with others from different backgrounds online because of his personal experiences. When he gets his VPN to work, he surfs English language sites on LGBTQ topics. He has browsed Wikipedia and read what people around the world have posted, but these stories do not really relate to the situation in China and his experiences. He has never contributed there or on the public forums of the Shanghai centre. He admires people who are out and active, but he just cannot make himself to go beyond looking at sites. He would like to compose a song or a post about being gay, but it is far too risky.

The social and cultural resources that underpin ideas about content production are more important for active content creation than for consumption and passive content creation (Litt & Hargittai, 2014; Robles, Molina, & De Marco, 2012). Those who feel vulnerable, alienated, or isolated are less likely to feel comfortable and motivated to share their thoughts and creations publicly online. These online patterns replicate those in the offline world (McLure Wasko & Faraj, 2005; Rogers & Kincaid, 1981). To contribute content, you need to feel that you have ideas that are worthwhile and that there are at least some people who will respond positively. If you have these beliefs about yourself, you will create and share content on public and private platforms. Those who are discriminated against, and have good support networks and feel they need to have a voice in wider society, will more likely use public spaces on and offline to share their creations and reshape public discourse, despite the risks. Those who have good support networks of people like them, but do not feel comfortable in wider societies, will use private spaces to share their creations. This way they maintain a positive sense of self (Nov, Naaman, & Ye, 2010). Those who are vulnerable but isolated and feel alienated from society are more likely to lurk in private spaces or post anonymously in public ones.

Consequences from digital inequalities in content creation

When examining the consequences of inequalities in the use of ICTs in content consumed and created, we can distinguish between quantitative, measurable outcomes of status – financial returns, number of fans, likes, views, and forwards – and qualitative, subjective aspects related to respect and feelings of belonging. Quantitatively measureable popularity does not always mean subjective benefits in terms of status and belonging. Your video could be the most popular on YouKu or TikTok, but the reactions might be negative or you might start to feel confused about who you are and about having to keep up appearances. Since popularity is easily quantifiable, there are more data on this and less on inequalities in the more qualitative aspects of the outcomes of content creation for people from different backgrounds.

Inequalities in popularity and fame in digital societies

Most studies on outcomes of popularity and representation perform content analyses to examine characteristics of the most popular posts or outputs. This methodological choice comes partly out of well-established representational studies in media and communications research. For example, the Bechdel test analyses how women are (under)represented in film and television series as independent characters in their own right (Garber, 2015). There is again very little research on everyday UGC, such as selfies, on whether what gets appreciated depends on who produces it or is depicted. The emphasis is often on the popular and the famous, less on moderately popular content, and nothing is known about those like JunWen whose creations get hardly any attention.

Open UGC platforms offer opportunities for those with a variety of identities to express and represent themselves in ways that they could not before. Indeed, more niche cultural forms, such as fan-fiction and home videos produced by young individuals, have gained prominence in public discourse (Jenkins et al., 2006; Shaw & Benkler, 2012). Yet, true fame is mostly obtained after content is promoted by mainstream media, such as radio, television, and newspapers (Keen, 2011). Getting into the inner-circle of pioneer bloggers, who relied a lot on traditional media to become famous in the early days, is the real road to success. After official stamps of approval from the traditional and digital establishment, likes and promotional deals pick up. This means that the popularity of UGC content still follows traditional patterns of inequalities (Carstensen, 2009).

In the UK, only seven out of the 50 most popular vloggers on YouTube are women (Bishop, 2018). Studies elsewhere find similarly low percentages of women among the most popular vloggers and bloggers (Schradie, 2015) – 10 per cent seems to be the norm (Harp & Tremayne, 2006). No similar research has been done for the ethnicity or class of those who are popular. Yet, McIlwain's (2017) research suggests that in the US, even when websites or content itself links to content created by a wide variety of producers, the general audience still gravitates towards the content produced by middle-class, white men.

Take JunWen. He won a prize for his music when he was 18, but he has not made a breakthrough online. He feels ignored and misunderstood as a musician. He did try once: '[When I] first bought my decks I sort of made a video of myself and I put that online.' But that did not get much reaction, and he does not know why. He sees that most of the artists on QQ or YouKu are based in Beijing and Shanghai, and feels like a country bumpkin in comparison to them. While he uploads songs, he does not feel he really understands what is required to be popular. He does not comply with the image that people have of mainstream electronic music artists online, and his visible and audible Tu heritage do not line up with Chinese ideals of male attractiveness. It might be that the only way you can be non-heterosexual online in China is performing in drag, since men playing caricatures of women has a long history in Chinese music theatre. But he does not identify with this. In the online gaming universe that he frequents, his avatar represents the kind of man he likes (i.e. burly, dark-skinned). He wonders if he might have received more requests to join quests if this avatar had represented mythical Chinese warriors who were lean, muscular, and with lighter skin colour. Research about sexism, racism, and homophobia in the gaming world suggests he might be right (Chess & Shaw, 2015; Gray, 2014).

JunWen is realising that to be discovered has always required more than talent. Knowing what audiences want and how the 'market' works have always been important. Socio-economic and socio-cultural resources also play a significant role in these skills.

Most musicians or artists who make a living were not discovered randomly – they knew the right people, and were in the right place at the right time (Accominotti, 2008; Reyes-Acosta, 2016). These network connections and socio-culturalsavviness are easier for people from middle- or upper-class milieus to obtain (Lutz, 2016). One of the things that is indicative of a person's class is their accent and how they use language. This seems to be no different online, where content creators are judged based on how they speak, and being mainstream and middle class is appreciated (Bishop, 2018). In fact, when JunWen includes voice in his tracks or when he is gaming, he is very careful not to let his Tu influences come out and he makes his Mandarin more 'coastal' (i.e. from Shanghai).

Who is alienated and who feels they belong in digital societies?

Popularity is often thought of as leading to only positive outcomes. Therefore, studies focus on people who are most popular and ignore those at the bottom of rankings. The lack of data on who is unheard and unliked – the 'invisible online' – is a gap in inequalities research. This gap is caused by an overemphasis on big data and content analysis, which draws researchers' and practitioners' eyes away from the less active, less popular producers. Nevertheless, negative outcomes of content creation should also consider how using ICTs makes individuals feel. The wrong kind of attention and a lack of attention can both result in feelings of discomfort, a lack of a sense of belonging, and questioning of one's identity. This cultural resource is not just social capital; you can have a strong network of friends and family but still feel that wider society discriminates against you (Chapter 2). If you do not have social resources, then a lack respect is even worse, leading to individual and societal isolation.

Feelings of belonging and a sense of identity are not directly related to the externally assigned sense of popularity. Those who become popular online might not be the ones who feel that they have a place in the digital society they inhabit. It might not be important that the majority recognises and validates your creations, as long as the right people do – people like you, people whose opinions and tastes you value. This last section is about inequalities in whether creating content and observing others' reactions to it makes one feel welcome, understood, and appreciated in digital spaces, independent of where you rank on the digital charts.

People from historically discriminated gender, ethnic, religious, and LGBTQ groups who create content receive more negative reactions than their advantaged peers. We should keep in mind that exposure to negative content does not automatically lead to harm (Global Kids Online, 2020; Livingstone et al., 2011). While the ideal solution is for there to be no hate speech, we should examine which people are most likely to be negatively impacted in the face of hate speech directed at them. There are nearly no data on this aspect of socio-digital inequalities, and evidence about sexism, racism, and homophobia comes almost exclusively from the US and Europe, and the required intersectional approach is completely missing from how these aspects are studied. The Global Kids Online study has added evidence from countries in the Global South on negative cultural outcomes (e.g. harassment) for the youngest generations of ICT users. New DiSTO projects are also starting to explore these issues in relation to socio-economic and socio-cultural characteristics.

To avoid these negative outcomes, marginalised communities create their own spaces online where outsiders are not welcome. In the Dutch DiSTO study with adults, we find no link between education and employment and positive cultural outcomes, such as a sense of belonging or understanding of identity (Van Deursen et al., 2017). Those who are socio-economically disadvantaged have lower levels of the skills needed to engage with ICTs. But when they gain skills, they are more likely to share content with and learn about people like them. Nevertheless, disadvantaged individuals are overall less likely to achieve positive outcomes when it comes to personal development than their more advantaged peers.

There are small variations on these trends of fewer positive and more negative outcomes depending on the population and the generations under investigation. For example, there were no inequalities among youth in the positive outcomes such as self-actualisation. Yet, other research indicates that marginalised youth growing up under tough circumstances are more likely to have negative outcomes, such as social or physical violence or institutionalisation, because the content that they post is considered anti-social or non-normative (Lim, Vadrevu, Chan, & Basnyat, 2012). In London and Los Angeles, those who were outside the labour market were less likely to have positive and negative outcomes in relation to how ICTs made them feel about themselves and the groups to which they belong. The data thus again paint a contradictory picture around inequalities in cultural outcomes of ICT based on socio-economic inequalities.

Issues such as sexism, racism, and homophobia online are widely discussed in the second decade of the 21st century. Yet, it is unclear if instances of it have increased, because these issues have not been monitored consistently. The Global Kids Online study finds that in countries where children are broad users of ICTs and intense users of social media, 40 per cent of young people have encountered hate speech online, which makes it much more common than, for example, encountering suicide or self-harm information. In terms of negative outcomes of participating online, those who come from backgrounds or who have characteristics that make it more likely that they are bullied, harassed, and discriminated offline are also more likely to be bullied online (d'Haenens & Ogan, 2013; Gorzig et al., 2017). Studies tend to suggest that being cyberbullied or harassed continues throughout the lifetime and is prevalent among adults (European Parliament, 2016). Even so, boys are more likely to be threatened online than older men, and older teens more likely to have seen something that upset them and are more likely to be bullied than younger teens (Global Kids Online, 2020).

Many studies focus on gender inequalities in relation to bullying and harassment. Their findings tend to paint a dystopian picture. Figures differ per country, but the patterns are pretty consistent. Among younger individuals, the rate of negative reactions to content posted is not that different, but consequences of this type of harassment are unequally distributed. The European Net Children Go Mobile (2020) study findings and the Global Kids Online (2020) studies show similar findings. The gender differences for preteens were almost absent while they were large among teenagers. This means teenage girls are most likely to have seen upsetting UGC (35 per cent) and to have been bullied (20 per cent). The overall level of cyberbullying could not be explained by the skills or use levels.

This suggests that the emphasis on higher levels of ICT use leading to more negative outcomes should be contested. It is not necessarily the use that determines whether outcomes are negative or not.

Girls and women are more likely to be at the receiving end of reputational attacks, psychological harassment, and sexual violence. They also find these attacks more upsetting than boys and men (Duggan, 2017; Patchin, 2019). However, boys and men are more often harassed through threats of physical violence and ideological political slurs. For women, their gender is more often explicitly the subject of the harassment than with men. Boys and men are more likely to be bullies in almost all studies (d'Haenens & Ogan, 2013; Global Kids Online, 2020; Patchin, 2019). All of this culminates, in the US at least, with women thinking that online harassment and bullying is a large problem and supporting the prioritising of feeling safe online, while men privilege free speech of any kind online (Duggan, 2017).

Research on harassment shows that people coming from ethnic minority backgrounds, especially women, are more likely to have been made to feel uncomfortable and unsafe online (Duggan, 2017). Conversely, social media, discussion platforms, and blogs can be used by these same people to challenge misrepresentation and harassment. The same tools used for harassment can cohere social support networks and communities online that are not available offline except among close family and friends (Gabriel, 2016). We know little about the real-life advantages and risks of being ranked or viewed highly (McIlwain, 2017). It might be the case that more exposure means more negative reactions, especially for these groups. There is evidence of sexism and heteronormativity in gaming: identity-targeted bullying leads to a higher likelihood of withdrawal from games, or hiding one's identity in digital spaces (Fox & Tang, 2017; Ingersoll, 2019). For example, there is no way JunWen would tell his gamer friends he is gay.

McKenna and Bargh's (1998) study showed that people whose minority or disadvantaged status was not visible offline were more likely to feel at home in digital spaces, sometimes more so than in offline public spaces. Nevertheless, those whose identity was salient (e.g. ethnicity, visible physical disability) were less likely to find comfort in online public spaces. It is important, then, to emphasise the positive aspects of segregated, online safe spaces. People from sexual and religious minorities are more likely to achieve a sense of self and comfort with their identity and a greater feeling of belonging through this use of ICTs (Helland, 2002; Lutz & Hoffmann, 2017).

These findings do not replicate everywhere. Analyses of DiSTO data for London show that people from ethnic minority backgrounds are more likely to feel a sense of belonging and a strengthening of their identity by engaging with ICTs. Yet, differences based on ethnic background or immigrant status are not significant in either the Netherlands or Los Angeles. When they have the same digital skill and engagement levels, there are no inequalities in cultural outcomes found between men and women, older and younger people, and those with and without a disability. The only inequality that is significant in both waves of the Dutch study is disability. Those with a disability that marginalised them feel their use of ICTs leads to a greater sense of belonging to society than others.

Sequentiality of cultural digital inequalities

There is a recurring theme of intersectionality in this book: inequalities in belonging and respectful treatment between different socio-economic or socio-cultural groups is not explained by any single socio-economic or socio-cultural characteristic. Let's examine how compound and sequential disadvantage in terms of skills and differences in use stand at the basis of inequalities in negative cultural outcomes.

The premise of the Corresponding Fields model is that specific resources, skills, and uses are linked to corresponding outcomes (Chapter 2). That is, individuals who come from socio-economic or socio-cultural groups who have traditionally had lower resources in a particular domain will have lower digital resources in that domain. For the cultural domain, examined in this chapter, this means that people with less status and symbolic capital are less likely to have the digital resources that allow them to express themselves and be recognised by others in a positive way in digital environments. Yet, they might be more aware of and engaged with defining this identity because they are 'other' and are constantly reminded of this by the dominant groups. In that sense, they have more cultural resources (i.e. a distinct sense of identity and group belonging) and more critical digital literacy. Therefore, when they have more technical and strategic skills, they are more likely to become aware of, seek out, and produce content that allows them to increase a sense of belonging (Buchi et al., 2018). The flipside of this is that more content creation and more exposure to UGC are linked to more negative reactions.

Increasing skills training for groups that have a greater need to belong and who have been traditionally discriminated against might mean that those designing these interventions see an increase in harassment and bullying for these particular groups. Indeed, young

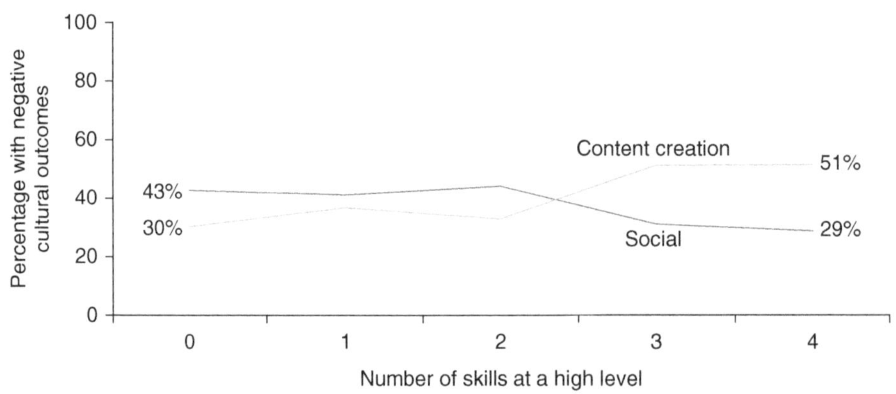

Figure 7.5 Inequalities in negative cultural outcomes based on digital content creation and social skills

Source: DiSTO NEETs project data (Helsper & Smirnova, 2016). Original analysis for this chapter.

Base: Young people (16-25) in the UK (N=1026 Non-NEETs and N=318 NEETs).

Note: Negative cultural outcomes refers to strongly or somewhat agreeing that you were confronted with others online who make you feel uncomfortable about certain aspects of your identity.

people who have the worst outcomes in terms of harassment based on their identity are those who have high content creation skills or low social skills (Figure 7.5).

Those with high levels of social skills are the least likely to have negative social outcomes. This suggests that skills training that aims to decrease encountering hateful content should include a broader understanding of how to use ICTs in socially constructive ways among the general population. If critical media literacy training only focuses on the creative part – teaching people how to make beautiful content and distribute it – this might allow the disempowered to have their voices out there, but not avoid the negative backlash that could come from it based on historical patterns of sexism, racism, and homophobia.

Conclusions and recommendations

Digital content creation is the online activity that could potentially impact not just on our own life-worlds, but our shared digital futures. The content we create and promote through our online activities is our legacy. It shapes the world for those who come after us. Therefore, it influences who feels welcome and has a chance to build on what we have done. It is through online activities that we express ourselves by creating representations of cultures, norms, and values that will be observed and studied for decades to come. It is one of the areas where ICTs have generated the most opportunities for a shift in the balance of power towards ordinary citizens by providing easy access to open sharing platforms with global audiences.

Nevertheless, content creation is one of the regionally most unequally distributed types of digital engagement. Content produced in large metropolitan areas and content about the Global South tends to be shaped by individuals from the Global North. This chapter presented evidence that the most prolific producer countries reflect historical and colonial distributions of economic and cultural capital. That is, the same regions that have dominated cultural industries and determined tastes world-wide have symbolic power to shape the digital world. Nevertheless, we lack data on everyday content creation through active, conscious production of original material, such as uploading photos. Similarly, we know little about inequalities in consuming or promoting certain types of content and not others, which feeds data into the algorithms that shape the digital world. Therefore, conclusions on inequalities in everyday non-professional User Generated Content (UGC) cannot be drawn.

At the beginning of this chapter I asked two questions: Who is most likely to produce what kind of digital content? And what type of content, produced by whom, is most likely to be consumed and valued?

The best answer comes from taking a process-based sequential approach. People who live in environments that provide autonomy and 'the right kind' of symbolic capital are more likely to develop technical and strategic skills, even though they are less likely to have more critical literacy. Thus, it is important that we teach not only technical digital content creation skills around how to create good-looking content, but we should also strategically teach critical literacy and resilience in dealing with negative reactions. Of course, this is not the responsibility of the discriminated and harassed; others must be made aware of the potential impact of the content they produce in their own image online.

Inequalities in content consumption, promotion, and creation do not always take the shape economists, sociologists, or policy makers expect. This complex digital landscape can be summarised as: those who grow up and live in rich environments with personal freedom that stimulates creativity and where their contributions are valued, develop more creative digital skills and confidence. They are more likely to create different types of content on a variety of open and private platforms (Hoffmann et al., 2015). On the other hand, discriminated groups might be more highly motivated to reach out actively to others. However, because of negative reactions and silencing on public platforms, they turn to sharing content privately with people like themselves. Simultaneously, they still consume diverse broadcast content that promotes content produced and valued by the dominant majority. There is room for optimism, since confident individuals from disadvantaged groups with collective, sharing cultures are more likely to want to use public platforms to produce and promote content that represents them. Potentially, this could turn amplification of identity-based inequalities into normalisation of symbolic capital of non-mainstream groups. Nevertheless, on public platforms it remains the case that upper-middle-class, young, or middle-aged men with greater feelings of belonging and confidence in their identity are more intense consumers. Accordingly, they are more valued as producers of cultural materials. This means they leave their mark on the digital landscape by making these types of content more popular. When algorithms incorporate and designers note these preferences, they also draw conclusions as to what the general population likes, and push to create more content along those lines.

The second question asked whether inequalities in the production, consumption, and valuation of digital content relate to inequalities in who is respected, and our sense of belonging in digital societies.

In answering this question, it is important to note that people experience the same things differently based on who they are. For example, negative reactions to content created online are shrugged off by white men, while these have a more negative impact on feelings of belonging and psycho-social well-being of women, ethnic, and sexual minorities. It is the persistence of everyday sexism, racism, and homophobia that makes these experiences more detrimental for groups with histories of discrimination and alienation. The consequence of this is the amplification of inequalities even when content creation leads to greater visibility and gives voice to marginalised groups. Negative reactions that perpetuate inequalities in power dynamics have existed for centuries. This pushes people into digital hiding; they are more likely to connect with others like themelves in safe, private spaces where they can control reactions to the content they create. The result is digital segregation. Everyone might become famous but, in a reformulation of the quote that opened this chapter, people are likely to be 'famous for fifteen people' very similar to them, especially marginalised groups. When there are no safe (private) spaces, when there are no networks of support, or when the person wants to make a change, individuals might feel they have no other option than to stay in these public spaces and suffer the abuse or be silenced, turning into consumers rather than producers of content. This segregation into separate digital spaces results in the disappearance of marginalised voices from open, mainstream platforms and public discourse.

Content creation online cannot be compared with the traditional arts or music industries, especially not when it comes to inequality in production. We need more data on how this happens for everyday non-professional content creators in different contexts to understand whether inequalities are amplified or overcome. Evidence is emerging about the lack of autonomy disadvantaged groups have in terms of non-voluntary data production: they indeed have less choice over providing and analysing their data. Yet, more research is needed on inequalities in more voluntary data production, which works through the consuming and promoting of materials produced by others (e.g. clicking and liking). These things shape what the digital world looks like for others who visit these spaces, and nudge them to decide whether or not to contribute to our digital world. Any platform, organisation, or regulator interested in reducing harm from online participation has to start paying attention to these low-involvement, data-generating activities which exacerbate inequalities.

While still speculative because of a lack of data, I conclude that the process from traditional to digital content creation inequalities seems to run as follows: the traditionally privileged few are more likely to feel like they are individually capable, respected in, and belong to the society they live in. This drives them to produce and share their own ideas and creations, feeding back into a validation and appreciation of their tastes and lifeworlds. They become motivated to continue to produce content in their own image. This may unwittingly silence others, who do not see themselves represented, and who receive negative or no feedback on the content they create. In particular, for the domain of cultural production and consumption of content, we require a long-term vision. Some of the consequences will only be seen after years of invisibility, self-censoring, and micro-aggressions.

CONCLUSIONS: RETHINKING SOCIO-DIGITAL INEQUALITIES

Much has happened since I started writing this book about inequalities in digital societies. The COVID-19 pandemic has pushed Information and Communication Technologies (ICTs) into the fabric of everyday life. This event achieved what infrastructure rollout, mass user uptake, and digital-by-default policies could not. At first, this led to optimism among those working on digital inclusion – surely the problem would be solved now that everyone had to go online for the basic necessities and connecting with loved ones. Nevertheless, it soon became clear that many were not able to take advantage of ICTs, and particular people were dropping out or disengaging. To those studying the full spectrum of socio-digital inequalities, this has not come as a surprise.

In this concluding chapter, I revise the lessons learned from socio-digital inequalities research and practice so far. Yet, because things continue to move quickly in this field, I also cast an eye towards the future. Therefore, I finish this book by suggesting how we can rethink inequalities research and redesign policy and interventions. I am hopeful that we can pre-empt some of the inequality challenges that lie ahead with the arrival of invisible, embedded ICTs.

The road travelled: Lessons learned about socio-digital inequalities

Socio-digital inequalities exist when people from particular backgrounds are systematically more likely to benefit and others are systematically more likely to suffer harm

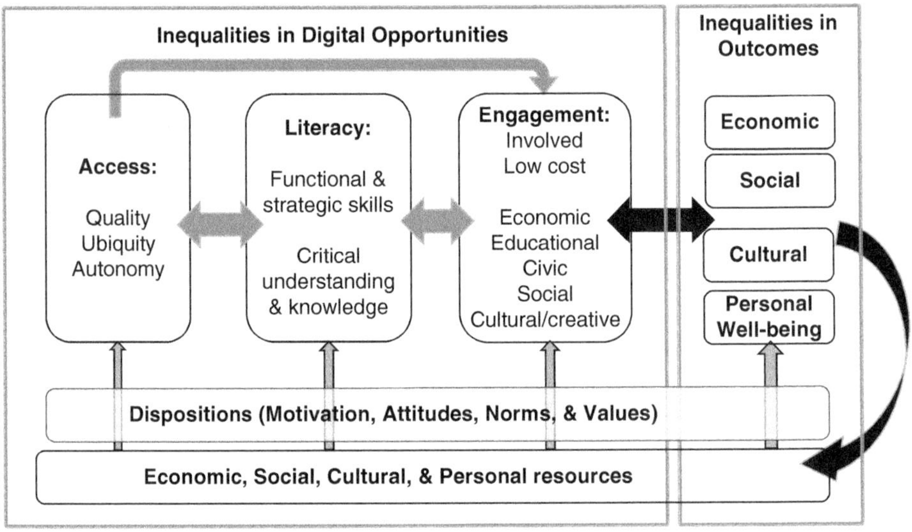

Figure X.1 Model of socio-digital inequalities in digital opportunities and outcomes

due to the digitisation of society. To examine these processes, the Corresponding Fields (CF) model was my guide. This meant exploring the links between corresponding historical and digital inequalities for five domains: economic (Chapter 3), educational (Chapter 4), civic (Chapter 5), social (Chapter 6), and cultural (Chapter 7) inequalities (Figure X.1).

By using this process-based model, I take the following as given:

- Socio-digital inequalities are not about divides between 'haves' and 'have nots' but about different types and levels of socio-digital inequalities.
- Dealing with first-level, infrastructure, and access inequalities is insufficient to guarantee well-being and participation in digital societies. Overcoming second-level inequalities in awareness, skills, and content provision is essential.

From equality of digital opportunity to equality of socio-digital well-being

Let me recap how the study of digital inequalities has gained complexity and nuance in the last two decades. The approach illustrated in Figure X.1, reflects an increasing breadth in what are considered important inequalities in digital societies (see Figure 2.1 for earlier model). For all five domains of inequality, digital resources (access, skills, and engagement types) played slightly different roles. But no matter what domain a chapter grappled with, first-level (access) and second-level (skills and use types) inequalities influenced outcomes of digital engagement. This reflects the sequential nature of digital inequalities. It is easier to develop skills if you have access, and you engage more broadly when you are more literate. The digital world differs based on your starting point. We enter through different doors, so we differ in how we navigate different digital worlds and inhabit different digital spaces.

Each chapter illustrates how digital inequalities are compound as well as sequential. People are multiply disadvantaged across and within digital resource types. People are disconnected based on the quality, ubiquity, and autonomy of their access (Chapter 3). Those who lack the functional, technical skills often also lack the strategic, critical skills that allow them to navigate digital worlds to achieve their goals (Chapter 4). Finally, socio-digital inequalities express themselves in public and private digital spaces, in involved and low-cost forms of engagement, and in the production, promotion, and consumption of different types of content (Chapters 5–7). These sequential and compound processes can entrench disconnect in digital societies, making it difficult to escape a situation of disadvantage.

The lesson learned from sequential and compounded digital inequalities is that first-level (access), second-level (skills and engagement), and third-level (outcome) digital inequalities should always be studied and combatted together.

I want to make four critical side notes to the insights that existing research and policy have provided. First, in understanding and tackling these inequalities, certain aspects of access (i.e. speed), literacy (i.e. functional-technical skills), and engagement (i.e. public, involved interactions and professional content creation) are overemphasised. Important types of inequalities are overlooked, meaning we remain ignorant of significant barriers to participation in digital societies. For example, at the first level, people such as Ben (Chapter 3) have mobile but not high-quality and autonomous access. At the second level, there are people like Ana. They have critical literacy but lack functional skills (Chapter 4). Finally, people such as Priya (Chapter 5) engage actively within specific communities and activities but are pushed to the sidelines in others.

My second critique regards the prevailing assumption that equalities in digital opportunities (i.e. similar access, skills, and use) lead to equality of outcomes. This is not the case for any of the domains of inequalities. For example, Carol (Chapter 6) has access to tech and uses Instagram and WhatsApp, but is more likely to be bullied than her equally-connected peers.

Third, inequalities in well-being, rather than economic and functional outcomes, are not sufficiently considered by socio-digital inequalities scholars and practitioners.

My fourth critique is that social and digital inequalities should be studied as mutually constitutive (Chapter 2), continuously feeding from and flowing back into each other. Subsequently, I used the common sequential approach, which starts with traditional inequalities leading to access, skills, and uses, and finally to outcome inequalities. This linear thinking was hard to maintain, and is why in the revised model (Figure X.1) all arrows are double-sided. Use leads back into skills acquisition, higher skill levels lead to the acquisition of better access, and experiences lead to different types of use and skill development. The latter relationship is severely understudied.

From social to digital inequalities and back again

I have so far described different understandings of digital inequalities but have not touched on their social causes and consequences. Clearly, traditional socio-economic and socio-cultural inequalities continue to shape digital inequalities at all levels. Equality in access and skills is a long way off, complicating meritocratic ideals which require full diffusion of infrastructure and training to improve prospects for employment, income, and education. More disheartening is that, even in countries with few of these material resource barriers to connecting, well-being is not achieved for all. Here, I highlight three general principles for socio-digital inequality feedback loops using concepts of traditional inequalities.

First, as we move from well-researched economic, learning, and civic engagement inequalities into lesser-explored socio-digital inequalities, such as social interaction, belonging, and empowerment, factors other than class gain importance. Material, objective resources, such as wealth, occupation, and formal education, are important for access, functional skills, and economic domains of engagement. Yet, inequalities in embodied resources, such as socialisation into distinct tastes, norms, and values based on education, ethnic, gender, and other backgrounds, take prominence in relation to inequalities in strategic, critical literacy, and non-economic types of engagement.

Second, although amplification dominates, there are positive signs of normalisation and even leapfrogging of traditional inequalities. In informal social and civic types of engagement, once people overcome access and skills barriers, traditionally disadvantaged people, such as ethnic minorities, women, and disadvantaged youth, are likely to engage more with issues of public interest and establish community relationships. Consequentially, they often have positive subjective well-being outcomes. They feel heard and empowered, building social capital within the digital spaces they inhabit.

Third, in interactive public spaces, people who are vulnerable socially (i.e. low status) and personally (i.e. low self-esteem) are exposed to negative outcomes or harms from engaging. As a result, they are more likely to be silenced. Due to discriminatory practices, well-being outcomes – in terms of status and power to shape the public world – are unequally distributed and disadvantaged people desert these public socio-digital spaces. The result is that engagement by historically disadvantaged people becomes restricted to closed communities or follows stereotypical patterns in public.

> The final outcome of these feedback loops between social and first-, second-, and third-level digital inequalities is the amplification of inequalities in terms of symbolic capital (i.e. influence) and expansion of formal social capital (i.e. status).

An intersectional perspective is largely absent in socio-digital inequalities research, with some exceptions for inequalities in access and skills. Research that looks at either class, gender, ethnicity, or health dominates over research that considers how all these interact and together create different inequalities within digital societies. The emphasis on vertical inequalities between socio-demographic groups, or between regions with different 'developmental statuses', overlooks horizontal or compound inequalities within socio-demographic groups and regions. Many groups (e.g. women) and regions (e.g. the Global South) are treated as digitally homogeneous. In socio-digital inequalities research, a good example of this concerns the elderly. Older age is indeed a consistent predictor of lower levels of engagement. Nevertheless, combinations of economic precarity, deteriorating health, limited support networks, and lack of ICT experience help explain disengagement better than age alone. By focusing on generational differences, the impact of economic and personal resources within generations are ignored, leading to the wrong assumption that the problem will disappear as 'digital dinosaurs' die out.

I wove intersectional perspectives into the book. For example, employment and education disadvantages accumulate, making it harder for people to achieve positive economic outcomes from ICT use (Chapters 3 and 4). Ben's (Chapter 3) and Ana's (Chapter 4) vignettes illustrate how compound disadvantage in their personal and family resources affect their choices for jobs and continuing educating. Age, gender, and socio-economic background together determine levels of engagement with social issues, and how individuals' interests are valued within online civic forums (Chapter 5). Priya faces gender inequalities and ideological polarisation when using ICTs to engage with social issues, even when she is socio-economically privileged. Carol's (Chapter 6) and JunWen's (Chapter 7) experiences show how gender, ethnicity, sexual orientation, and social isolation work together in complex ways to determine who feels empowered, connected, and appreciated in digital societies.

Socio-digital inequalities are, in other words, complicated. These social intersections, compounded by multiple levels of digital disadvantage, are hard to disentangle. It would be easy to give up and think that nothing can be done about them. That is not what I advocate with this book! The socio-digital inequalities research presented is not a mere academic exercise. Rather, it leads us to potential solutions.

From causes and consequences to solutions

The approach taken to explaining socio-digital inequalities is important, because proposed solutions depend on how socio-digital inequalities are framed. Because much existing research is based in neoliberal, Marxist, or Bourdieusian principles, we have made headway in mapping out structural socio-digital inequalities rooted in wealth, capital, and class. Consequently, this led to prioritising certain consequences of socio-digital inequality (i.e. unemployment, poverty, physical health) and privileging specific solutions (i.e. market regulation, skills training, awareness campaigns). Let me briefly review some potential solutions based on the theory and evidence for individual micro-individual and macro-level drivers.

Individual, agentic, intrinsic, and motivation-based solutions

Even though I critique a pure equality of opportunity approach, it is undeniable that people need it to participate in society. To give people agency and choice to participate in digital societies, we must prioritise access, skills, and services for people who lack them. Seeing inequalities in wealth and capital as root causes of socio-digital inequalities translates into solutions such as free or subsidised infrastructure and devices with low connection costs (Chapter 3). When a lack of functional, strategic, or critical skills are regarded as the culprit, accessible and affordable training should be provided (Chapter 4). If there is an undersupply of fundamental services or content catering to particular people, regulation should be put in place to make them cognitively and physically accessible. These solutions – lowering barriers to entry into the digital world – suit neoliberal democracies aiming to achieve equality of opportunity through market competition and government regulation. This is easy for wealthy countries, but poorer countries also have initiatives where access is provided to poor households with varying levels of success. The reason some of these programmes failed is that they used top-down approaches without learning lessons from capabilities-based approaches. These demonstrate that working with local communities to learn what people need, in social and digital terms, is fundamental to making interventions effective.

> People are eager to take up online opportunities that are useful and gratifying to them, once they overcome first- and second-level access and skills barriers. This suggests individualistic and agentic interventions can be successful.

The analyses of subjective aspects of socio-digital inequalities shows that interventions for all areas – from access to skills to use – will only work if people consider the digital to be relevant to their everyday lives. That is, people need to be intrinsically motivated. Therefore, raising awareness about the benefits of ICT use is another way to confront digital inequalities. Here, the relativity of disadvantage becomes important, because intrinsic motivation to digitally engage is established when we compare our own situation to that of others. If people who have a high-end mobile phone, extensively engage in social networking, or use health tracker apps are completely different from us, we will not consider these activities relevant or attainable. Without this intrinsic motivation to overcome inequalities, people do not feel like they can change the situation, no matter how serious the disconnect seems to an outsider. They might instead accept socio-digital inequalities as given and justified. For example, people evaluate their skills as reasonable because they compare themselves to people like them, even if these are insufficient to find a job (Chapter 4). Or they evaluate their skill levels as low in comparison to someone of a different background, but accept these inequalities because they believe someone like them will never be skilled. Two examples from the book's vignettes are instructive. Priya feels that she should not engage in public discussions because she is an upper-caste, Hindi woman. Similarly, Ben does not see the point of buying a high-end phone, because he prefers hanging out with his friends at the pub and does not see them benefitting from having one.

> Public awareness campaigns and interventions trying to nudge people into the digital world should ensure that the people who demonstrate the risks and benefits of digital engagement are similar to the people they are trying to reach.

I am critical of the individualistic framing of interventions used in motivational public awareness campaigns and individual skills training. They put the onus on individuals to realise that they are disadvantaged and should engage. It creates the idea that, once knowledge and opportunities are available, engagement is a matter of individual choice and effort (Mummendey, Kessler, Klink, & Mielke, 1999). In other words, if people judge digitisation not to be for them, this should be accepted. This is where the bottom-up equality of opportunity approach becomes tricky, because it could lead to complacency with technological fixes. Once tablets have been handed out, skills training has been made available, and services pushed online, the job of policy makers is done. However, as shown in this book, systematic inequalities in outcomes of ICT use between people from different backgrounds remain given equal levels of individual motivation, access, skills, and use. This means that providing equality of these digital opportunities is essential but not sufficient to alleviate social inequalities. There must be other inequalities to address.

Structural, systemic, attitude-based solutions

Digitisation does not happen in a vacuum. ICTs are created and used in societies with long histories of norms and values that position people unequally. This means that the kinds of choices available to us are structurally restricted. That is, we are socialised into thinking and behaving in certain ways that allow us to function comfortably in society. As this book shows, the introduction of ICTs often amplifies these patterns because these processes are less visible or we are less conscious of them. Our digital preferences are adaptive, just like our social ones. If society continues to be sexist, racist, and ableist, interventions focusing on only changing the digital will not make a difference.

There is not enough awareness that individuals from certain backgrounds systematically have worse outcomes from digital engagement, which has little to do with their skills or motivation levels. More awareness of the structural socio-cultural and socio-economic inequalities that underpin these differences in outcomes is needed for real societal change. One example is the classist and gendered perception and socialisation about digital literacy. For example, programmes focusing on teaching disadvantaged youth digital skills, such as uploading CVs, does not help if the labour market is biased against them or online job-seeking platforms are not designed in ways that allow them to demonstrate their skills

(Chapter 4). Carol might get passed over for jobs because employers inaccurately assume, as a woman from Manaus, that she does not have the digital skills needed. If this was more widely understood, women's rights campaigners would be on the case, for example, making this type of discrimination part of women and human rights and equal employment rights campaigns. Another example is who becomes popular on and listened to on social and entertainment media. JunWen is not popular on gaming platforms and his music does not appear under recommendations because his creations conform to neither stereotypes around masculinity nor 'gay appropriate' behaviour. Awareness could lead to a #YoureSoHeteroNormative campaign being set up to make us realise how we are perpetuating discrimination in digital spaces. Chapters 6 and 7 suggest that communicators, consumers, and creators can generate social change by shining a light on the ways we behave online.

The burden of responsibility to be 'positively connected' thus lies not with isolated individuals, but with civil society and social institutions. Inequalities in digital societies not based on tangible things such as access or technical skills have been off the radar of those fighting for the rights of vulnerable and disadvantaged groups. If their offline work starts to embrace the digital realm as intimately interlinked with the wider issues they are looking at, their campaigns for justice will be more effective. Awareness must be created that digital inequalities exacerbate the non-digital inequalities that governing bodies, third sector, and commercial sector organisations are trying to tackle. Civil society needs to become more aware of how certain technological designs and affordances can exacerbate inequalities. Similarly, corporate social responsibility policies should always include a commitment to creating digitally-equal spaces and taking responsibility if the design of their digital products and services leads to inequalities in people's well-being.

Missing data mean missing solutions

We need three types of data that are currently missing to make targeted and effective evidence-based interventions at the micro or macro level possible. First, research is still descriptive and economistic, rather than theoretically and socially grounded. We know who lacks access, skills, or engagement, but cannot explain why they do not, even when economic barriers are removed. Improving digital resources does not tackle the underlying structural issues that cause the unequal distribution of resources. For socio-digital inequalities that are lower on the policy agenda, such as everyday content creation and social and civic participation, we lack basic data on inequalities, let alone the solutions that are essential to shaping our future digital worlds. Second, a lack of longitudinal research that examines relationships between a variety of traditional and digital inequalities means that we do not know which inequalities are getting worse and which inequalities are getting better, let alone why. Third, most research, especially that which goes beyond access, comes from the Global North. In the Global North, gender, ethnicity, class, and health are likely to intersect for digital as much as social inequalities. In Priya's India, religion in combination with gender and caste is likely to shape people's access to and engagement with ICTs.

In JunWen's China, sexuality, family structure, and location might be more important. Yet, because of a lack of research on the Global South, we do not know whether observed patterns are universal or which aspects are important in shaping socio-digital inequalities across different contexts.

Notwithstanding these limitations of the evidence available, we can still draw conclusions about what effective and high-quality interventions and policy look like. Sustainable solutions to tackling systematic inequalities in socio-economic, socio-cultural, and personal well-being as a result of digitisation must be implemented at the same level as the cause of the problem. To achieve full participation in digital societies, this means changing underlying economic and socio-cultural structures through collective action, while simultaneously providing individuals with the digital resources that they might lack.

Three futures: Digital inequalities in research, practice, and technology

Socio-digital inequalities research and practice has wised up to the idea that disadvantage is multidimensional, sequential, compound, and interlaced with existing inequalities. This is a welcome development. Nevertheless, there is more to be done to improve our understanding and ability to combat inequalities in future digital societies. This requires rethinking our approaches to research, redesigning policy and practice, and pre-empting the potential impact of new ICTs that are sneaking into everyday life.

The missing middle: Rethinking inequalities research in socio-digital ecology terms

When scholars and practitioners explain why some people are less likely to fully engage with ICTs, they take individual characteristics as the start and end point of analyses. They assume that stable features such as socio-economic or socio-cultural characteristics consistently influence how individuals engage with ICTs. Very few examine how our kaleidoscope of everyday interactions and relationships influence how we see our digital selves and the world around us, or how we change as we move from one environment to the next.

The issue is that people do not live in society or in isolation with purely individual needs and abilities. Rather, we all live within specific relationships and environments. National regulatory and cultural landscapes are the most abstract, and there is little comparative research into how they influence socio-digital inequalities. More striking is the lack of consistent theorisation around how the characteristics of the people around us, and of the neighbourhoods and households that we work and live in, shape inequalities.

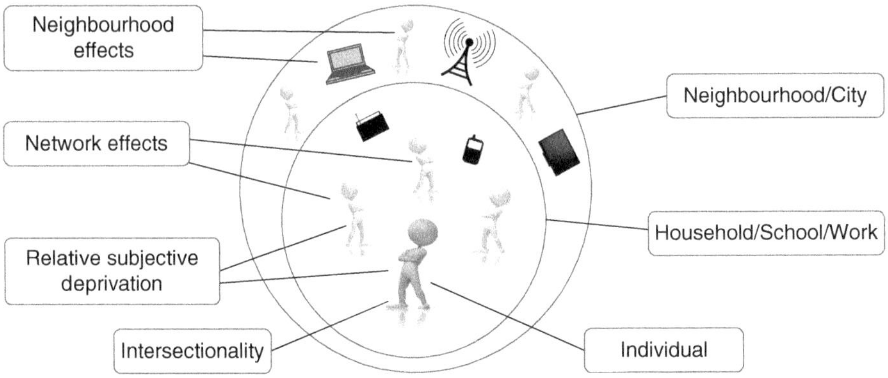

Figure X.2 Illustration of socio-ecological theories and meso-contextual levels of analysis

Note: Each context consists of individuals (with behaviours, norms, and values) and material objects/infrastructures.

These meso- and community-level causes – explored in the traditional inequalities literature – shape socio-digital inequalities more than macro-structural or micro-personal characteristics. I have already discussed why our lack of understanding of who we compare ourselves with determines whether our digital engagement is problematic. Here, I pick up on structuration-based ecological frameworks from traditional inequalities literature (Chapter 1) that have not been extensively used to study socio-digital inequalities (Figure X.2).

These socio-digital ecology approaches are derived from life-course, network, neighbourhood effects, and domestication studies. Their combination allows for hypotheses about how our daily experiences shape people's digital resources and their disposition to change socio-digitally unequal societies. In the DiSTO studies, we are using them to explain why things like poverty, education, gender, and personality relate to digital inequalities in different ways for different people in different countries and neighbourhoods (see Helsper, 2017b, 2019b; Helsper, 2021).

Life-course studies and structuration

In inequalities research, the life-course approach recognises social structuration based on general societal inequalities. Yet, they add the idea of biographical structuration that can exacerbate or ameliorate these structural processes (Schafer, Ferraro, & Mustillo, 2011). The main idea is that childhood and young adult experiences determine how characteristics of a person and their household express themselves in disadvantage throughout their lifetime. Experiences and characteristics often accumulate in negative ways for disadvantaged people, making them feel helpless in the face of new challenges. On the other hand, early positive experiences can lift people out of desperate situations and give them confidence to overcome challenges. Early childhood experiences thus structure our agency – how we adapt our preferences and expectations to fit the realities we have grown up in. How someone interprets experiences in the digital world, and whether they think they should change their digital resources and habits, is going to depend on these earlier experiences. This book hints at the importance of early childhood experiences shaping self- and social esteem and later interactions with others online for disadvantaged teens and people like Carol (Chapter 6). Ben's experience of rejection from an early age means he sees a lack of response from online employers as a confirmation that it does not matter what he does, giving up further attempts at finding a job online (Chapter 3). Thus, our understanding of why people might not engage positively in digital societies could benefit from life-course approaches.

Networks, neighbourhoods, and households shaping dispositions through extrinsic motivation

There is a group of ecological theories that focuses on how our social and physical environments shape our ability to change unequal societies. These theories have core principles, such as homogeneity/diversity, hierarchy/power structures, and mobility, which are not fully understood or applied in socio-digital inequalities research. Yet, there are hints of their importance in existing research around inequalities in digital support networks, between neighbourhoods, and in household dynamics.

Network effects research examines how people around us influence our dispositions and behaviours. Rather than who we are and what our characteristics are, it is the characteristics of the people we interact with and relate to that shape what we do and think. These extrinsic motivators mean that people with the same characteristics acquire different digital skills and engagement patterns, and have different outcomes, because they are part of social networks with different structures and norms, and not because they are demographically different (Van Dijk, 2020). This book hinted at how, in collectivist cultures, influence from close networks might dominate (e.g. Carol in Brazil, Priya in India, JunWen in China). People in more individualistic cultures might experience more pressure from friends and influencers (e.g. Ben in the UK, Ana in the US). This underexplored area of research could explain who is most likely to drive change in others.

Equally unexplored are basic network theory concepts such as the externalities and homogeneity of networks, and how they influence our digital habits and values (DiMaggio & Garip, 2012). It is very likely that if people in your network are digitally well resourced and engaged, you are more likely to be too. In Ben's network, only two people have a latest model smartphone, while only two people in JunWen's network do not. Due to these externalities, mobile digital skills, activities, and understandings will spread much more quickly in JunWen's network. Resources, behaviours, and beliefs also spread more quickly in networks that are homogeneous, or are made of individuals with similar characteristics. We know that networks of disadvantaged people tend to be more digitally homogeneous, with fewer resources and expertise (Helsper & Van Deursen, 2017). In addition, if these networks are culturally homogeneous and socially close, people with few resources are less likely to be connected than people in heterogeneous, dispersed networks.

From social geography come neighbourhood effects approaches that theorise how differences in the characteristics of everyday living environments lead to inequalities in resources and dispositions between neighbourhoods and regions. These neighbourhoods create 'landscapes of opportunities for action' through infrastructure, service provision, and behaviours displayed in them (Sampson, 2017). In digital inequalities research, the infrastructure part has been taken up by researchers studying inequalities within large, unequal metropolitan urban areas (Chapter 3). Most of this research focuses on infrastructure, access, and inequalities in economic outcomes, rather than literacy, use, and other resource domains (Helsper, 2019b).

Rarely are key neighbourhood effects principles, such as segregation and mobility, applied in this research. Researchers prefer to describe average socio-economic and socio-demographic neighbourhood characteristics. In the DiSTO heatmap studies, evidence is emerging that segregation into ethnically, professionally, and financially homogeneous neighbourhoods without much mobility or interaction between residents of these different areas entrenches intra-city inequalities. In homogeneous white neighbourhoods with higher digital literacy and ICT-positive, techno-utopian dispositions, small tech businesses are more likely to appear (Mossberger et al., 2021). This results in a concentration of digital infrastructure, skills, and learning opportunities in wealthier, more highly educated neighbourhoods. If a person who is lower-educated and poor lives in these neighbourhoods – or if they are mobile and move through these neighbourhoods – they are more likely to be aware of disparities and become digitally savvy and engaged than when they live in a less digitised neighbourhood.

Domestication approaches theorise how ICT dispositions and behaviours are shaped and consolidated within smaller ecologies (Chapter 2). They describe a four-step process where households or organisations adopt technologies through continuous negotiation about the appropriate use and value of ICTs among inhabitants (Haddon, 2011). Network and neighbourhood effects theories predict which broader social and physical environments facilitate the development, growth, and acceleration of positive digital dispositions among the people who live, study, and work in these spaces (DiMaggio & Garip, 2012; Mossberger et al., 2021).

Together, these ecological frameworks allow us to understand the ideal circumstances that empower people to make informed decisions about whether to engage and how to achieve positive outcomes from digitisation.

Collective action: Rethinking policy and practice

These ideal circumstances, theorised through socio-digital ecology theories, can be enabled through policy and practices that create collective action, instigating change from the bottom up. The close-knit nature of networks of many disadvantaged people can be turned into a policy and intervention advantage. In these networks, small changes among well-connected, influential people have knock-on effects for all others in the networks. This means identifying influencers and designing interventions for local communities and requires an understanding of the hierarchies, norms, and values that circulate within these particular collectives. Not understanding these principles can lead to potentially beneficial outcomes of courses or public awareness campaigns being undone by more influential private interactions or community environments that reject these norms or display different behaviours.

Ecological theories suggest that the visibility of technology and infrastructures shapes our dispositions and practices around ICTs. When we live in neighbourhoods and work in offices where technology is embedded in every café, shop, school, and workplace – and people are seen to be engaging with ICTs – we are more likely to connect ourselves. If we live in an environment where technologies are invisible or where the majority of people like us are not using ICTs in clear, beneficial ways, we are less likely to perceive digital engagement as important. If, besides rolling out infrastructure and providing skills training, interventions embed technologies in and stimulate the practices of residents, they can generate change. This change will happen among those who live in and move between these spaces, with spill-over effects for those who are not directly exposed to technology. This requires understanding what important collective spaces are, what they look like, and working with residents to promote positive engagement.

Since early childhood role models and environments have knock-on effects for digital dispositions, skills, and behaviours later in life, this is where interventions can be effective and have lasting impacts. More should be done to create positive socio-digital environments for the youngest, without assuming they are all digital natives. Adults should not be forgotten, although we know that interventions mostly benefit those who have experienced empowerment early on despite being disadvantaged. For people who have suffered compound disadvantage and have had negative childhood experiences, having positive smaller digital experiences and general confidence-building should precede any digital intervention focusing on skills and broad engagement.

In all of this, it is important to remember that people's social and physical spaces are shaped by historical processes. Disadvantage is concentrated not only in people, but also in networks and locations. Local socio-digital ecologies are often manifestations of unequal systems and histories. This benefits interventions, because networks, neighbourhoods, and households are easier to change than society at large or isolated individuals. Creating awareness and behaviour change at this meso-level is effective, powerful, and long-lasting. Benefits accrue not just for the individuals who make up these collectives, but also by alleviating structural injustices. If we are confronted in our everyday lives with the fact that digital opportunities and social outcomes of digitisation are unequally distributed, then questions will be asked. Resistance will be more likely and structural change might be demanded.

> The digital future starts in a network or neighbourhood near us. How we use ICTs impacts not only our own lives, but also those of future generations and others in less fortunate positions. We are collectively responsible for making constructive contributions.

The digital future is invisible: Pre-empting inequalities in virtual societies

Our digital societies of the future are likely to be different from the ones we have barely got used to. This raises questions about whether the evidence and experiences we have gathered can be applied in the rapidly advancing world of invisible, embedded technologies such as the Internet of Things, artificial intelligence, and virtual and augmented reality (VR and AR). Will we have to start all over again? After reading this book, it should be clear that my answer is a resounding: No! I have argued that up until now we have only started to tap into the wealth that traditional inequalities research has to offer to help us to understand our current situation better. These theories will remain useful, no matter how extraordinary the future turns out to be. Let's recognise the new, but not be blinded by it.

The greatest risk is repeating the techno-utopianism that we have seen following the introduction of each new technology. Rather than creating level playing fields, emerging research suggests that people who are traditionally disadvantaged feel uncomfortable and unwelcome in developing digital spaces such as VR and AR, in ways that have nothing to do with a lack of skill or quality access (Outlaw, 2019).

However, we also should not get lost in ungrounded moral panics. We will not disappear into completely virtual worlds. Our own physicality – our need to eat, drink, sleep, and love in physical places – ties us to this analogue planet. If anything, the COVID-19 crisis has shown that the desire to hug loved ones and engage in face-to-face discussion is, in many ways, preferable to virtual connections and meetings. Nevertheless, we have become so used to ICTs that we do not question them. In the future, our brick and mortar world will increasingly intermingle with bits and bytes, the digital indistinguishable from organic and physical matter. This book has shown how the digital and the social are already difficult to separate, and this will be increasingly true. Ironically, this means that the social will be the most important site of intervention in invisibly digital societies. If certain people are systematically not benefitting or experiencing harms, we will have to make changes to the social processes that push digitisation to lead to these outcomes.

The reason why I use the term 'digital engagement' rather than 'ICT use' throughout this book is to counter a tendency for technologies to be embedded and invisible. We engage with them, but they seemingly function independently from our use. They exist in the background, animated by our voices and shaped by our behavioural inputs, outside our awareness. The inequalities in passive, low-cost types of engagement should be a warning (Chapter 7). They threaten a future where our access and technical skills will be less important than our awareness of how algorithms shape unequal experiences. We will have to make conscious decisions about when and how to contribute, not only for ourselves, but also for others. The ability to decide not to use ICTs is already unequally distributed; 'digital detoxes' are the privilege of the few who will not lose their jobs, social benefits, or support networks if they disconnect. As we move to digital societies, these power differentials are likely to become worse.

We must remember that ICTs do not come out of nowhere; they are designed, adapted, and adopted by humans. We need to take control over and accept our responsibility in shaping the digital future. Every move we make and thought we express when connected has an impact on what the digital world will look like in the future. Certain people, likely those reading this book, are more likely to be designing these algorithms, which pick up on certain things as normal and desirable. The digital world of the future will be shaped in their image.

Concluding remarks

Digital societies will not become equitable until traditional socio-economic and socio-cultural inequalities are tackled. Nor will we stop the amplification of existing inequalities unless we consider the impact of an unequal distribution of digital resources (i.e. access, literacy, and engagement types). Only by considering evidence from both sides – by improving social and digital inequalities – will we be able to design policies, interventions, and campaigns that cultivate a more just future. This means that digital opportunity – in the sense of affordable access and high skill levels and a diversity of content and services – is essential, but not sufficient for equality in well-being in digital societies. If societies are fundamentally unequal, and some have more power than others to shape their own and others' lives, and if people are socialised to accept the unequal status quo, then digital opportunity will still mean an unjust social reality.

This book on disconnect has shown that socio-digital inequalities cannot be understood by simply looking at personal merit or motivation. Individual skills training and awareness raising around the opportunities and risks that digital engagement provides leads to short-term change for that person, but will not deal with systemic issues – thus amplifying societal inequalities. That inequalities in non-material outcomes, such as civic participation, well-being, and status, are more unequally distributed and harder to tackle through techno-centric interventions seems to play into the hands of socio-constructivist pessimists. It is easy to put our heads in our hands and laments that things can only get worse. Nevertheless, there are exceptions that hint at how ICTs have helped people overcome entrenched disadvantages. There must be a middle road between blaming the victim and blaming the system for inequalities in increasingly digital societies. The evidence shows that neither perspective will help bring about real lasting change.

We need a change of perspective in socio-digital inequalities research and practice. We should design research and interventions around lived realities, where individual characteristics and structural factors that shape disadvantage come together. Inequalities in digital societies manifest through our everyday actions in digital and social spaces. I hope this book raises awareness of how our everyday behaviours, beliefs, institutions, and practices contribute to systematic inequalities in digital societies. Not all is despair. The fact that we all play a role in shaping socio-digital environments also means that we can collectively create a more just socio-digital future. The equality of this future depends on generating awareness about the causes and consequences of socio-digital inequalities and modifying our own digital practices.

REFERENCES

Abbas, R., & Mesch, G. (2018). Do rich teens get richer? Facebook use and the link between offline and online social capital among Palestinian youth in Israel. *Information Communication & Society, 21*(1), 63–79. doi:10.1080/1369118x.2016.1261168

Accominotti, F. (2008). Marché et hiérarchie: La structure sociale des décisions de production dans un marché culturel. *Histoire & Mesure, 23*(2), 177–218. Retrieved from www.jstor.org/stable/24566814

Alper, M., Katz, V. S., & Schofield Clark, L. (2016). Researching children, intersectionality, and diversity in the digital age. *Journal of Children and Media, 10*(1), 107–114. doi:10.1080/17482798.2015.1121886

Alzouma, G. (2005). Myths of digital technology in Africa: Leapfrogging development? *Global Media and Communication, 1*(3), 339–356. doi:10.1177/1742766505058128

American Psychiatric Association. (2017). Internet gaming. Retrieved from www.psychiatry.org/patients-families/internet-gaming

Ames, M. G. (2019). *The charisma machine: The life, death, and legacy of one laptop per child.* Cambridge, MA: MIT Press.

Amichai-Hamburger, Y., Kaplan, H., & Dorpatcheon, N. (2008). Click to the past: The impact of extroversion by users of nostalgic websites on the use of Internet social services. *Computers in Human Behavior, 24*(5), 1907–1912. doi:10.1016/j.chb.2008.02.005

Amichai-Hamburger, Y., McKenna, K. Y. A., & Tal, S.-A. (2008). E-empowerment: Empowerment by the Internet. *Computers in Human Behavior, 24*(5), 1776–1789. doi:10.1016/j.chb.2008.02.002

Anderson, M. (2018). *About a quarter of rural Americans say access to high-speed internet is a major problem.* Washington, DC: Pew Research Center. Retrieved from www.pewresearch.org/fact-tank/2018/09/10/about-a-quarter-of-rural-americans-say-access-to-high-speed-internet-is-a-major-problem/

Aneez, Z., Neyazi, T. A., Kalogeropoulos, A., & Kleis Nielsen, R. (2019). *India Digital News Report 2019.* Oxford: Oxford University Press. Retrieved from https://reutersinstitute.politics.ox.ac.uk/sites/default/files/2019-03/India_DNR_FINAL.pdf

Annenberg Centre for the Digital Future. (2020). *Digital Future Project.* Los Angeles (CA). Retrieved from www.digitalcenter.org/

Araque, J. C., Maiden, R. P., Bravo, N., Estrada, I., Evans, R., Hubchik, K., … Reddy, M. (2013). Computer usage and access in low-income urban communities. *Computers in Human Behavior, 29*(4), 1393–1401. doi:10.1016/j.chb.2013.01.032

Archer, M. S. (2010). Morphogenesis versus structuration: on combining structure and action. *British Journal of Sociology, 61*(s1), 225–252. doi:10.1111/j.1468-4446.2009.01245.x

Arora, P. (2012). The leisure divide: Can the 'Third World' come out to play? *Information Development, 28*(2), 93–101. doi:10.1177/0266666911433607

Atkinson, A. B. (2015). *Inequality: What can be done?* Cambridge, MA: Harvard University Press.

Bagozzi, R. P. (2007). The legacy of the technology acceptance model and a proposal for a paradigm shift. *Journal of the Association for Information Systems, 8*(4), 12. Retrieved from https://aisel.aisnet.org/jais/vol8/iss4/12

Banaji, S. (2017). *Children and media in India: Narratives of class, agency and social change.* New York: Routledge.

Banaji, S., & Moreno-Almeida, C. (2019). Politicising participatory culture at the margins: The significance of class, gender and online media for the practices of youth networks in the MENA region. *Global Media and Communication.* Retrieved from http://eprints.lse.ac.uk/101475/

Banks, M. (2017). *Creative justice: Cultural industries, work and inequality.* London: Rowman & Littlefield.

Barberá, P., Wang, N., Bonneau, R., Jost, J. T., Nagler, J., Tucker, J., & González-Bailón, S. (2015). The critical periphery in the growth of social protests. *Plos One, 10*(11), e0143611. doi:10.1371/journal.pone.0143611

Barker, R. G. (1968). *Ecological psychology: Concepts and methods for studying the environment of human behavior.* Stanford, CA: Stanford University Press.

Baym, N. K. (2015). *Personal connections in the digital age* (2nd ed.). Cambridge, UK: Polity Press.

Beane, J. A. (1997). *Curriculum integration: Designing the core of democratic education.* Williston, VT: Teachers College Press.

Bechmann, A. (2019). Inequality in posting behaviour over time: A study of Danish Facebook users. *Nordicom Review, 40*(s1), 31–49. doi:10.2478/nor-2019-0012

Bennett, W. L., & Segerberg, A. (2012). The logic of connective action. *Information, Communication & Society, 15*(5), 739–768. doi:10.1080/1369118X.2012.670661

Bishop, S. (2018). Anxiety, panic and self-optimization: Inequalities and the YouTube algorithm. *Convergence: The International Journal of Research into New Media Technologies, 24*(1), 69–84. doi:10.1177/1354856517736978

Blank, G. (2013). Who creates content? Stratification and content creation on the Internet. *Information Communication & Society, 16*(4), 590–612. doi:10.1080/1369118x.2013.777758

Blank, G. (2016). The digital divide among Twitter users and its implications for social research. *Social Science Computer Review, 35*(6), 679–697. doi:10.1177/0894439316671698

Blank, G., Dutton, W. H., & Lefkowitz, J. (2020). *Oxis 2019: Digital divides in Britain are narrowing but deepening.* Oxford: Oxford University Press. Retrieved from https://oxis.oii.ox.ac.uk/blog/digital-divides-in-britain-are-narrowing-but-deepening/

Blank, G., & Groselj, D. (2014). Dimensions of Internet use: Amount, variety, and types. *Information Communication & Society, 17*(4), 417–435. doi:10.1080/1369118x.2014.889189

Boase, J., & Wellman, B. (2006). Personal relationships: On and off the Internet. In A. L. Vangelisti & D. Perlman (Eds.), *The Cambridge handbook of interpersonal relationships* (pp. 709–726). Cambridge: Cambridge University Press.

Bolin, G. (2012). The labour of media use. *Information, Communication & Society, 15*(6), 796–814. doi:10.1080/1369118X.2012.677052

Bossert, W., D'Ambrosio, C., & Peragine, V. (2007). Deprivation and social exclusion. *Economica, 74*(296), 777–803.

Boulianne, S. (2016). Online news, civic awareness, and engagement in civic and political life. *New Media & Society, 18*(9), 1840–1856. doi:10.1177/1461444815616222

Boulianne, S. (2019). Revolution in the making? Social media effects across the globe. *Information Communication & Society, 22*(1), 39–54. doi:10.1080/1369118x.2017.1353641

Bourdieu, P. (1986). The forms of capital. In J. C. Richards (Ed.), *Handbook of theory and research for sociology of education* (pp. 241–258). New York: Greenwood Press.

Bourdieu, P. (1990). Structures, habitus, practices. In P. Bourdieu (Ed.), *The logic of practice* (pp. 52–79). Stanford, CA: Stanford University Press.

Bourdieu, P. (2010). *Distinction: A social critique of the judgement of taste.* London: Routledge.

boyd, d. (2012). White flight in networked publics? How race and class shaped American teen engagement with MySpace and Facebook. In L. Nakamura & P. A. Chow-White (Eds.), *Race after the internet* (pp. 203–222). NewYork: Routledge.

Bozkurt, A., Honeychurch, S., Singh, L., & Koutropoulos, A. (2017). Learners on the periphery: Lurkers as invisible learners. *European Journal of Open, Distance and E-Learning, 20*(1), 191–211. doi:10.1515/eurodl-2017-0012

Brake, D. R. (2014). Are we all online content creators now? Web 2.0 and digital divides. *Journal of Computer-Mediated Communication, 19*(3), 591–609. doi:10.1111/jcc4.12042

Bronfenbrenner, U. (1979). *The ecology of human development: Experiments by nature and design.* Cambridge, MA: Presidents of Harvard College.

Broos, A., & Roe, K. (2006). The digital divide in the playstation generation: Self-efficacy, locus of control and ICT adoption among adolescents. *Poetics, 34*(4–5), 306–317. doi:10.1016/j.poetic.2006.05.002

Bruns, A. (2019). *Filter Bubbles and Echo Chambers: Debunking the Myths.* Cambridge, UK: Polity

Buchanan, S., & Tuckerman, L. (2016). The information behaviours of disadvantaged and disengaged adolescents. *Journal of Documentation, 72*(3), 527–548. doi:10.1108/JD-05-2015-0060

Buchi, M., Festic, N., & Latzer, M. (2018). How social well-being is affected by digital inequalities. *International Journal of Communication, 12,* 3686–3706. Retrieved from https://ijoc.org/index.php/ijoc/article/view/8780

Buchi, M., Just, N., & Latzer, M. (2016). Modeling the second-level digital divide: A five-country study of social differences in Internet use. *New Media & Society, 18*(11), 2703–2722. doi:10.1177/1461444815604154

Buckingham, D. (2005). *Media education: Literacy, learning and contemporary culture.* Cambridge, UK: Polity Press.

Buckingham, D. (2007). Digital media literacies: Rethinking media education in the age of the Internet. *Research in Comparative and International Education, 2*(1), 43–55. doi:10.2304/rcie.2007.2.1.43

Buglass, S. L., Binder, J. F., Betts, L. R., & Underwood, J. D. M. (2017). Motivators of online vulnerability: The impact of social network site use and FOMO. *Computers in Human Behavior, 66,* 248–255. doi:10.1016/j.chb.2016.09.055

Burchardt, T., & Hick, R. (2018). Inequality, advantage and the capability approach. *Journal of Human Development and Capabilities, 19*(1), 38–52. doi:10.1080/19452829.2017.1395396

Burke, P. J., & Briggs, A. (2001). *A social history of the media.* Cambridge, UK: Polity Press.

Byrne, D. (2005). *Social exclusion.* New York: Open University Press.

Byrne, D. (2008). The future of (the) 'race': Identity, discourse and the rise of computer-mediated public spheres. In A. Everett (Ed.), *Learning race and ethnicity: Youth and digital media.* (pp. 15–38). Cambridge, MA: MIT Press.

Byrne, J., Kardefelt-Winther, D., Livingstone, S., & Stoilova, M. (2016). *Global Kids Online research synthesis, 2015–2016*. Retrieved from: www.globalkidsonline.net/synthesis

Cabinet Office, & Government Digital Services. (2012). *Digital efficiency report*. London: Cabinet Office. Retrieved from www.gov.uk/government/publications/digital-efficiency-report/digital-efficiency-report

Camerini, A. L., Schulz, P. J., & Jeannet, A. M. (2018). The social inequalities of Internet access, its use, and the impact on children's academic performance: Evidence from a longitudinal study in Switzerland. *New Media & Society, 20*(7), 2489–2508. doi:10.1177/1461444817725918

Cammaerts, B. (2018). *The circulation of anti-austerity protest*. London: Palgrave Macmillan.

Carpentier, N. (2015). Differentiating between access, interaction and participation. *Conjunctions: Transdisciplinary Journal of Cultural Participation, 2*(2), 7–28. doi:10.7146/tjcp.v2i2.23117

Carstensen, T. (2009). Gender trouble in Web 2.0: Gender perspectives on social network sites, wikis and weblogs. *International Journal of Science Gender and Technology, 1*(1), 18. Retrieved from http://genderandset.open.ac.uk/index.php/genderandset/article/view/18

Casemajor, N., Couture, S., Delfin, M., Goerzen, M., & Delfanti, A. (2015). Non-participation in digital media: Toward a framework of mediated political action. *Media, Culture & Society, 37*(6), 850–866. doi:10.1177/0163443715584098

Caspi, A., Houts, R. M., Belsky, D. W., Harrington, H., Hogan, S., Ramrakha, S., Poulton, R., & Moffitt, T. E. (2016). Childhood forecasting of a small segment of the population with large economic burden. *Nature Human Behaviour, 1*(1), 5. doi:10.1038/s41562-016-0005

Castells, M. (2000). Towards a sociology of the Network Society. *Contemporary Sociology, 29*(5), 693–699. doi:10.2307/2655234

Castells, M. (2013). *Communication power* (2nd ed.). Oxford: Oxford University Press.

CEBR. (2018). *The economic impact of Digital Inclusion in the UK: A report for Good Things Foundation*. London: CEBR. Retrieved from www.goodthingsfoundation.org/sites/default/files/research-publications/the_economic_impact_of_digital_inclusion_in_the_uk_final_submission_stc_0.pdf

CGI.br. (2019). *Analise dos resultados domicilios 2018 In Pesquisa sobre o uso das Tecnologias de Informação e Comunicação nos domicílios brasileiros -TIC Domicílios 2018* [*ICT Households Survey on the Use of Information and Communication Technologies in Brazilian Households*] (pp. 101–252). Sao Paolo, Brazil: Núcleo de Informação e Coordenação do Ponto BR.

Chakravarty, S. R., & D'Ambrosio, C. (2006). The measurement of social exclusion. *Review of Income and Wealth, 52*(3), 377–398.

Chattoo, C. B. (2018). Oscars so white: Gender, racial, and ethnic diversity and social issues in US documentary films (2008–2017). *Mass Communication and Society, 21*(3), 368–394. doi:10.1080/15205436.2017.1409356

Chen, W. H., Lee, K. H., Straubhaar, J. D., & Spence, J. (2014). Getting a second opinion: Social capital, digital inequalities, and health information repertoires. *Journal of the Association for Information Science and Technology, 65*(12), 2552–2563. doi:10.1002/asi.23130

Chess, S., & Shaw, A. (2015). A conspiracy of fishes, or, how we learned to stop worrying about #GamerGate and embrace hegemonic masculinity. *Journal of Broadcasting & Electronic Media, 59*(1), 208–220. doi:10.1080/08838151.2014.999917

Cho, J., Gil de Zúñiga, H., Rojas, H., & Shah, D. v. (2003). Beyond access: The digital divide and Internet uses and gratifications. *IT & Society, 1*(4), 46–72. Retrieved from www.stanford.edu/group/siqss/itandsociety/v01i04/v01i04a05.pdf

Christensen, H. S. (2011). Political activities on the Internet: Slacktivism or political participation by other means? *First Monday, 16*(2). doi:10.5210/fm.v16i2.3336

Clarke, A. Y., & McCall, L. (2013). Intersectionality and social explanation in social science research. *Du Bois Review-Social Science Research on Race, 10*(2), 349–363. doi:10.1017/s1742058x13000325

Cohen, G. A. (1995). The Pareto argument for inequality. *Social Philosophy and Policy, 12*(1), 160–185. doi:10.1017/S026505250000460X

Cohen, G. A. (2008). *Rescuing justice and equality*. Cambridge, MA: Harvard University Press.

Cole, H., & Griffiths, M. D. (2007). Social interactions in massively multiplayer online role-playing gamers. *Cyberpsychology & Behavior, 10*(4), 575–583. doi:10.1089/cpb.2007.9988

Coleman, J. S. (1990). *Foundations of social theory*. Cambridge, MA: Harvard University Press.

Collins, P. H. (2015). Intersectionality's definitional dilemmas. *Annual Review of Sociology, 41*, 1–20. doi:10.1146/annurev-soc-073014-112142

Condor, C. N. Q., Rojas, J. J. O., & Ccora, C. R. Q. (2019). Analysis of a One Laptop Per Child program in educational institutions in exclusion and poverty zones: Peru case. *Revista Iberoamericana De Educacion, 79*(1), 71–95. doi:10.35362/rie7913391

Conor, B., Gill, R., & Taylor, S. (2015). Gender and creative labour. *Sociological Review, 63*, 1–22. doi:10.1111/1467-954x.12237

Cooper, M. N. (2010). Broadband in America: A policy of neglect is not benign. In *Networking and Telecommunications: Concepts, Methodologies, Tools, and Applications* (pp. 990–1017). Hershey, PA: Information Resources Management Association.

Correa, T. (2010). The participation divide among 'Online Experts': Experience, skills and psychological factors as predictors of college students' web content creation. *Journal of Computer-Mediated Communication, 16*(1). doi:10.1111/j.1083-6101.2010.01532.x

Correa, T. (2016). Digital skills and social media use: How Internet skills are related to different types of Facebook use among 'digital natives'. *Information Communication & Society, 19*(8), 1095–1107. doi:10.1080/1369118x.2015.1084023

Correa, T., Hinsley, A. W., & de Zúñiga, H. G. (2010). Who interacts on the Web? The intersection of users' personality and social media use. *Computers in Human Behavior, 26*(2), 247–253. doi:10.1016/j.chb.2009.09.003

Correa, T., & Jeong, S. H. (2011). Race and online content creation. *Information, Communication & Society, 14*(5), 638–659. doi:10.1080/1369118X.2010.514355

Cote, J. E., & Levine, C. G. (2002). *Identity, formation, agency, and culture*. Mahwah, NJ: Lawrence Earlbaum.

Couldry, N., Fotopoulou, A., & Dickens, L. (2016). Real social analytics: A contribution towards a phenomenology of a digital world. *The British Journal of Sociology, 67*(1), 118–137. doi:10.1111/1468-4446.12183

Crenshaw, K. W. (1991). Mapping the margins: Intersectionality, identity politics, and violence against women of color. *Stanford Law Review, 43*(6), 1241–1299. doi:10.2307/1229039

Cristia, J., Ibarrarán, P., Cueto, S., Santiago, A., & Severín, E. (2017). Technology and child development: Evidence from the One Laptop per Child program. *American Economic Journal: Applied Economics, 9*(3), 295–320. doi:10.1257/app.20150385

Cross, J. (2007). *Informal learning: Rediscovering the natural pathways that inspire innovation and performance*. San Francisco, CA: Pfeiffer/John Wiley & Sons.

Cummings, J. N., & Kraut, R. (2002). Domesticating computers and the Internet. *Information Society, 18*(3), 221–231. doi:10.1080/01972240290074977

D'Haenens, L., & Ogan, C. (2013). Internet-using children and digital inequality: A comparison between majority and minority Europeans. *Communications-European Journal of Communication Research, 38*(1), 41–60. doi:10.1515/commun-2013-0003

Dahlgren, P. (2002). In search of the talkative public: Media, deliberative democracy and civic culture. *Javnost-the Public, 9*(3), 5–25. doi:10.1080/13183222.2002.11008804

Dash, A. (2016). Network inequality. *Humane Tech, 2020*. doi:10.1080/13691 18X.2019.1593484

Davies, H. C., Eynon, R., & Wilkin, S. (2017). Neoliberal gremlins? How a scheme to help disadvantaged young people thrive online fell short of its ambitions. *Information Communication & Society, 20*(6), 860–875. doi:10.1080/1369118x.2017.1293131

de Melo, G., Machado, A., & Miranda, A. (2017). The impact on learning of a One Laptop per Child program. Evidence from Uruguay. *Trimestre Economico, 84*(334), 383–409. doi:10.20430/ete.v84i334.305

De Vuyst, S. (2017). Shifting gender gaps in journalism? A longitudinal study on gender segregation in a converging media environment. *Catalan Journal of Communication & Cultural Studies, 9*(2), 249–263. doi:10.1386/cjcs.9.2.249_1

Desjarlais, M., & Willoughby, T. (2010). A longitudinal study of the relation between adolescent boys and girls' computer use with friends and friendship quality: Support for the social compensation or the rich-get-richer hypothesis? *Computers in Human Behavior, 26*(5), 896–905. doi:10.1016/j.chb.2010.02.004

Digital Europe. (2019). *The voice of digitally transforming industries*. Retrieved from www.digitaleurope.org/

DiMaggio, P., & Garip, F. (2012). Network effects and social inequality. *Annual Review of Sociology, 38*(1), 93–118. doi:10.1146/annurev.soc.012809.102545

DiMaggio, P., Hargittai, E., Celeste, C., & Shafer, S. (2004). *From unequal access to differentiated use: A Literature review and agenda for research on digital inequality*. Retrieved from https://pdfs.semanticscholar.org/4b80/e96eb81f92eeacc978a48436c0ed9b820b6f.pdf

DiSTO partners. (2020). *From digital skills to tangible outcomes*. London: London School of Economics. Retrieved from www.lse.ac.uk/media-and-communications/research/research-projects/disto

Dixon, L. J., Correa, T., Straubhaar, J., Covarrubias, L., Graber, D., Spence, J., & Rojas, V. (2014). Gendered space: The digital divide between male and female users in internet public access sites. *Journal of Computer-Mediated Communication, 19*(4), 991–1009. doi:10.1111/jcc4.12088

Donner, J. (2015). *After access: Inclusion, development, and a more mobile Internet*. Cambridge, MA: MIT Press.

Drabowicz, T. (2014). Gender and digital usage inequality among adolescents: A comparative study of 39 countries. *Computers & Education, 74*, 98–111. doi:10.1016/j.compedu.2014.01.016

Drabowicz, T. (2017). Social theory of internet use: Corroboration or rejection among the digital natives? Correspondence analysis of adolescents in two societies. *Computers & Education, 105*, 57–67. doi:10.1016/j.compedu.2016.10.004

Duggan, M. (2017). *Online harassment 2017*. Washington, DC: Pew Research Center. Retrieved from www.pewinternet.org/2017/07/11/online-harassment-2017/

Dutton, W. H., & Blank, G. (2015). Cultural stratification on the internet: Five clusters of values and beliefs among users in Britain. In L. Robinson, S. R. Cotten, J. Schulz, T. M. Hale, & A. Williams (Eds.), *Communication and information technologies annual: Digital distinctions and inequalities* (Vol. 10, pp. 3–28). Bingley, UK: Emerald.

Dutton, W. H., & Shepherd, A. (2006). Trust in the Internet as an experience technology. *Information, Communication & Society, 9*(4), 433–451. doi:10.1080/13691180600858606

Ebbers, W. E., Jansen, M. G. M., & van Deursen, A. (2016). Impact of the digital divide on e-government: Expanding from channel choice to channel usage. *Government Information Quarterly, 33*(4), 685–692. doi:10.1016/j.giq.2016.08.007

Ellemers, N., Spears, R., & Doosje, B. (2002). Self and social identity. *Annual Review of Psychology, 53*, 161–186.

England, P. (2016). Sometimes the social becomes personal: Gender, class, and sexualities. *American Sociological Review, 81*(1), 4–28. doi:10.1177/0003122415621900

Ellison, N. B., Steinfield, C., & Lampe, C. (2011). Connection strategies: Social capital implications of Facebook-enabled communication practices. *New Media & Society, 13*(6), 873–892. doi:10.1177/1461444810385389

Elwood, S., & Leszczynski, A. (2018). Feminist digital geographies. *Gender, Place & Culture, 25*(5), 629–644. doi:10.1080/0966369X.2018.1465396

Esping-Andersen, G. (2007). More inequality and fewer opportunities? Structural determinants and human agency in the dynamics of income distribution. In D. Held & A. Kaya (Eds.), *Global inequalities* (pp. 216–251). Malden, MA: Polity Press.

EU Kids Online. (2019). *Enhancing knowledge of European children's online opportunities, risks and safety*. Retrieved from www.lse.ac.uk/media-and-communications/research/research-projects/eu-kids-online

Eubanks, V. (2011). *Digital dead end: Fighting for social justice in the information age*. Cambridge, MA: MIT Press.

European Commission. (2017). *My region, my Europe, our future: The seventh report on economic, social and territorial cohesion*. (SWD (2017) 330 final PART 3/13). Brussels: European Commission. Retrieved from https://eur-lex.europa.eu/resource.html?uri=cellar:d7ee4ad5-ada0-11e7-837e-01aa75ed71a1.0001.02/DOC_13&format=PDF

European Commission. (2020). *EU's Digital Economy and Society Index*. Brussels: European Commission. Retrieved from https://ec.europa.eu/digital-single-market/en/desi

European Parliament. (2016). *Cyberbullying among young people*. Brussels: European Parliament. Retrieved from www.europarl.europa.eu/RegData/etudes/STUD/2016/571367/IPOL_STU(2016)571367_EN.pdf

Eurostat. (2018a). *Digital economy and society statistics – households and individuals*. Retrieved from https://ec.europa.eu/eurostat/statistics-explained/index.php?title=Digital_economy_and_society

Eurostat. (2018b). *Individuals using mobile devices to access the internet on the move: % of individuals aged 16 to 74*. Retrieved from https://ec.europa.eu/eurostat/tgm/graph.do?tab=graph&plugin=1&pcode=tin00083&language=en&toolbox=data

Eurostat. (2019a). *Community survey on ICT usage in households and by individuals*. Retrieved from https://circabc.europa.eu/sd/a/28e0bbb8-af94-455d-93de-94985f62ade7/Model%20Questionnaire%202019%20v%201.1%20-%20after%20WG.pdf

Eurostat. (2019b). *ICT usage in households and by individuals*. Retrieved from https://ec.europa.eu/eurostat/web/digital-economy-and-society/data/database

Ewing, T. (2008). Forum – Participation cycles and emergent cultures in an online community. *International Journal of Market Research, 50*(5), 575–590. doi:10.2501/s1470785308200043

Eynon, R., & Helsper, E. J. (2015). Family dynamics and Internet use in Britain: What role do children play in adults' engagement with the Internet? *Information Communication & Society, 18*(2), 156–171. doi:10.1080/1369118x.2014.942344

Fajkowska, M., & Kreitler, S. (2018). Status of the trait concept in contemporary personality psychology: Are the old questions still the burning questions? *Journal of Personality, 86*(1), 5–11. doi:10.1111/jopy.12335

Feng, G., Zhang, Y., & Lin, Z. (2019). A meta-analysis of the effects of sociodemographic factors on social media adoption. *International Journal of Communication, 13*, 30. Retrieved from https://ijoc.org/index.php/ijoc/article/view/10088

Fletcher, E. K., Pande, R., & Troyer Moore, C. (2017). Women and work in India: Descriptive evidence and a review of potential policies. *HKS Faculty Research Working Paper Series, 18*(4). Retrieved from https://scholar.harvard.edu/files/rpande/files/women_and_work_in_india_indiaflfp_workingpaper.pdf

Fotopoulou, A. (2016). Digital and networked by default? Women's organisations and the social imaginary of networked feminism. *New Media & Society, 18*(6), 989–1005. doi:10.1177/1461444814552264

Fox, J., & Tang, W. Y. (2017). Women's experiences with general and sexual harassment in online video games: Rumination, organizational responsiveness, withdrawal, and coping strategies. *New Media & Society, 19*(8), 1290–1307. doi:10.1177/1461444816635778

Franklin, U. M. (2004). *The real world of technology* (revised ed.). Toronto, ON: House of Anansi Press.

Fraser, N. (2007). Reframing justice in a globalizing world. In D. Held & A. Kaya (Eds.), *Global inequalities* (pp. 252–272). Malden, MA: Polity Press.

Freire, P., & Macedo, D. (1987). *Literacy: Reading the word and the world*. South Handley, MA: Bergin and Garvey.

Friederici, N., Ojanperä, S., & Graham, M. (2017). The impact of connectivity in Africa: Grand visions and the mirage of inclusive digital development. *The Electronic Journal of Information Systems in Developing Countries, 79*(1), 1–20. doi:10.1002/j.1681-4835.2017.tb00578.x

Friedman, S., & Savage, M. (2019). Time, accumulation and trajectory: Bourdieu and social mobility. In S. Lawler & G. Payne (Eds.), *Social mobility for the 21st century: Everyone a winner?* London: Routledge.

Fuchs, C. (2009). The role of income inequality in a multivariate cross-national analysis of the digital divide. *Social Science Computer Review, 27*(1), 41–58. doi:10.1177/0894439308321628

Gabriel, D. (2016). Blogging while Black, British and female: A critical study on discursive activism. *Information Communication & Society, 19*(11), 1622–1635. doi:10.1080/1369118x.2016.1146784

Galperin, H., Bar, F., & Helsper, E. J. (2019). *Connecting Skid Row*. Retrieved from https://homelessness.usc.edu/usc-initiative-news/connecting-skid-row/

Galperin, H., Bar, F., & Kim, A. (2017). *Mapping digital exclusion in Los Angeles County*. Los Angeles, CA: Retrieved from http://arnicusc.org/publications/mapping-digital-exclusion-in-los-angeles-county/

Gangadharan, S. P. (2017). The downside of digital inclusion: Expectations and experiences of privacy and surveillance among marginal Internet users. *New Media & Society, 19*(4), 597–615. doi:10.1177/1461444815614053

Garber, M. (2015). Call it the 'Bechdel-Wallace Test'. *The Atlantic, 8*. Retrieved from www.theatlantic.com/entertainment/archive/2015/08/call-it-the-bechdel-wallace-test/402259/

Gecas, V. (1989). The social psychology of self-efficacy. *Annual Review of Sociology, 15*(8), 291–316.

Gerbaudo, P. (2012). *Tweets and the streets: Social media and contemporary activism*. London: Pluto Press.

Ghodes, A. R. (2018). Reflections on digital technologies, repression, and resistance: Epilogue. *State Crime Journal, 7*(1), 141–144. doi:10.13169/statecrime.7.1.0141

Gibson, J. J. (2015). *The ecological approach to visual perception* (Classic ed.). New York: Psychology Press.

Giddens, A. (1990). *The consequences of modernity*. Cambridge, UK: Polity Press.

Gil de Zúñiga, H., & Valenzuela, S. (2011). The mediating path to a stronger citizenship: Online and offline networks, weak ties, and civic engagement. *Communication Research, 38*(3), 397–421. doi:10.1177/0093650210384984

Glaumann, M., & Bohlin, E. (2013). *Analyzing the effect of broadband on GDP an Ericsson report*. Retrieved from Stockholm (SE): https://www.ericsson.com/49e75a/assets/local/about-ericsson/sustainability-and-corporate-responsibility/documents/download/socioeconomic-effect-of-broadband-speed.pdf

Global Commission on Internet Governance. (2016). *One Internet*. London: Global Commission on Internet Governance. Retrieved from www.cigionline.org/initiatives/global-commission-internet-governance

Global Kids Online. (2019). *Children's rights in the digital age*. Retrieved from http://globalkidsonline.net/

Global Kids Online. (2020). *Global Kids Online: Comparative report*. Retrieved from http://globalkidsonline.net/

Goldfinch, S., Gauld, R., & Herbison, P. (2009). The participation divide? Political participation, trust in government, and e-government in Australia and New Zealand. *Australian Journal of Public Administration, 68*(3), 333–350. doi:10.1111/j.1467-8500.2009.00643.x

Goldthorpe, J. H. (1996). Class analysis and the reorientation of theory: The case of persisting differences in educational attainment. *The British Journal of Sociology, 47*(3), 481–505.

Gonzales, A. (2016). The contemporary US digital divide: From initial access to technology maintenance. *Information Communication & Society, 19*(2), 234–248. doi:10.1080/1369118x.2015.1050438

Gorski, P. (2016). Rethinking the role of 'Culture' in educational equity: From cultural competence to equity literacy. *Multicultural Perspectives, 18*(4), 221–226. doi:10.1080/15210960.2016.1228344

Gorzig, A., Milosevic, T., & Staksrud, E. (2017). Cyberbullying victimization in context: The role of social inequalities in countries and regions. *Journal of Cross-Cultural Psychology, 48*(8), 1198–1215. doi:10.1177/0022022116686186

Graham, M., & Zook, M. (2011). Visualizing global cyberscapes: Mapping user-generated placemarks. *Journal of Urban Technology, 18*(1), 115–132. doi:10.1080/10630732.2011.578412

Granovetter, M. (1983). The strength of weak ties: A network theory revisited. *Sociological Theory, 1*(1), 201–233.

Gray, K. L. (2014). *Deviant acts: Racism and sexism in virtual gaming communities*. Waltham, MA: Anderson.

Gray, T. J., Gainous, J., & Wagner, K. M. (2017). Gender and the digital divide in Latin America. *Social Science Quarterly, 98*(1), 326–340. doi:10.1111/ssqu.12270

Gregson, N. (1987). Structuration theory: Some thoughts on the possibilities for empirical research. *Environment and Planning D: Society and Space*, *5*(1), 73–91. doi:10.1068/d050073

Grenfell, M. J. (2014). *Pierre Bourdieu: Key concepts*. Abingdon: Routledge.

Haddon, L. (2011). Domestication analysis, objects of study, and the centrality of technologies in everyday life. *Canadian Journal of Communication*, *36*(2), 311–323. doi:10.22230/cjc.2011v36n2a2322

Halsey, A. H., Heath, A. F., & Ridge, J. M. (1980). *Origins and destinations: Family, class, and education in modern Britain*. Oxford: Clarendon Press.

Halupka, M. (2018). The legitimisation of clicktivism. *Australian Journal of Political Science*, *53*(1), 130–141. doi:10.1080/10361146.2017.1416586

Hargittai, E. (2002). Second level digital divide: Differences in people's online skills. *First Monday*, *7*(4). Retrieved from www.firstmonday.dk/issues/issue7_4/hargittai/

Hargittai, E. (2010). Digital Na(t)ives? Variation in Internet skills and uses among members of the 'Net Generation' *Sociological Inquiry*, *80*(1), 92–113. doi:10.1111/j.1475-682X.2009.00317.x

Hargittai, E., & Litt, E. (2011). The tweet smell of celebrity success: Explaining variation in Twitter adoption among a diverse group of young adults. *New Media & Society*, *13*(5), 824–842. doi:10.1177/1461444811405805

Hargittai, E., & Shaw, A. (2013). Digitally savvy citizenship: The role of Internet skills and engagement in young adults' political participation around the 2008 presidential election. *Journal of Broadcasting & Electronic Media*, *57*(2), 115–134. doi:10.1080/08838151.2013.787079

Hargittai, E., & Shaw, A. (2015). Mind the skills gap: The role of Internet know-how and gender in differentiated contributions to Wikipedia. *Information Communication & Society*, *18*(4), 424–442. doi:10.1080/1369118x.2014.957711

Hargittai, E., & Walejko, G. (2008). The participation divide: Content creation and sharing in the digital age. *Information communication and society*, *11*(2), 239–256. doi:10.1080/13691180801946150

Harlow, S., & Guo, L. (2014). Will the revolution be tweeted or Facebooked? Using digital communication tools in immigrant activism. *Journal of Computer-Mediated Communication*, *19*(3), 463–478. doi:10.1111/jcc4.12062

Harp, D., & Tremayne, M. (2006). The gendered blogosphere: Examining inequality using network and feminist theory. *Journalism & Mass Communication Quarterly*, *83*(2), 247–264. doi:10.1177/107769900608300202

Hays, S. (1994). Structure and agency and the sticky problem of culture. *Sociological Theory*, *12*(1), 57–72. doi:10.2307/202035

Haythornthwaite, C. (2002). Strong, weak, and latent ties and the impact of new media. *The Information Society*, *18*(5), 385–401. doi:10.1080/01972240290108195

Heft, H. (2005). *Ecological psychology in context: James Gibson, Roger Barker, and the legacy of William James's radical empiricism*. London: Routledge.

Held, D., & Kaya, A. (2007). *Global inequalities*. Malden, MA: Polity Press.

Helland, C. (2002). Surfing for salvation. *Religion*, *32*(4), 293–302. doi:10.1006/reli.2002.0406

Helsper, E. J. (2010). Gendered Internet use across generations and life stages. *Communication Research*, *37*(3), 352–374. doi:10.1177/0093650209356439

Helsper, E. J. (2011). *The emergence of a digital underclass: Digital policies in the UK and evidence for inclusion*. Retrieved from http://eprints.lse.ac.uk/38615/

Helsper, E. J. (2012). A Corresponding Fields model for the links between social and digital exclusion. *Communication Theory, 22*(4), 403–426. doi:10.1111/j.1468-2885.2012.01416.x

Helsper, E. J. (2017a). The social relativity of digital exclusion: Applying relative deprivation theory to digital inequalities. *Communication Theory, 27*(3), 223–242. doi:10.1111/comt.12110

Helsper, E. J. (2017b). A socio-digital ecology approach to understanding digital inequalities among young people. *Journal of Children and Media, 11*(2), 256–260. doi:10.1080/17482798.2017.1306370

Helsper, E. J. (2018). Digital inequalities policies in Latin America are mostly words and little accountability, just like in Europe. Retrieved from http://blogs.lse.ac.uk/latamcaribbean/2018/01/23/digital-inequalities-policies-in-latin-america-are-mostly-words-and-little-accountability-just-like-in-europe/

Helsper, E. J. (2019a). Digital inequalities amongst digital natives. In L. Haddon & L. Green (Eds.), *Routledge companion to digital media and children*. London: Routledge.

Helsper, E. J. (2019b). Why location-based studies offer new opportunities for a better understanding of socio-digital inequalities. [Por que estudos baseados em localização oferecem novas oportunidades para uma melhor compreensão das desigualdades sociodigitais?] In NIC.br (Ed.), *Desigualdades digitais no espaco urbano: Um estudo sobre o acesso e o uso da Internet na cidade de São Paulo* (pp. 19–44). Sao Paolo, Brazil: NIC.br.

Helsper, E. J. (2020). *Cyberscene: Report on the production of the theatre play Cookies*. Retrieved from www.lse.ac.uk/media-and-communications/research/research-projects/disto/Publications

Helsper, E. J. (2021). Network and neighborhood effects in digital skills. In E. Hargittai (Ed.), *Handbook of digital inequality*. Cheltenham, UK: Edward Elgar.

Helsper, E. J., & Eynon, R. (2013). A skills framework to understanding digital engagement. Paper presented at the 63rd Annual ICA Conference, London (UK).

Helsper, E. J., & Galacz, A. (2009). Understanding the links between social and digital inclusion in Europe. In G. Cardoso, A. Cheong, & J. Cole (Eds.), *The world wide Internet: Changing societies, economies and cultures* (pp. 146–178). Taipa: University of Macau Press.

Helsper, E. J., & Reisdorf, B. C. (2013). A Quantitative Examination of Explanations for Reasons for Internet Nonuse. *Cyberpsychology Behavior and Social Networking, 16*(2), 94–99. doi:10.1089/cyber.2012.0257

Helsper, E. J., & Reisdorf, B. C. (2017). The emergence of a 'digital underclass' in Great Britain and Sweden: Changing reasons for digital exclusion. *New Media & Society, 19*(8), 1253–1270. doi:10.1177/1461444816634676

Helsper, E. J., & Smahel, D. (2019). Excessive internet use by young Europeans: Psychological vulnerability and digital literacy? *Information, Communication & Society*, 1–19. doi:10.1080/1369118X.2018.1563203

Helsper, E. J., & Smirnova, S. (2016). *Slipping through the net report: Are disadvantaged young people being further left behind in the digital era?* Retrieved from www.lse.ac.uk/media@lse/research/DiSTO/Pdf/Slipping-through-the-Net-December-2016.PDF

Helsper, E. J., & Smirnova, S. (2018). *Digital Reach Insights report*. Retrieved from https://socialtechtrust.org/wp-content/uploads/2018/06/SME834-Digital-Reach-Insights-report-FINAL.pdf

Helsper, E. J., & Van Deursen, A. J. A. M. (2017). Do the rich get digitally richer? Quantity and quality of support for digital engagement. *Information Communication & Society, 20*(5), 700–714. doi:10.1080/1369118x.2016.1203454

Helsper, E. J., & Van Deursen, A. J. A. M. (2018). Chapter 2. ICT Skills for the Future. In *Measuring the Information Society* (pp. 21–50). Geneva (CH): International Telecommunications Union.

Helsper, E. J., Van Deursen, A. J. A. M., & Eynon, R. (2015). *Tangible outcomes of Internet use*. Retrieved from www.lse.ac.uk/media@lse/research/DiSTO.aspx

Hesmondhalgh, D. (2006). Bourdieu, the media and cultural production. *Media, Culture & Society, 28*(2), 211–231. doi:10.1177/0163443706061682

Hilbert, M. (2016). The bad news is that the digital access divide is here to stay: Domestically installed bandwidths among 172 countries for 1986–2014. *Telecommunications Policy, 40*(6), 567–581. doi:10.1016/j.telpol.2016.01.006

Hirzalla, F., van Zoonen, L., & de Ridder, J. (2011). Internet use and political participation: Reflections on the mobilization/normalization controversy. *Information Society, 27*(1), 1–15. doi:10.1080/01972243.2011.534360

Hodgson, G. M. (2014). What is capital? Economists and sociologists have changed its meaning: Should it be changed back? *Cambridge Journal of Economics, 38*(5), 1063–1086. doi:10.1093/cje/beu013

Hodgson, G. M. (2015). *Conceptualizing capitalism: Institutions, evolution, future*. Chicago, IL: University of Chicago Press.

Hoffmann, C. P., Lutz, C., & Meckel, M. (2015). Content creation on the Internet: A social cognitive perspective on the participation divide. *Information Communication & Society, 18*(6), 696–716. doi:10.1080/1369118x.2014.991343

Hofstede, G. (2015). National differences in communication culture. In D. Brzozowska & W. Chlopicki (Eds.), *Cultures software: Communication Styles* (pp. 1–15). Newcastle-upon-Tyne, UK: Cambridge Scholars Publishing.

Hofstra, B., Corten, R., van Tubergen, F., & Ellison, N. B. (2017). Sources of segregation in social networks: A novel approach using Facebook. *American Sociological Review, 82*(3), 625–656. doi:10.1177/0003122417705656

Hollingshead, A. B. (1996). Information suppression and status persistence in group decision making: The effects of communication media. *Human Communication Research, 23*(2), 193–219. doi:10.1111/j.1468-2958.1996.tb00392.x

Homero, G. d. Z., Trevor, D., Brigitte, H., & James, L. (2017). Personality traits and social media use in 20 countries: How personality relates to frequency of social media use, social media news use, and social media use for social interaction. *Cyberpsychology, Behavior, and Social Networking, 20*(9), 540–552. doi:10.1089/cyber.2017.0295

Hong, S. J., Thong, J. Y. L., & Tam, K. Y. (2006). Understanding continued information technology usage behavior: A comparison of three models in the context of mobile internet. *Decision Support Systems, 42*(3), 1819–1834. doi:10.1016/j.dss.2006.03.009

Houston, R. D., & Erdelez, S. (2002). The digital divide: Who really benefits from the proposed solutions for closing the gap? *Proceedings of the American Society for Information Science and Technology, 39*(1), 99–106. doi:10.1002/meet.1450390111

Howarth, C., Campbell, C., Cornish, F., Franks, B., Garcia-Lorenzo, L., Gillespie, A., … Tennant, C. (2013). Insights from societal psychology: The contextual politics of change. *Journal of Social and Political Psychology, 1*(1). doi:10.5964/jspp.v1i1.64

Huang, K. T., Cotten, S. R., & Rikard, R. V. (2017). Access is not enough: The impact of emotional costs and self-efficacy on the changes in African-American students' ICT use patterns. *Information Communication & Society, 20*(4), 637–650. doi:10.1080/1369118x.2016.1203456

Hunt, J. (2005). Combating social exclusion: The EU's contribution. *Journal of Social Welfare and Family Law, 27*(1), 113–120. doi:10.1080/09649060500085974

Ignatow, G., & Robinson, L. (2017). Pierre Bourdieu: Theorizing the digital. *Information Communication & Society, 20*(7), 950–966. doi:10.1080/1369118x.2017.1301519

Indaco, A., & Manovich, L. (2016). *Urban social media inequality: Definition, measurements, and application.* Retrieved from https://arxiv.org/abs/1607.01845

Indian Government. (2020). Digital India. Retrieved from https://digitalindia.gov.in/

Ingersoll, C. (2019). *Free to play? Hate, harassment and positive social experiences in online games.* Retrieved from www.adl.org/media/13139/download

International Standards Organisation (ISO). (2020) *Country codes.* Retrieved from Online Browsing Platform: www.iso.org/obp/ui/#search

International Telecommunications Union (ITU). (2014). *The state of broadband 2014.* Geneva: ITU. Retrieved from www.itu.int/pub/S-POL-BROADBAND

ITU. (2015). *ICT facts and figures: The world in 2015* [Press release]. Geneva: ITU. Retrieved from www.itu.int/en/ITU-D/Statistics/Documents/facts/ICTFactsFigures2015.pdf

ITU. (2016). *Measuring the information society.* Geneva: ITU. Retrieved from www.itu.int/en/ITU-D/Statistics/Pages/publications/mis2016.aspx

ITU. (2017a). *ICT Development Index.* Geneva: ITU. Retrieved from www.itu.int/net4/ITU-D/idi/2017/index.html

ITU. (2017b). *ICT facts and figures 2017.* Geneva: ITU. Retrieved from www.itu.int/en/ITU-D/Statistics/Pages/facts/default.aspx

ITU. (2017c). *Measuring the information society.* Geneva: ITU. Retrieved from www.itu.int/en/ITU-D/Statistics/Pages/publications/mis2017.aspx

ITU. (2018). *ICT Development Index.* Geneva: ITU. Retrieved from www.itu.int/net4/ITU-D/idi/2017/index.html

Jackson, L. A., Von Eye, A., Biocca, F. A., Barbatsis, G., Zhao, Y., & Fitzgerald, H. E. (2006). Does home Internet use influence the academic performance of low-income children? *Developmental Psychology, 42*(3), 429–435.

Jackson, L. A., & Wang, J. L. (2013). Cultural differences in social networking site use: A comparative study of China and the United States. *Computers in Human Behavior, 29*(3), 910–921. doi:10.1016/j.chb.2012.11.024

James, J. (2016). *The impact of mobile phones on poverty and inequality in developing countries.* Tilburg, NL: Springer.

Janmaat, J. G. (2013). Subjective inequality: A review of international comparative studies on people's views about inequality. *Archives Europeennes De Sociologie, 54*(3), 357–389. doi:10.1017/s0003975613000209

Jenkins, H. (2013). From new media literacies to new media expertise. In P. Fraser & J. Wardle (Eds.), *Current perspectives in media education: Beyond the manifesto* (pp. 110–127). Basingstoke, UK: Palgrave Macmillan.

Jenkins, H., & Carpentier, N. (2013). Theorizing participatory intensities: A conversation about participation and politics. *Convergence – the International Journal of Research into New Media Technologies, 19*(3), 265-286. doi:10.1177/1354856513482090

Jenkins, H., Clinton, K., Purushotma, R., Robison, A., & Weigel, M. (2006). *Confronting the challenges of participatory culture: Media education for the 21st century.* Retrieved from www.macfound.org/media/article_pdfs/JENKINS_WHITE_PAPER.PDF

Joinson, A. N. (2003). *Understanding the psychology of Internet behaviour: Virtual worlds, real lives.* New York: Palgrave.

Juris, J. S. (2012). Reflections on #Occupy everywhere: Social media, public space, and emerging logics of aggregation. *American Ethnologist, 39*(2), 259–279. doi:10.1111/j.1548-1425.2012.01362.x

Kaminski, G. (1989). The relevance of ecologically oriented conceptualizations to theory building in environment and behavior research. In E. H. Zube & G. T. Moore (Eds.), *Advance in environment, behavior, and design* (Volume 2, pp. 3–36). Boston, MA: Springer US.

Kanbur, R., & Stiglitz, J. E. (2016). Dynastic inequality, mobility and equality of opportunity. *Journal of Economic Inequality, 14*(4), 419–434. doi:10.1007/s10888-016-9328-4

Kardefelt-Winther, D. (2017). Conceptualizing Internet use disorders: Addiction or coping process? *Psychiatry and Clinical Neurosciences, 71*(7), 459–466. doi:10.1111/pcn.12413

Karpf, D. (2010). Online political mobilization from the advocacy group's perspective: Looking beyond clicktivism. *Policy & Internet, 2*(4), 7–41. doi:10.2202/1944-2866.1098

Katz, R. L. (2009). Estimating broadband demand and its economic impact in Latin America. Paper presented at the third ACORN-REDECOM Conference, Mexico City, Mexico. Retrieved from www.acorn-redecom.org/papers/acornredecom2009katz.pdf

Keane, M. (2016). *Handbook of cultural and creative industries in China*. Cheltenham, UK: Edward Elgar.

Keen, A. (2011). *The Cult of the Amateur: How blogs, MySpace, YouTube and the rest of today's user-generated media are killing our culture and economy* (new ed.). London: Nicholas Brealey.

Keipi, T., Rasanen, P., Oksanen, A., Hawdon, J., & Nasi, M. (2018). Exposure to online hate material and subjective well-being: A comparative study of American and Finnish youth. *Online Information Review, 42*(1), 2–15. doi:10.1108/oir-05-2016-0133

Kelly, T., & Rossotto, C. M. (2012). *Broadband strategies handbook*. Washington, DC: World Bank. Retrieved from https://openknowledge.worldbank.org/handle/10986/6009

Kendall, D. (2011). *Framing class: Media representations of wealth and poverty in America* (2nd ed.). Lanham, MD: Rowman & Littlefield.

Kostin, D. (2020). *S&P 500 Index analysis*. Retrieved from www.cnbc.com/2020/02/18/outside-of-the-big-5-tech-companies-earnings-growth-is-zero.html

Kraemer, K. L., Dedrick, J., & Sharma, P. (2009). One Laptop Per Child: Vision vs. reality. *Communications of the Acm, 52*(6), 66–73. doi:10.1145/1516046.1516063

Kral, I. (2014). Shifting perceptions, shifting identities: Communication technologies and the altered social, cultural and linguistic ecology in a remote indigenous context. *Australian Journal of Anthropology, 25*(2), 171–189. doi:10.1111/taja.12087

Kreckel, R. (2005). Rethinking inequalities. *Paper presented at the seventh Congress of the European Sociological Association, Torun, Poland*. Retrieved from www2.soziologie.uni-halle.de/emeriti/kreckel/docs/elite.pdf

Kuhn, P., & Mansour, H. (2014). Is Internet job search still ineffective? *The Economic Journal, 124*(581), 1213–1233. doi:10.1111/ecoj.12119

Kushner, S. (2016). Read only: The persistence of lurking in Web 2.0. *First Monday, 21*(6). doi:10.5210/fm.v21i6.6789

Kuttan, A., & Peters, L. (2003). *From digital divide to digital opportunity*. Lanham, MD: Scarecrow Press.

Kuznets, S. (1955). Economic growth and income inequality. *The American Economic Review, 45*(1), 1–28. Retrieved from www.jstor.org/stable/1811581

Kvasny, L. (2005). The role of the habitus in shaping discourses about the digital divide. *Journal of Computer Mediated Communication, 10*(2). doi:10.1111/j.1083-6101.2005.tb00242.x

Kvasny, L., Trauth, E. M., & Morgan, A. J. (2009). Power relations in IT education and work: The intersectionality of gender, race, and class. *Journal of Information, Communication and Ethics in Society, 7*(2/3), 96–118. doi:10.1108/14779960910955828

Labour Party. (2019). British Broadband: Labour sets out mission to connect communities across Britain by delivering free full-fibre broadband for all [Press release]. Retrieved from https://labour.org.uk/press/british-broadband-labour-sets-out-mission-to-connect-communities-across-britain-by-delivering-free-full-fibre-broadband-for-all/

Lane, D. S., & Dal Cin, S. (2018). Sharing beyond Slacktivism: The effect of socially observable prosocial media sharing on subsequent offline helping behavior. *Information, Communication & Society, 21*(11), 1523–1540. doi:10.1080/1369118X.2017.1340496

Lawler, S. (2011). Symbolic capital. In D. Southerton (Ed.), *Encyclopedia of consumer culture* (Volume 1, pp. 1418–1420). doi:10.4135/9781412994248

Lee, C. P., Chen, D. Y., & Huang, T. Y. (2014). The interplay between digital and political divides: The case of e-petitioning in Taiwan. *Social Science Computer Review, 32*(1), 37–55. doi:10.1177/0894439313497470

Lee, S. J. (2009). Online communication and adolescent social ties: Who benefits more from Internet use? *Journal of Computer-Mediated Communication, 14*(3), 509–531. doi:10.1111/j.1083-6101.2009.01451.x

Leigh-Hunt, N., Bagguley, D., Bash, K., Turner, V., Turnbull, S., Valtorta, N., & Caan, W. (2017). An overview of systematic reviews on the public health consequences of social isolation and loneliness. *Public Health, 152*, 157–171. doi:10.1016/j.puhe.2017.07.035

Lessig, L. (2005). *Code: And other laws of cyberspace, version 2.0.* New York: Basic Books.

Liff, S., & Stewart, F. (2001). Community e-gateways: Locating networks and learning for social inclusion. *Information, Communication and Society, 4*(3), 317–340.

Lim, S. S., Vadrevu, S., Chan, Y. H., & Basnyat, I. (2012). Facework on Facebook: The online publicness of juvenile delinquents and youths-at-risk. *Journal of Broadcasting & Electronic Media, 56*(3), 346–361. doi:10.1080/08838151.2012.705198

Lin, N., & Erickson, B. H. (2008). Theory, measurement, and the research enterprise on social capital. In N. Lin & B. H. Erickson (Eds.), *Social capital an international research programme*. Oxford: Oxford University Press.

Literat, I. (2016). Interrogating participation across disciplinary boundaries: Lessons from political philosophy, cultural studies, art, and education. *New Media & Society, 18*(8), 1787–1803. doi:10.1177/1461444816639036

Litt, E. (2013). Measuring users' internet skills: A review of past assessments and a look toward the future. *New Media & Society, 15*(4), 612–630. doi:10.1177/1461444813475424

Litt, E., & Hargittai, E. (2014). Smile, snap, and share? A nuanced approach to privacy and online photo-sharing. *Poetics, 42*, 1–21. doi:10.1016/j.poetic.2013.10.002

Liu, D., Ainsworth, S. E., & Baumeister, R. F. (2016). A meta-analysis of social networking online and social capital. *Review of General Psychology, 20*(4), 369–391. doi:10.1037/gpr0000091

Livingstone, S. (2003). The changing nature and uses of media literacy. In R. Gill, Pratt, A., Rantanen, T. & Couldry, N. (Eds.), *Media@LSE electronic working papers* (Volume 4). London: London School of Economics.

Livingstone, S. (2013). Online risk, harm and vulnerability: Reflections on the evidence base for child internet safety policy. *ZER: Journal of Communication Studies, 18*, 13–28.

Livingstone, S., Burton, P., Cabello, P., Helsper, E. J., Kanchev, P., Kardefelt-Winther, D., … Yu, S.-H. (2017). Media and information literacy among children on three continents: Insights into the measurement and mediation of well-being. In UNESCO (Ed.), *MILID Yearbook 2017*. Göteborg: NORDICOM.

Livingstone, S., Haddon, L., Görzig, A., & Ólafsson, K. (2011). Risks and safety on the internet: The perspective of European children. *Full findings and policy implications from the EU Kids Online survey of 9–16 year olds and their parents in 25 countries*. London. Retrieved from http://eprints.lse.ac.uk/33731/

Livingstone, S., & Helsper, E. J. (2010). Balancing opportunities and risks in teenagers' use of the internet: The role of online skills and internet self-efficacy. *New Media & Society, 12*(2), 309–329. doi:10.1177/1461444809342697

Livingstone, S., & Millwood-Hargrave, A. (2006). *Harm and offence in media content: A review of the evidence*. Bristol: Intellect Press.

Livingstone, S., Ólafsson, K., Helsper, E. J., Lupianez-Villanueva, F., Veltri, G. A., & Folkvord, F. (2017). Maximizing opportunities and minimizing risks for children online: The role of digital skills in emerging strategies of parental mediation. *Journal of Communication, 67*(1), 82–105. doi:10.1111/jcom.12277

Looker, E. D., & Naylor, T. D. (2010). *Digital diversity: Youth, equity, and information technology*. Ontario, ON: Wilfried Laurier University Press.

Lovink, G., & Rossiter, N. (2018). *Organization after social media*. Colchester, UK: Minor Compositions.

LSE Commission on Truth Trust and Technology. (2019). *Tackling the information crisis: A policy framework for media system resilience*. London: London School of Economics. Retrieved from www.lse.ac.uk/media-and-communications/truth-trust-and-technology-commission/The-report

Luke, A. (2012). Critical literacy: Foundational notes. *Theory into Practice, 51*(1), 4–11. doi: 10.1080/00405841.2012.636324

Lupiáñez-Villanueva, F., Gaskell, G., Veltri, G., Theben, A., Folkford, F., Bonatti, L., … Codagnone, C. (2016). *Study on the impact of marketing through social media, online games and mobile applications on children's behaviour*. Brussels: European Commission. Retrieved from https://ec.europa.eu/info/sites/info/files/online_marketing_children_final_report_en.pdf

Lutz, C. (2016). A social milieu approach to the online participation divides in Germany. *Social Media + Society, 2*, 1–14. doi:10.1177/2056305115626749

Lutz, C., & Hoffmann, C. P. (2017). The dark side of online participation: Exploring non-, passive and negative participation. *Information Communication & Society, 20*(6), 876–897. doi:10.1080/1369118x.2017.1293129

Lutz, C., Hoffmann, C. P., & Meckel, M. (2014). Beyond just politics: A systematic literature review of online participation. *Political Studies Review, 16*(2), 148–157. doi:10.5210/fm.v19i7.5260

Luyt, B. (2006). Defining the digital divide: The role of e-readiness indicators. *Aslib Proceedings, 58*(4), 276–291. doi:10.1108/00012530610687669

Lyons, A., Zuchetti, A., Kass-Hanna, J., & Cobo, C. (2019). *Bridging the gap between digital skills and employability for vulnerable populations*. Montevideo, Uruguay: Fundacion Ceibal. Retrieved from https://digital.fundacionceibal.edu.uy/jspui/handle/123456789/291

Macaya, J. F. M., Alves, A. F., Meirelles, F., & Cunha, M. A. (2019). Digital by default: The use of service channels by citizens. Paper presented at the Electronic Government: 18th IFIP WG 8.5 International Conference, EGOV 2019, San Benedetto del Tronto, Italy.

Maccoby, E. F. (2007). Historical overview of socialization research and theory. In J. E. Crussec & P. D. Hastings (Eds.), *Handbook of socialization theory and research* (pp. 13–42). New York: Guilford Press.

Madianou, M., & Miller, D. (2012). *Migration and new media: Transnational families and polymedia*. Abingdon, UK: Routledge.

Mansell, R. (2012). *Imagining the Internet*. Oxford: Oxford University Press.

Marchi, R. (2017). News translators: Latino immigrant youth, social media, and citizenship training. *Journalism & Mass Communication Quarterly, 94*(1), 189–212. doi:10.1177/1077699016637119

Mare, A. (2018). Politics unusual? Facebook and political campaigning during the 2013 harmonised elections in Zimbabwe. *African Journalism Studies, 39*(1), 90–110. doi:10.1080/23743670.2018.1425150

Marinetti, F. T. (1909). The Futurist Manifesto. *Le Figaro*, 20 February. Retrieved from https://391.org/manifestos/1909-the-futurist-manifesto-f-t-marinetti/

Martin, S. P., & Robinson, J. P. (2014). The income digital divide: Trends and predictions for levels of Internet use. *Social Problems, 54*(1), 1–22. doi:10.1525/sp.2007.54.1.1

Martinez-Cantos, J. L. (2017). Digital skills gaps: A pending subject for gender digital inclusion in the European Union. *European Journal of Communication, 32*(5), 419–438. doi:10.1177/0267323117718464

Marwick, A. E. (2015). Status update: Celebrity, publicity, and branding in the social media age. New Haven, CT: Yale University Press.

Mascheroni, G., & Ólafsson, K. (2016). The mobile Internet: Access, use, opportunities and divides among European children. *New Media & Society, 18*(8), 1657–1679. doi:10.1177/1461444814567986

McChesney, R. W. (2013). *Digital disconnect: How capitalism is turning the Internet against democracy*. New York: The New Press.

McIlwain, C. (2017). Racial formation, inequality and the political economy of web traffic. *Information Communication & Society, 20*(7), 1073–1089. doi:10.1080/1369118x.2016.1206137

McInroy, L. B. (2016). Pitfalls, potentials, and ethics of online survey research: LGBTQ and other marginalized and hard-to-access youths. *Social Work Research, 40*(2), 83–93. doi:10.1093/swr/svw005

McKenna, K. Y. A., & Bargh, J. A. (1998). Coming out in the age of the Internet: Identity 'demarginalization' through virtual group participation. *Journal of Personality and Social Psychology, 75*(3), 681–694. doi:10.1037/0022-3514.75.3.681

McLure Wasko, M., & Faraj, S. (2005). Why should I share? Examining social capital and knowledge contribution in electronic networks of practice. *MIS Quarterly, 29*(1), 35–57. doi:10.2307/25148667

McMillan Cottom, T. (2017). Black cyberfeminism: Ways forward for intersectionality and digital sociology. In J. Daniels, K. Gregory, & T. McMillan Cottom (Eds.), *Digital sociologies*. Bristol, UK: Policy Press.

Mendonca, S., Crespo, N., & Simoes, N. (2015). Inequality in the network society: An integrated approach to ICT access, basic skills, and complex capabilities. *Telecommunications Policy, 39*(3–4), 192–207. doi:10.1016/j.telpol.2014.12.010

Meneses, J., & Momino, J. M. (2010). Putting digital literacy in practice: How schools contribute to digital inclusion in the network society. *Information Society, 26*(3), 197–208. doi:10.1080/01972241003712231

Meng, B. C. (2012). Underdetermined globalization: Media consumption via P2P networks. *International Journal of Communication, 6*, 467–483. Retrieved from https://ijoc.org/index.php/ijoc/article/view/1258

Mervyn, K., & Allen, D. K. (2012). Sociospatial context and information behavior: Social exclusion and the influence of mobile information technology. *Journal of the American Society for Information Science and Technology, 63*(6), 1125–1141. doi:10.1002/asi.22626

Mesch, G. S. (2012). Minority status and the use of computer-mediated communication: A test of the social diversification hypothesis. *Communication Research, 39*(3), 317–337. doi:10.1177/0093650211398865

Meza-Cordero, J. A. (2017). Learn to play and play to learn: Evaluation of the One Laptop Per Child program in Costa Rica. *Journal of International Development, 29*(1), 3–31. doi:10.1002/jid.3267

Micheli, M. (2016). Social networking sites and low-income teenagers: Between opportunity and inequality. *Information Communication & Society, 19*(5), 565–581. doi:10.1080/1369118x.2016.1139614

Micheli, M., Lutz, C., & Buchi, M. (2018). Digital footprints: An emerging dimension of digital inequality. *Journal of Information Communication & Ethics in Society, 16*(3), 242–251. doi:10.1108/jices-02-2018-0014

Milanović, B. (2016). *Global inequality: A new approach for the age of globalization.* Cambridge, MA: The Belknap Press of Harvard University Press.

Miles, S. (2018). Still getting it on online: Thirty years of queer male spaces brokered through digital technologies. *Geography Compass, 12*(11). doi:10.1111/gec3.12407

Minges, M. (2015). *Exploring the relationship between broadband and economic growth.* Retrieved from http://pubdocs.worldbank.org/en/391452529895999/WDR16-BP-Exploring-the-Relationship-between-Broadband-and-Economic-Growth-Minges.pdf

Molina-Guzman, I. (2016). #OscarsSoWhite: How Stuart Hall explains why nothing changes in Hollywood and everything is changing. *Critical Studies in Media Communication, 33*(5), 438–454. doi:10.1080/15295036.2016.1227864

Momus. (1991). Pop Stars? *Nein Danke!* Retrieved from http://imomus.com/index499.html

Morozov, E. (2009). From slacktivism to activism. *Foreign Policy, 19*(5). Retrieved from https://foreignpolicy.com/2009/09/05/from-slacktivism-to-activism/

Mortensen, T. E. (2018). Anger, fear, and games: The long event of #GamerGate. *Games and Culture, 13*(8), 787–806. doi:10.1177/1555412016640408

Mossberger, K., Tolbert, C. J., & Franko, W. (2013). *Digital cities the Internet and the geography of opportunity*. New York: Oxford University Press.

Mossberger, K., Tolbert, C. J., & Lacombe, S. (2021). *Choosing the future: Technology and opportunity in communities*. New York (NY): Oxford University Press.

Mossberger, K., Tolbert, C. J., & McNeal, R. S. (2007). *Digital citizenship: The Internet, society, and participation*. Cambridge, MA: MIT Press.

Mouzelis, N. (1989). Restructuring structuration theory. *The Sociological Review, 37*(4), 613–635. doi:10.1111/j.1467-954X.1989.tb00047.x

Mummendey, A., Kessler, T., Klink, A., & Mielke, R. (1999). Strategies to cope with negative social identity: Predictions by social identity theory and relative deprivation theory. *Journal of Personality and Social Psychology, 76*(2), 229–245. doi:10.1037/0022-3514.76.2.229

Naidu, S. C. (2016). Domestic labour and female labour force participation. *Economic & Political Review Weekly, 51*(44–45). Retrieved from https://epw.in/journal/2016/44-45/special-articles/domestic-labour-and-female-labour-force-participation.html

Nakamura, L., & Chow-White, P. A. (2013). *Race after the Internet.* New York: Routledge.

Nam, T. (2012). Dual effects of the internet on political activism: Reinforcing and mobilizing. *Government Information Quarterly, 29*(1), S90–S97. doi:10.1016/j.giq.2011.08.010

Napoli, P. M., & Obar, J. A. (2014). The emerging mobile internet underclass: A critique of mobile internet access. *Information Society, 30*(5), 323–334. doi:10.1080/01972243.2014.944726

Navarro, V. (2000). Development and quality of life: A critique of Amartya Sen's development as freedom. *International Journal of Health Services, 30*(4), 661–674. doi:10.2190/10xk-uyuc-e9p1-clfx

Net Children Go Mobile. (2020). *Net children go mobile.* Retrieved from http://netchildrengomobile.eu/

Newholm, T., Keeling, K., McGoldrick, P., Macaulay, L., & Doherty, J. (2008). The digital divide and the theory of optimal slack. *New Media & Society, 10*(2), 295–319. doi:10.1177/1461444807086475

Newman, N., Fletcher, R., Kalogeropoulos, A., & Kleis Nielsen, R. (2019). *Digital News Report 2019.* Oxford: Oxford University Press. Retrieved from https://reutersinstitute.politics.ox.ac.uk/sites/default/files/2019-06/DNR_2019_FINAL_1.pdf

Newman, R. (2017). *Digital communities.* London: DotEveryone. Retrieved from https://projects.doteveryone.org.uk/digitalcommunities/index.html

NIC.br. (2019). *Desigualdades digitais no espaço urbano: Um estudo sobre o acesso e o uso da Internet na cidade de São Paulo.* São Paulo, Brazil: Comitê Gestor da Internet no Brasil.

Norris, P. (2001). *Digital divide: Civic engagement, information poverty, and the internet worldwide.* Cambridge: Cambridge University Press.

Nov, O., Naaman, M., & Ye, C. (2010). Analysis of participation in an online photo-sharing community: A multidimensional perspective. *Journal of the American Society for Information Science and Technology 61*(3), 555–566. doi:10.1002/asi.v61:3

Nowland, R., Necka, E. A., & Cacioppo, J. T. (2018). Loneliness and social internet use: Pathways to reconnection in a digital world? *Perspectives on Psychological Science, 13*(1), 70–87. doi:10.1177/1745691617713052

Nussbaum, M. C. (2000). *Women and human development: The capabilities approach.* Cambridge: Cambridge University Press.

OECD. (2007). *Participative web: User created content: Web 2.0, Wikis and social networking.* Paris: OECD.

OECD. (2015a). *PISA in focus: Who are the best online readers?* Geneva: OECD. Retrieved from www.oecd.org/pisa/pisaproducts/pisainfocus/pisa-in-focus-n55-(eng)-final.pdf

OECD. (2015b). *Students, computers and learning: Making the connection.* Paris: OECD. Retrieved from www.oecd.org/publications/students-computers-and-learning-9789264239555-en.htm

OECD. (2018). *PISA 2018 Reading Literacy Framework.* Geneva: OECD. Retrieved from www.iprase.tn.it/documents/20178/344196/Pisa+2018+reading+literacy+framework+_final.pdf/14f3abfc-966c-46b1-a8d8-4d962193ecfd

OECD. (2019). *OECD Skills Survey: PIAAC.* Paris: OECD. Retrieved from https://piaacdataexplorer.oecd.org/ide/idepiaac/

Ofcom. (2016a). *Media literacy audit: Report on adult media literacy.* London: Ofcom. Retrieved from www.ofcom.org.uk/advice/media_literacy/medlitpub/medlitpubrss/medialit_audit/

Ofcom. (2016b). *Smart phone by default qualitative research report.* London: Ofcom. Retrieved from www.ofcom.org.uk/advice/media_literacy/medlitpub/medlitpubrss/medialit_audit/

Ofcom. (2019). *Adults: Media use and attitudes report.* London: Ofcom. Retrieved from www.ofcom.org.uk/__data/assets/pdf_file/0021/149124/adults-media-use-and-attitudes-report.pdf

Olsaretti, S. (2014). Freedom's value: Some persisting questions for Amartya Sen's capability approach. *Jurisprudence, 5*(2), 369–375. doi:10.5235/20403313.5.2.369

Olssen, M. (2016). Neoliberal competition in higher education today: Research, accountability and impact. *British Journal of Sociology of Education, 37*(1), 129–148. doi: 10.1080/01425692.2015.1100530

Olssen, M., & Peters, M. A. (2005). Neoliberalism, higher education and the knowledge economy: From the free market to knowledge capitalism. *Journal of Education Policy, 20*(3), 313–345. doi:10.1080/02680930500108718

ONS. (2003–2014). *The Omnibus Survey*. London: Office for National Statistics. Retrieved from https://gss.civilservice.gov.uk/archive/about/surveys/the-omnibus-survey/index.html

ONS. (2020). *Consumer price inflation basket of goods and services: 2020*. London: Office for National Statistics. Retrieved from www.ons.gov.uk/economy/inflationandpriceindices/articles/ukconsumerpriceinflationbasketofgoodsandservices/2020

Outlaw, J. (2019). *Why women don't like Virtual Reality: A study of safety, usability and self-expression in social VR*. Retrieved from https://extendedmind.io/social-vr

Oyedemi, T. (2015). Participation, citizenship and internet use among South African youth. *Telematics and Informatics, 32*(1), 11–22. doi:10.1016/j.tele.2014.08.002

Pagani, L., Argentin, G., Gui, M., & Stanca, L. (2016). The impact of digital skills on educational outcomes: Evidence from performance tests. *Educational Studies, 42*(2), 137–162. doi:10.1080/03055698.2016.1148588

Papacharissi, Z., & Rubin, A. M. (2000). Predictors of Internet use. *Journal of Broadcasting & Electronic Media, 44*(2), 175–196. doi:10.1207/s15506878jobem4402_2

Parker, J. (2000). *Structuration*. Buckingham, UK: Open University Press.

Patchin, J. W. (2019). *2019 cyberbullying data*. Retrieved from https://cyberbullying.org/2019-cyberbullying-data

Pearce, K. E., & Rice, R. E. (2017). Somewhat separate and unequal: Digital divides, social networking sites, and capital-enhancing activities. *Social Media + Society, 3*(2). doi:10.1177/2056305117716272

Petronio, S. (2002). *Boundaries of privacy: Dialectics of disclosure*. Albany, NY: State University of New York Press.

Pew Internet & American Life Project. (2018). *Core Trends Survey*. Washington, DC: Pew Research Center. Retrieved from www.pewinternet.org/dataset/jan-3-10-2018-core-trends-survey/

Pew Research Center. (2017). *Science and News Survey*. Washington, DC: Pew Research Center. Retrieved from www.journalism.org/dataset/2017-pew-research-center-science-and-news-survey/

Pick, J. B., Sarkar, A., & Rosales, J. (2015). A spatial and regression analysis of social media in the United States counties. Paper presented at the ICIS 2015 Pre-Conference Workshop Proceedings 3, Fort Worth, TX, US.

Piketty, T. (2013). *Capital in the twenty-first century*. Cambridge, MA: Harvard University Press.

Piketty, T. (2020). *Capital and ideology*. Cambridge, MA: Harvard University Press.

Pinnock, A. (2019). The menace of meritocracy: Unmasking inequality in the creative and cultural industries. *Cultural Trends, 28*(2–3), 249–260. doi:10.1080/09548963.2019.1617947

Pogge, T. W. (2007). Why inequality matters. In D. Held & A. Kaya (Eds.), *Global inequalities* (pp. 132–148). Malden, MA: Polity Press.

Poley, M. E. M., & Luo, S. H. (2012). Social compensation or rich-get-richer? The role of social competence in college students' use of the Internet to find a partner. *Computers in Human Behavior, 28*(2), 414–419. doi:10.1016/j.chb.2011.10.012

Polizzi, G. (2020). Digital literacy and the National Curriculum for England: Learning from how the experts engage with and evaluate online content. *Computers & Education, 152*(103859). doi:10.1016/j.compedu.2020.103859

Pon, B. (2016). *Winners and losers in the global app economy*. Farnham, UK: Caribou Digital. Retrieved from www.cariboudigital.net/wp-content/uploads/2019/01/Caribou-Digital-Winners-and-Losers-in-the-Global-App-Economy-2016.pdf

Portes, A. (1998). Social capital: Its origins and applications in modern sociology. *Annual Review of Sociology, 24*, 1–24.

Prevost, A. K., & Schaffner, B. F. (2008). Digital divide or just another absentee ballot? Evaluating internet voting in the 2004 Michigan democratic primary. *American Politics Research, 36*(4), 510–529. doi:10.1177/1532673X08318586

Prieger, J. E. (2013). The broadband digital divide and the economic benefits of mobile broadband for rural areas. *Telecommunications Policy, 37*(6–7), 483–502. doi:10.1016/j.telpol.2012.11.003

Przybylski, A. K., & Bowes, L. (2017). Cyberbullying and adolescent well-being in England: A population-based cross-sectional study. *Lancet Child & Adolescent Health, 1*(1), 19–26. doi:10.1016/s2352-4642(17)30011-1

Pulos, A. (2013). Confronting heteronormativity in online games: A critical discourse analysis of LGBTQ sexuality in *World of Warcraft*. *Games and Culture, 8*(2), 77–97. doi:10.1177/1555412013478688

Putnam, R. D. (2002). *The dynamics of social capital*. Oxford: Oxford University Press.

Quandt, T. (2012). What's left of trust in a network society? An evolutionary model and critical discussion of trust and societal communication. *European Journal of Communication, 27*(1), 7–21. doi:10.1177/0267323111434452

Ragnedda, M. (2018). Conceptualizing digital capital. *Telematics and Informatics, 35*(8), 2366–2375. doi:10.1016/j.tele.2018.10.006

Ragnedda, M., & Muschert, G. W. (2018). *Theorizing digital divides*. London: Routledge.

Rainie, L., & Wellman, B. (2012). *Networked: The new social operating system*. Cambridge, MA: MIT Press.

Rains, S. A., & Tsetsi, E. (2017). Social support and digital inequality: Does Internet use magnify or mitigate traditional inequities in support availability? *Communication Monographs, 84*(1), 54–74. doi:10.1080/03637751.2016.1228252

Ravallion, M. (2003). The debate on globalization, poverty and inequality: Why measurement matters. *International Affairs, 79*(4), 739–753. doi:10.1111/1468-2346.00334

Rawls, J. (1971). *A theory of justice*. Cambridge, MA: Presidents and Fellows Harvard College.

Reporters Without Borders. (2019). *World Press Freedom Index*. Retrieved from https://rsf.org/en/ranking

Reyes-Acosta, C. (2016). Digitally mediated social ties and achieving recognition in the field of creative and cultural production: Unravelling the online social networking mystery. (PhD thesis). *The London School of Economics and Political Science (LSE)*, London. Retrieved from http://etheses.lse.ac.uk/3604/

Rice, E., & Barman-Adhikari, A. (2014). Internet and social media use as a resource among homeless youth. *Journal of Computer-Mediated Communication, 19*(2), 232–247. doi:10.1111/jcc4.12038

Risman, B. J. (2004). Gender as a social structure: Theory wrestling with activism. *Gender & Society, 18*(4), 429–450. doi:10.1177/0891243204265349

Robeyns, I. (2005). Selecting capabilities for quality of life measurement. *Social Indicators Research 74*(191), 191–215. doi:10.1007/s11205-005-6524-1

Robinson, L. (2009). A taste for the necessary: A Bourdieuian approach to digital inequality. *Information Communication & Society, 12*(4), 488–507. doi:10.1080/13691180902857678

Robinson, L. (2018). The identity curation game: Digital inequality, identity work, and emotion management. *Information Communication & Society, 21*(5), 661–680. doi:10.1080/1369118x.2017.1411521

Robinson, L., & Gran, B. K. (2018). No kid is an island: Privacy scarcities and digital inequalities. *American Behavioral Scientist, 62*(10), 1413–1430. doi:10.1177/0002764218787014

Robinson, L., Wiborg, O., & Schulz, J. (2018). Interlocking inequalities: Digital stratification meets academic stratification. *American Behavioral Scientist, 62*(9), 1251–1272. doi:10.1177/0002764218773826

Robinson, Z. F. (2018). Intersectionality and gender theory. In B. J. Risman, C. M. Froyum, & W. J. Scarborough (Eds.), *Handbook of the sociology of gender* (2nd ed., pp. 69–80). New York: Springer US.

Robles, J. M., Molina, O., & De Marco, S. (2012). Digital political participation and the political digital divide in Spain: A study of digital inequalities. *Arbor-Ciencia Pensamiento Y Cultura, 188*(756), 795–810. doi:10.3989/arbor.2012.756n4012

Rogers, E. M. (1995). *Diffusion of innovations*. New York: The Free Press.

Rogers, E. M., & Kincaid, D. L. (1981). *Communication networks: Toward a new paradigm for research*. New York: The Free Press.

Rose, R. (2005). A global diffusion model of e-governance. *Journal of Public Policy, 25*(1), 5–27. Retrieved from https://www.jstor.org/stable/4007783

Ruggiero, T. E. (2000). Uses and gratifications theory in the 21st century. *Mass Communication and Society, 3*(1), 3–37. doi:10.1207/S15327825MCS0301_02

Russo, S., & Amna, E. (2016). The personality divide: Do personality traits differentially predict online political engagement? *Social Science Computer Review, 34*(3), 259–277. doi:10.1177/0894439315582487

Salahuddin, M., Tisdell, C., Burton, L., & Alam, K. (2016). Does internet stimulate the accumulation of social capital? A macro-perspective from Australia. *Economic Analysis and Policy, 49*, 43–55. doi:10.1016/j.eap.2015.11.011

Sampson, R. J. (2017). Urban sustainability in an age of enduring inequalities: Advancing theory and ecometrics for the 21st-century city. *Proceedings of the National Academy of Sciences*. doi:10.1073/pnas.1614433114

Sandel, M. (2020). *The tyranny of merit*. London: Penguin Press.

Saranto, K., & Hovenga, E. J. S. (2004). Information literacy: What it is about? Literature review of the concept and the context. *International Journal of Medical Informatics, 73*(6), 503–513. doi:10.1016/j.ijmedinf.2004.03.002

Savage, M. (2015). *Social class in the 21st century*. London: Pelican Randomhouse.

Schafer, M. H., Ferraro, K. F., & Mustillo, S. A. (2011). Children of misfortune: Early adversity and cumulative inequality in perceived life trajectories. *American Journal of Sociology, 116*(4), 1053–1091. doi:10.1086/655760

Schradie, J. (2011). The digital production gap: The digital divide and Web 2.0 collide. *Poetics, 39*(2), 145–168. doi:10.1016/j.poetic.2011.02.003

Schradie, J. (2012). The trend of class, race, and ethnicity in social media inequality. Who still cannot afford to blog? *Information Communication & Society, 15*(4), 555–571. doi:10.1080/1369118x.2012.665939

Schradie, J. (2015). The gendered digital production gap: Inequalities of affluence. In *Communication and information technologies annual* (Volume 9, pp. 185–213). Bingley, UK: Emerald.

Schroeder, R. (2010). Mobile phones and the inexorable advance of multimodal connectedness. *New Media & Society, 12*(1), 75–90. doi:10.1177/1461444809355114

Schumacher, P., & Morahan-Martin, J. (2001). Gender, Internet and computer attitudes and experiences. *Computers in Human Behavior, 17*(1), 95–110. doi:10.1016/S0747-5632(00)00032-7

Schwabach, A. (2014). *Buy Internet and the law: Technology, society, and compromises* (2nd ed.). Santa Barbabara, CA: ABC-CLIO.

Sefton-Green, J. (2006). *Literature review in informal learning with technology outside school.* Bristol, UK: NFER. Retrieved from www.nfer.ac.uk/publications/FUTL72/FUTL72.pdf

Selwyn, N. (2005). The social processes of learning to use computers. *Social Science Computer Review, 23*(1), 122–135.

Selwyn, N. (2006). Digital division or digital decision? A study of non-users and low-users of computers, *Poetics, 34*(4–5), 273–292.

Selwyn, N. (2008). O uso das TIC na educação e a promoção de inclusão social: Uma perspectiva crítica do Reino Unido. *Educação & Sociedade, 29*, 815–850. Retrieved from www.scielo.br/scielo.php?script=sci_arttext&pid=S0101-73302008000300009&nrm=iso

Selwyn, N. (2009). The digital native – myth and reality. *Aslib Proceedings, 61*(4), 364–379. doi:10.1108/00012530910973776

Selwyn, N. (2013). 'Empowering the world's poorest children'? A critical examination of One Laptop Per Child. In N. Selwyn & K. Facer (Eds.), *Politics of education and technology: Conflicts, controversies, and connections* (pp. 101–125). New York: Palgrave Macmillan.

Selwyn, N., Gorard, S., Furlong, J., & Madden, L. (2003). Older adults' use of information and communications technology in everyday life. *Ageing and Society, 23*(5), 561–582. doi:10.1017/S0144686X03001302

Sen, A. (1997). Human capital and human capability. *World Development, 25*(12), 1959–1961. doi:10.1016/s0305-750x(97)10014-6

Sen, A. (2002). Development, capabilities, and freedom: Response to commentaries. *Studies in Comparative International Development, 37*(2), 78–86. doi:10.1007/bf02686264

Sen, A. (2004). Capabilities, lists, and public reason: Continuing the conversation. *Feminist Economics, 10*(3), 77–80. doi:10.1080/1354570042000315163

Sen, A. (2008). Capability and well-being. In D. M. Hausman (Ed.), *Philosophy of economics: An anthology* (3rd ed., pp. 270–293). New York: Cambridge University Press.

Servon, L. J. (2002). *Bridging the digital divide: Technology, community and public policy.* Oxford: Blackwell Publishers.

Shaban, A. R. A. (2019). Twitter backlash after Ethiopia PM's internet 'not water or air' threat. *Africa News*, 3 August. Retrieved from www.africanews.com/2019/08/03/twitter-backlash-after-ethiopia-pm-s-internet-not-water-or-air-threat//

Shahin, S. (2018). Facing up to Facebook: How digital activism, independent regulation, and mass media foiled a neoliberal threat to net neutrality. *Information Communication & Society, 22*(1), 1–17. doi:10.1080/1369118x.2017.1340494

Shaw, A., & Benkler, Y. (2012). A tale of two blogospheres: Discursive practices on the left and right. *American Behavioral Scientist, 56*(4), 459–487. doi:10.1177/0002764211433793

Short, E. C. (1986). A historical look at curriculum design. *Theory Into Practice, 25*(1), 3–9. doi:10.1080/00405848609543191

Simmons, R., & Thompson, R. (2011). Education and training for young people at risk of becoming NEET: Findings from an ethnographic study of work-based learning programmes. *Educational Studies, 37*(4), 447–450.

Sinpeng, A. (2017). Participatory inequality in online and offline political engagement in Thailand. *Pacific Affairs, 90*(2), 253–274. doi:10.5509/2017902253

Skoric, M. M., Zhu, Q. F., Goh, D., & Pang, N. (2016). Social media and citizen engagement: A meta-analytic review. *New Media & Society, 18*(9), 1817–1839. doi:10.1177/1461444815616221

Slavina, A., & Brym, R. (2019). Demonstrating in the Internet age: A test of Castells' theory. *Social Movement Studies, 19*(2), 201–221. doi:10.1080/14742837.2019.1627866

Smith, H., & Pettigrew, T. (2015). Advances in Relative Deprivation Theory and research. *Social Justice Research, 28*(1), 1–6. doi:10.1007/s11211-014-0231-5

Soyer, E., Cornelissen, G., & Karelaia, N. (2013). Clicktivism or slacktivism? Impression management and moral licensing. In G. Cornelissen, E. Reutskaja, & A. Valenzuela (Eds.), *European advances in consumer research* (Volume 10, pp. 244–244). Duluth, MN: Association for Consumer Research.

Srinagar. (2019). Restrictions will be eased after August 15: Jammu and Kashmir governor. *Times of India*. Retrieved from https://timesofindia.indiatimes.com/india/restrictions-will-be-eased-after-august-15-jammu-and-kashmir-governor/articleshow/70667056.cms

Statista. (2018). *China data period 2007–2018*. Retrieved from www.statista.com/statistics/278566/urban-and-rural-population-of-china/ and www.statista.com/statistics/265154/internet-users-in-china-in-urban-and-rural-regions/

Steinfield, C., Ellison, N. B., & Lampe, C. (2008). Social capital, self-esteem, and use of online social network sites: A longitudinal analysis. *Journal of Applied Developmental Psychology, 29*(6), 434–445. doi:10.1016/j.appdev.2008.07.002

Stiglitz, J. E. (2015). *The price of inequality: How today's divided society endangers our future*. New York: W. W. Norton & Co.

Stones, R. (2005). *Structuration theory*. Basingstoke, UK: Palgrave Macmillan.

Straubhaar, J. D., Castro, D., Duarte, L. G., & Spence, J. (2019). Class, pay TV access and Netflix in Latin America: Transformation within a digital divide. *Critical Studies in Television, 14*(2), 233–254. doi:10.1177/1749602019837793

Straubhaar, J. D., Tufekci, Z., Spence, J., & Rojas, V. (2012). *Digital inequity in the Austin technopolis: Race, class, gender, and the digital divide in Austin*. Austin, TX: University of Texas Press.

Straus Jacob, R. (2016). Congressional social media communications: Evaluating Senate Twitter usage. *Online Information Review, 40*(5), 643–659. doi:10.1108/OIR-10-2015-0334

Suttcliffe, B. (2007). The unequalled and unequal twentieth century. In D. Held & A. Kaya (Eds.), *Global inequalities* (pp. 50–72). Malden, MA: Polity Press.

Suzuki, L., & Aronson, J. (2005). The cultural malleability of intelligence and its impact on the racial/ethnic hierarchy. *Psychology Public Policy and Law, 11*(2), 320–327. doi:10.1037/1076-8971.11.2.320

Taneja, H., & Webster, J. G. (2016). How do global audiences take shape? The role of institutions and culture in patterns of web use. *Journal of Communication, 66*(1), 161–182. doi:10.1111/jcom.12200

Taylor, K., & Silver, L. (2019). *Smartphone ownership is growing rapidly around the world, but not always equally*. Washington, DC: Pew Research Center. Retrieved from www.pewresearch.org/global/wp-content/uploads/sites/2/2019/02/Pew-Research-Center_Global-Technology-Use-2018_2019-02-05.pdf

Telegeography. (2019). *Submarine cable map*. Retrieved from www.submarinecablemap.com

Teo, T. S. H., Lim, V. K. G., & Lai, R. Y. C. (1999). Intrinsic and extrinsic motivation in Internet usage. *Omega, 27*(1), 25–37. doi:10.1016/S0305-0483(98)00028-0

Therborne, G. (2013). *The killing fields of inequality*. Cambridge, UK: Polity Press.

Thiessen, V., & Looker, E. D. (2008). Cultural centrality and information and communication technology among Canadian youth. *Canadian Journal of Sociology/Cahiers Canadiens De Sociologie, 33*(2), 311–336.

Thiessen, V., & Looker, E. D. (2010). Bridging and bonding social capital: Computer and Internet use among youth in relation to their cultural identities. In E. D. Looker & T. D. Naylor (Eds.), *Digital diversity: Youth equity and information technology* (pp. 59–86). Ontario, ON: Wilfried Laurier University Press.

Thomas, J. (2018). Thanks to social media, the pandemics of the future could be psychological. *The National*. Retrieved from www.thenational.ae/opinion/comment/thanks-to-social-media-the-pandemics-of-the-future-could-be-psychological-1.755042

Thompson, G. F. (2007). Global inequality the 'Great Divergence' and supranational regionalization. In D. Held & A. Kaya (Eds.), *Global inequalities* (pp. 176–203). Malden, MA: Polity Press.

Thorson, K., Xu, Y., & Edgerly, S. (2018). Political inequalities start at home: Parents, children, and the socialization of civic infrastructure online. *Political Communication, 35*(2), 178–195. doi:10.1080/10584609.2017.1333550

Thurow, L. C. (2000). Globalization: The product of a knowledge-based economy. *Annals of the American Academy of Political and Social Science, 570*, 19–31. doi:10.1177/0002716200570001002

Torenli, N. (2006). The 'other' faces of digital exclusion: ICT gender divides in the broader community. *European Journal of Communication, 21*(4), 435–455. doi:10.1177/0267323106070010

Totura, C. M. W., MacKinnon-Lewis, C., Gesten, E. L., Gadd, R., Divine, K. P., Dunham, S., & Kamboukos, D. (2009). Bullying and victimization among boys and girls in middle school. The influence of perceived family and school contexts. *Journal of Early Adolescence, 29*(4), 571–609. doi:10.1177/0272431608324190

Tufekci, Z. (2012). Past and future divides: Social mobility, inequality and digital divides in Austin during the tech boom. In J. Straubhaar, J. Spence, Z. Tufekci, & R. G. Lentz (Eds.), *Inequity in the technopolis: Race, class, gender, and the digital divide in Austin* (pp. 85–108). Austin, TX: University of Austin Press.

UK Government. (2017a). *Digital skills and inclusion policy*. London: UK Government. Retrieved from www.gov.uk/government/publications/digital-inclusion-and-skills-policy/digital-skills-and-inclusion-policy

UK Government. (2017b). PART 1 access to digital services: Universal service broadband obligations. In *Digital Economy Act 2017*. London: UK Government.

UN Department of Economics and Social Affairs. (2018). *E-Government Survey 2018: Gearing e-government to support transformation towards sustainable and resilient societies*. Retrieved from https://publicadministration.un.org/egovkb/en-us/Reports/UN-E-Government-Survey-2018

UNDP. (2019). *Human Development Reports*. Oxford: UNDP. Retrieved from http://hdr.undp.org/en/data

United Nations. (2018). *Reduced inequalities: Why it matters*. New York: UN. Retrieved from www.un.org/sustainabledevelopment/inequality/

Valkenburg, P. M., Koutamanis, M., & Vossen, H. G. M. (2017). The concurrent and longitudinal relationships between adolescents' use of social network sites and their social self-esteem. *Computers in Human Behavior, 76*, 35–41. doi:10.1016/j.chb.2017.07.008

Valkenburg, P. M., Schouten, A. P., & Peter, J. (2005). Developing a model of adolescent friendship formation on the Internet. *Cyberpsychology & Behavior, 8*(5), 423–430. doi:10.1089/cpb.2005.8.423

Van Deursen, A. J. A. M., & Helsper, E. J. (2015). The third level digital divide: Who benefits most from being online? In L. Robinson, S. R. Cotten, J. Schulz, T. M. Hale, & A. Williams (Eds.), *Communication and information technologies annual: Digital distinctions and inequalities* (Volume 10, pp. 29–52). Bingley (UK): Emerald.

Van Deursen, A. J. A. M., & Helsper, E. J. (2017). Collateral benefits of Internet use: Explaining the diverse outcomes of engaging with the Internet. *New Media & Society, 20*(7), 2333–2351. doi:10.1177/1461444817715282

Van Deursen, A. J. A. M., Helsper, E. J., & Eynon, R. (2016). Development and validation of the Internet Skills Scale (ISS). *Information Communication & Society, 19*(6), 804–823. doi:10.1080/1369118x.2015.1078834

Van Deursen, A. J. A. M., Helsper, E. J., Eynon, R., & Van Dijk, J. A. G. M. (2017). The compoundness and sequentiality of digital inequality. *International Journal of Communication, 11*, 452–473. Retrieved from https://ijoc.org/index.php/ijoc/article/view/5739

Van Deursen, A. J. A. M., & Mossberger, K. (2018). Any thing for anyone? A new digital divide in Internet-of-Things skills. *Policy and Internet, 10*(2), 122–140. doi:10.1002/poi3.171

Van Deursen, A. J. A. M., & Van Dijk, J. A. G. M. (2008). Measuring digital skills: Performance tests of operational, formal, information and strategic Internet skills among the Dutch population. Paper presented at the ICA Conference, Montreal, Canada, 22–26 May.

Van Deursen, A. J. A. M., & Van Dijk, J. A. G. M. (2014). The digital divide shifts to differences in usage. *New Media & Society, 16*(3), 507–526. doi:10.1177/1461444813487959

Van Deursen, A. J. A. M., & Van Dijk, J. A. G. M. (2015). Internet skill levels increase, but gaps widen: A longitudinal cross-sectional analysis (2010–2013) among the Dutch population. *Information Communication & Society, 18*(7), 782–797. doi:10.1080/1369118x.2014.994544

Van Deursen, A. J. A. M., Van Dijk, J. A. G. M., & Ten Klooster, P. M. (2015). Increasing inequalities in what we do online: A longitudinal cross-sectional analysis of Internet activities among the Dutch population (2010–2013) over gender, age, education, and income. *Telematics and Informatics, 32*(2), 259–272. doi:10.1016/j.tele.2014.09.003

van Dijck, J. (2009). Users like you? Theorizing agency in user-generated content. *Media Culture & Society, 31*(1), 41–58. doi:10.1177/0163443708098245

Van Dijk, J. A. G. M. (2005). *The deepening divide: Inequality in the Information Society*. Thousand Oaks, CA: Sage.

Van Dijk, J. A. G. M. (2020). *The digital divide*. Oxford: Polity Press.

Van Dijk, J. A. G. M., & Hacker, K. (2003). The digital divide as a complex and dynamic phenomenon. *The Information Society, 19*(4), 315–326.

Van Dijk, J. A. G. M., & Van Deursen, A. J. A. M. (2014). *Digital skills, unlocking the information society*. New York: Palgrave Macmillan.

Van Laar, E., Van Deursen, A. J. A. M., Van Dijk, J. A. G. M., & de Haan, J. (2017). The relation between 21st-century skills and digital skills: A systematic literature review. *Computers in Human Behavior, 72*, 577–588. doi:10.1016/j.chb.2017.03.010

Venkatesh, V. (2000). Determinants of perceived ease of use: Integrating control, intrinsic motivation, and emotion into the Technology Acceptance Model. *Information Systems Research, 11*(4), 342–365. doi:10.1287/isre.11.4.342.11872

Venkatesh, V., & Sykes, T. A. (2013). Digital divide initiative success in developing countries: A longitudinal field study in a village in India. *Information Systems Research, 24*(2), 239–260. doi:10.1287/isre.1110.0409

Vera-Sanso, P., Barrientos, A., Damodaran, L., Gilhooly, K., Goulding, A., Hennessy, C., … Walford, N. (2014). Participation and social connectivity. In A. Walker (Ed.), *The new science of aging* (pp. 181–208). Bristol, UK: Policy Press.

Viard, V. B., & Economides, N. (2015). The effect of content on global internet adoption and the global 'Digital Divide'. *Management Science, 61*(3), 665–686. doi:10.1287/mnsc.2013.1875

Villanueva-Mansilla, E., Nakano, T., & Evaristo, I. (2015). From divides to capitals: An exploration of digital divides as expressions of social and cultural capital In L. Robinson, S. R. Cotten, J. Schulz, T. M. Hale, & A. Williams (Eds.), *Communication and information technologies annual: Digital distinctions and inequalities* (Volume 10, pp. 89–117). Bingley (UK): Emerald.

Vochocova, L. (2018). Witty divas, nice mothers and tough girls in a sexist world: Experiences and strategies of female influencers in online political debates. *Media Culture & Society, 40*(4), 535–550. doi:10.1177/0163443717729211

Vuorikari, R., Punie, Y., Carretero Gomez, S., & Van Den Brande, G. (2016). *DigComp 2.0*. Brussels: European Commission. Retrieved from https://ec.europa.eu/jrc/en/digcomp

Vuyk, K. (2017). *Oude en nieuwe ongelijkheid: Over het failliet van het verheffingsideaal*. Utrecht, NL: Klement.

Walby, S. (2007). Complexity theory, systems theory, and multiple intersecting social inequalities. *Philosophy of the Social Sciences, 37*(4), 449–470. doi:10.1177/0048393107307663

Walby, S. (2011). Globalization and multiple inequalities. In E. N. L. Chow, M. T. Segal, & L. Tan (Eds.), *Analyzing gender, intersectionality, and multiple inequalities: Global, transnational and local contexts* (Volume 15, pp. 17–33). Bingley, UK: Emerald.

Walker, I., & Smith, H. J. (2002). *Relative deprivation: Specification, development, and integration*. New York: Cambridge University Press.

Walzer, M. (1985). *Spheres of justice: A defence of pluralism and equality*. Oxford: Blackwell.

Warschauer, M. (2003). *Technology and social inclusion: Rethinking the digital divide*. Cambridge, MA: MIT Press.

Wei, K. K., Teo, H. H., Chan, H. C., & Tan, B. C. Y. (2011). Conceptualizing and testing a social cognitive model of the digital divide. *Information Systems Research, 22*(1), 170–187. doi:10.1287/isre.1090.0273

Wei, L. (2012). Number matters: The multimodality of internet use as an indicator of the digital inequalities. *Journal of Computer-Mediated Communication, 17*(3), 303–318. doi:10.1111/j.1083-6101.2012.01578.x

Weidman, A. C., Fernandez, K. C., Levinson, C. A., Augustine, A. A., Larsen, R. J., & Rodebaugh, T. L. (2012). Compensatory internet use among individuals higher in social anxiety and its implications for well-being. *Personality and Individual Differences, 53*(3), 191–195. doi:10.1016/j.paid.2012.03.003

Weimann, G., Weiss-Blatt, N., Mengistu, G., Tregerman, M. M., & Oren, R. (2014). Reevaluating 'The End of Mass Communication?' *Mass Communication and Society, 17*(6), 803–829. doi:10.1080/15205436.2013.851700

Wellman, B., Boase, J., & Chen, W. (2002). The networked nature of community on and off the Internet. *IT and Society, 1*(1), 151–165.

Whitacre, B. (2017). Fixed broadband or mobile: What makes us more civically engaged? *Telematics and Informatics, 34*(5), 755–766. doi:10.1016/j.tele.2017.02.006

Whitacre, B., Strover, S., & Gallardo, R. (2015). How much does broadband infrastructure matter? Decomposing the metro-non-metro adoption gap with the help of the National Broadband Map. *Government Information Quarterly, 32*(3), 261–269. doi:10.1016/j.giq.2015.03.002

White, D. (2016). *Digital participation and social justice in Scotland: Understanding and tackling the digital divide*. Dunfermline, Scotland: Carnegie Trust UK. Retrieved from www.carnegieuktrust.org.uk/publications/role-digital-exclusion-social-exclusion/

White, P., & Selwyn, N. (2013). Moving on-line? An analysis of patterns of adult internet use in the UK, 2002–2010. *Information Communication & Society, 16*(1), 1–27. doi:10.1080/1369118x.2011.611816

Whittaker, S., Terveen, L., Hill, W., & Cherny, L. (1998). The dynamics of mass interaction. Paper presented at the Proceedings of the 1998 ACM Conference on Computer Supported Cooperative Work, Seattle, WA.

Wikipedia. (2020). *Wikipedia: Statistics*. Retrieved from https://en.wikipedia.org/wiki/Special:Statistics

Williams, D. (2006). On and off the net: Scales for social capital in an online era. *Journal of Computer-Mediated Communication, 11*(2), 593–628. doi:10.1111/j.1083-6101.2006.00029.x

Wojcicki, S. (2020). *YouTube at 15: My personal journey and the road ahead*. Retrieved from https://youtube.googleblog.com/2020/02/youtube-at-15-my-personal-journey.html

World Bank. (2016). *The World Bank's Digital Adoption Index*. Washington, DC. Retrieved from www.worldbank.org/en/publication/wdr2016/Digital-Adoption-Index

World Bank. (2017). *World Bank Development Indicators*. Washington, DC. Retrieved from https://databank.worldbank.org/source/world-development-indicators

World Bank. (2018). *Poverty and shared prosperity 2018: Piecing together the poverty puzzle*. Washington, DC: World Bank.

World Bank, & International Telecommunications Union. (2020). World Telecommunication/ICT Indicators database. *Washington, DC*. Retrieved from https://data.worldbank.org/.

World Internet Project. (2018). *World Internet Project Report: Eighth edition (2017)*. Los Angeles, CA. Retrieved from www.worldinternetproject.com/publications.html

World Internet Project. (2019). *World Internet Project Report: Ninth edition (2018)*. Los Angeles, CA. Retrieved from www.worldinternetproject.com/publications.html

Wright, E. O. (2005). *Approaches to class analysis*. Cambridge: Cambridge University Press.

Xenos, M., Vromen, A., & Loader, B. D. (2014). The great equalizer? Patterns of social media use and youth political engagement in three advanced democracies. *Information Communication & Society, 17*(2), 151–167. doi:10.1080/1369118x.2013.871318

Xin, X. R., & Mossig, I. (2017). Co-evolution of institutions, culture and industrial organization in the film industry: The case of Shanghai in China. *European Planning Studies, 25*(6), 923–940. doi:10.1080/09654313.2017.1300638

Yao, M. Z., Rice, R. E., & Wallis, K. (2007). Predicting user concerns about online privacy. *Journal of the American Society for Information Science and Technology, 58*(5), 710–722. doi:10.1002/asi.20530

Yates, S. J., Kirby, J., & Lockley, E. (2015). 'Digital-by-default': Reinforcing exclusion through technology. In L. Foster, A. Brunton, C. Deeming, & T. Haux (Eds.), *In defence of welfare 2* (pp. 158–161). Bristol, UK: Policy Press.

Yosso, T. J. (2002). Critical race media literacy – challenging deficit discourse about Chicanas/os. *Journal of Popular Film and Television, 30*(1), 52–62. doi:10.1080/01956050209605559

Yu, W. T. (2018). Creative industries agglomeration and industrial efficiency in China. *Growth and Change, 49*(4), 677–695. doi:10.1111/grow.12255

Zhang, M. L. (2015). Internet use that reproduces educational inequalities: Evidence from big data. *Computers & Education, 86*, 212–223. doi:10.1016/j.compedu.2015.08.007

Zillien, N., & Hargittai, E. (2009). Digital distinction: Status-specific internet uses. *Social Science Quarterly, 90*(2), 274–291. doi:10.1111/j.1540-6237.2009.00617.x

Zimmermann, B. (2006). Pragmatism and the capability approach: Challenges in social theory and empirical research. *European Journal of Social Theory, 9*(4), 467–484. doi:10.1177/1368431006073014

Zook, M. (2005). *The geography of the Internet industry: Venture capital, dot-coms, and local knowledge*. Oxford: Blackwell.

INDEX